Handwriting

Handwriting

A KEY TO PERSONALITY

Klara G. Roman

PANTHEON BOOKS, NEW YORK

By the kind permission of Mrs. Kate Wolff, on behalf of her late husband Werner Wolff, and the publishers, fig. #16 is reproduced from an article by Werner Wolff in Collier's, May 22, 1948; figs. 242, 243, 245 are reproduced from DIAGRAMS OF THE UNCONSCIOUS, by Werner Wolff, Grune & Stratton, N.Y., 1949.

MANUFACTURED IN THE UNITED STATES OF AMERICA

Designed by Lucian Bernhard

Library of Congress Catalog Card No.: 52-7197
ISBN: 0-394-73091-7

987

PREFACE

A book on graphology is likely to be accorded a more appreciative reception today, both from the general public and in academic circles, than would have been possible a few years ago. The increasingly widespread acceptance of the dynamic theory of personality has laid the groundwork for a fuller understanding of graphology in America. Yet it is of interest to note that in Europe graphology is among the oldest psychological approaches for the study of personality, and was widely used before the advent of psychoanalysis, Gestalt theory, social anthropology, or projective techniques.

At the present time, the psychologist working with projective techniques and other tests is well equipped not only by a thorough knowledge of dynamic psychology but also by specific professional training. Unfortunately, the graphologist still labors in an undefinable limbo; no specific course of training, no set of academic standards, no degree or certificate in graphology exists to attest the scientific background and reliability of the handwriting analyst. In short, the graphologist is, of necessity, a self-made individual, learning more from his own efforts than from those of others. However, it is important for the graphologist to have dual skills: he must have specific knowledge, and beyond that a profound understanding of personality, if he is to be capable of synthesizing the facts as well as the intangibles into a true personality picture.

The author of this book had the privilege of working for more than two decades on research projects instituted by government agencies and clinical institutions in Europe, notably in Budapest. The present study is, however, not a recapitulation of the widely published results of those years. Rather, it is an attempt to make a modest contribution toward the many efforts directed to the study of personality in the United States. As regards data in this specific field, the author is grateful for the experi-

v

ence provided by work at Michael Reese Hospital in Chicago, to which she was called by Dr. Franz Alexander. Further excellent opportunities for observation and testing have been afforded her in the give and take of contact with her unusually mature students at the New School for Social Research, New York.

Students of any scientific subject should realize that the essential method is the same for all fields, yet each discipline is unique with respect to the nature of its data and the manner by which it is derived. Although graphologists have attempted to objectify handwriting analysis and to treat graphic factors psychometrically, these attempts have thus far provided only limited information, less valuable than that derived from the composite impression obtained from the writing pattern when viewed as a whole. Nevertheless, the need for further work of this sort is obvious, for there are many long-accepted graphological hypotheses that still carry an implied question mark. The verified answers for which we strive can be obtained, but it will take time. To be scientifically convincing, all conclusions must be checked and double-checked under adequately controlled conditions. In the meantime, we have to rely partly on hypotheses based upon substantial evidence and found to accord with verified psychological laws and principles.

The method of handwriting analysis presented in this book rests mainly upon psychometrically and experimentally verified observations and, further, on generalizations that promise future validation through use simultaneously with clinical and projective tests.

New York City   Klara G. Roman

September 1951

ACKNOWLEDGMENTS

It gives me pleasure to make some expression of thanks to those persons who have helped me in the preparation of this book. I am especially indebted to my students and co-workers, Mr. Leslie A. Behunek, Mr. Sol Levine, Mrs. Patricia A. Miller, Miss Tess Segel, Mrs. Sipora Van Praag, and Miss Dorly Wang. Their extensive familiarity with the field of psychology permitted them quickly to attain insight into and appreciation of the principles and potentialities of graphology. Their sustained interest, assistance, and numerous suggestions have been of inestimable aid to me in the completion of my book.

Thanks are also due Mrs. Lily Erlanger, Mrs. Ruth Guttman, and Miss Betty Roberg for their technical aid in the preparation of illustrations, charts, and diagrams.

Mr. John Rewald very kindly put at my disposal his collection of autographs of famous artists. The handwritings of Manet, Monet, Ingres, and Jacques Lipchitz in this book are reproduced from letters in his possession.

Finally, I should like to express my gratitude to two artists, Mr. Willy Pogany and Mr. Leon Dabo, who supplied me with specimens of handwritings of prominent artists. I am also indebted to Mr. Pogany for his aid and suggestions in constructing the more complicated charts.

C O N T E N T S

HISTORY: The French Pioneers—German Scientific Groundwork—Advances in Switzerland—The Hungarian School—American Developments

3-18

Part One: DEVELOPMENTAL STAGES IN HANDWRITING

I SCRIBBLING 21-39

Interpretation of Scribbles (23). The Riddle of the Doodle (29). Doodles and Psychotherapy (36).

II LEARNING TO WRITE 40-59

Association of Speaking, Reading, Writing (42). Eye-Hand Control (42). The Writing Model (44). Analyzing Children's Handwriting (47). Reversals and Left-Handedness (51). Stuttering (54). The Ungainly Hand (56).

III HANDWRITING IN PUBERTY
AND ADOLESCENCE 60-79

Graphic Reflection of Conflicts (61). Experimental and Statistical Studies (64). The Graphodyne (64). Developmental Sex Differences (67). Diagnostic Value of Graphic Indices (69). Writing Pressure in Adolescence (74). Graphic Indices of Behavior Disorders (77).

IV PERSONAL STYLE 80-103

The Linear and the Pictorial Pattern (82). The Spontaneous and the Artificial Hand (86). Consistency in Personal Style (90). Influences of Time and Place (90). The American Hand (95). Professional and Vocational Patterns (99).

Part Two: ANALYSIS AND INTERPRETATION

V THE STUDENTSHIP   107-112

Intuitive Perception (108). Empirical Generalizations (110).
The Specimen Collection (111).

VI MATERIAL AND PROCEDURE   113-133

The Overall-Impression (119). Differentiation, Ordering, and
Interpretation of Graphic Indices (124-130). Synthesis
(132). Ethics of the Graphologist (132).

VII SYMBOLISM OF THE WRITING SPACE   134-146

The Three Zones (137). Direction (140). Direction in
Ancient Writing (143). The Mythology of Right and Left
(145).

VIII EXPANSION OF THE WRITING PATTERN   147-183

Proportions (148). Vertical and Horizontal Expansion (150).
Capital Letters (161). The Capital "I" (163). Projection of
the Body Image (165). Zonal Interpretation of Size (166).
The Lower Loops (177).

IX SLANT   184-198

Fluctuations in Slant (192). Slant and Handedness (194).

X CONNECTIVE FORMS   199-220

The Garland (203). The Arcade (207). The Angular Connective Form (214). The Threadlike Connective Form
(216). The Mixed Connective Form (218).

XI CONTINUITY AND FLUENCY   221-239

Continuity of Stroke and Unity of Movement (224). Degrees of Connectedness and their Meaning (228). Fluency in
Speech and Writing (234). Disturbances in Flow of Speech
and Writing (235).

XII SPEED AND PERSONAL PACE   240-253

The Dynamics of Pace (242). Graphic Indices of Speed
(247). Factors Affecting Speed (250).

XIII WRITING PRESSURE   254-277

Pressure and Muscular Strength (261). Pressure and Psychic Energy (263). Displaced Pressure (270). Emphasis Revealed in Pressure (273).

XIV TENSION AND RELEASE   278-288

Graphodyne Study of Tension-Release Patterns (279). Psychosomatic Aspects (282). Expressive Significance (283).

XV ARRANGEMENT   289-310

Spacing (289). Alignment (292). Word Interspaces (300). Margins (303). The Writing on the Envelope (308).

XVI THE SIGNATURE   311-331

The Development of Self (311). Imaginative Projection (314). The Roots of Graphic Imagery (315). Congruence of Signature and Body Script (319). Relation of Given and Family Name (322). Personality Changes (323). Elaboration and Appendages (326). Placement (330).

SAMPLE ANALYSES WITH USE OF WORK SHEETS

Handwriting of a Young Woman Applicant for a Secretarial Position   335
Handwriting of an American Artist   340
Handwriting of a Delinquent Girl   345
Handwriting Analysis in a Criminal Case   352

BIBLIOGRAPHY   363

INDEX   371

ABOUT THE AUTHOR   383

The reader of this book should bear in mind that no reproduction of a handwriting can fully convey the emotional quality and vitality of the original script.

INTRODUCTORY

HISTORY

Interest in handwriting as an expression of personality is really as old as the use of writing itself.

Over three hundred years before the Christian Era, Aristotle observed: "Spoken words are the symbols of mental experience, and written words are the symbols of spoken words. Just as all men have not the same speech sounds, so all men have not the same writing." Another early observer was Suetonius Tranquillus, historian of the first twelve Caesars. Speaking of the handwriting of the Emperor Augustus, he said: "I have above all remarked the following in his writing. He does not separate his words, nor does he carry over to the next line any excess letters; instead, he places them under the final word and ties them to it with a stroke." A later Roman emperor, Justinian, records in his memoirs that he has been struck by the observation that an individual's handwriting changes with ill-health and age.

The first known systematic attempts to study and describe the relationship between handwriting traits and character traits were made in Italy at the beginning of the seventeenth century, when Alderisius Prosper published in Bologna a study entitled *Ideographia*. A physician, Camillo Baldo, followed him with a treatise presenting a method for judging the nature of a writer from his letters.[8] Both of these studies fell into oblivion. However, they must have attracted some contemporary readers, because subsequently it became a practice for itinerant magicians and other wonder workers to go from castle to castle giving consultations on character by means of handwriting interpretation.

3

In the eighteenth century, curiosity about the possible revelations to be found in handwriting began also to stir the minds of poets and philosophers. They were fascinated at discovering the intimate link between handwriting and character, and in studying scripts they came up with sharp observations and personality portraits of startling accuracy.

THE FRENCH PIONEERS

Around 1830, a strong interest in the disclosures to be obtained from handwriting arose in France. The Abbé Flandrin and his disciple, the Abbé Jean-Hippolyte Michon of Paris, spent their lives in studying handwritings. Their successes in interpretation soon became known throughout the country. Michon possessed a methodical mind, an extraordinary gift for observation, and a photographic memory. He collected thousands of handwriting specimens and studied them with attention to each of the minute details that he designated as "elements of the handwriting." He regarded each of these graphic elements as a "sign" to be interpreted as an outward index of an inner attribute.

After thirty years of intensive concentration on the subject, Michon published his system of handwriting analysis. He coined for it the name of "graphology," which became widely known and accepted after his publication of *Les mystères de l'écriture*[106] in 1872 and *La méthode pratique de graphologie*[107] in 1878. These books intrigued people in general and attracted artists and scholars to the study of handwriting. From the ranks of his disciples grew the *Société Graphologique*, which flourished up to the time of the second world war.

Michon was branded by later graphologists as a mere "interpreter of signs." He is said to have ascribed to each sign a definite and fixed meaning. Moreover, the absence of a given sign in a script was held to indicate a quality opposite to that which would be indicated by its presence. On the other hand, he formulated a "law of balance," stated in *La méthode pratique de graphologie* as follows: "One sign does not cancel the significance of another. The counterweight of opposing signs must be considered."

It is true that Michon's interest was focused mainly on the meaning of forms, in contrast to the orientation of those later graphologists who came to regard handwriting purely as "crystallized" expressive movement. Modern graphology, however, considers both movement and form as expressing and projecting the writer's inner life. Thus Michon's contribution in relation to the interpretation of graphic forms will have to be revised.

One of Michon's successors, J. Crépieux-Jamin, broke away from the "school of fixed signs," as this system was later called. He shifted emphasis from the elements of handwriting—such as the forms of *t* bars, *i* dots, hooks, and flourishes—to the over-all aspects. "The study of elements," he said, "is to graphology as study of the alphabet is to the reading of prose." He stressed the point that a handwriting must be perceived as a whole, to which each trait contributes in varying degree and with differing emphasis. This concept—in its approach much akin to the gestaltist point of view—lead him to a theory of "resultants" produced by the combination and interaction of many elements, i.e., traits.[22]

Crépieux-Jamin persuaded Alfred Binet, the founder of modern methods of intelligence testing, to examine into the realiability of handwriting analysis. The first problem was to test the assumption that specific character traits correlate with specific handwriting traits. The affirmative results with respect to the graphic indices of honesty and intelligence brought new esteem to graphology, which Pierre Janet hailed as a "science of the future." A further crucial aspect of the investigation turned on age and sex differences in handwriting, and it was demonstrated that neither the chronological age nor the sex of a writer can be ascertained from his script.[14] Crépieux-Jamin explained that it is the psychological and not the physiological personality that is revealed in handwriting, and ever since the time of these decisive experiments, graphologists have always requested information about the sex and age of a subject before undertaking a handwriting analysis.

#1

GERMAN SCIENTIFIC GROUNDWORK

During most of the nineteenth century, French investigators held the foremost place in theoretical and applied graphology. Toward the end of the century, German scientists took over the leadership. Though they based their first steps upon the work of Crépieux-Jamin, they later minimized the part he had played in founding scientific graphology. German treatises did not mention his name, though the standard German work, *Handschrift und Charakter*, by Ludwig Klages, even borrowed its title from the Frenchman's popular work, *L'écriture et le caractère*.[22]

The first penetrating insights regarding the phenomenon of writing came from the work of physiologists and psychiatrists, who instituted methodical investigations. Wilhelm Preyer, a professor of physiology at Jena, demonstrated the similarity of the writing patterns produced by use of different body members—the right hand, the left hand, the mouth, the toes.[126] Figure #1 shows the fluent and legible script of a man who had no arms or legs, and who, in Preyer's presence, used his mouth to direct the pen. The concept that handwriting is really "brain writing," a centrally organized function, was formulated by Preyer in 1895. His publications met with an unreceptive attitude on the part of his academic colleagues, who thought it pathetic "that a scientist of merit

6

should lose himself in the field of dangerous sciences, among which hypnosis and graphology belong."

Georg Meyer, a psychiatrist, made a further important contribution by undertaking to analyze writing movement.[105] One of his conclusions was that the character of a handwriting is determined not by the anatomy or the strength of the writer's hand but by his "psychomotor energies." While underlining what he considered the three main factors of writing movement—extension, speed, and pressure—Meyer regarded unity of expression as the decisive feature of psychomotor functioning. To demonstrate the relationship between writing movement and emotion, he conducted experiments with psychotic patients in states of mania, elation, and depression.

Furthermore, Meyer recognized that problems of expression cannot be treated apart from what he called the "character" of the writer. Graphologists, he believed, needed the help of a new science, "characterology," and a common vocabulary for the two fields, e.g., terms for denoting those intangible properties or traits of personality which almost defy definition. His suggestion was fully developed later by Klages,[81] and also independently by Theodor Lessing.[88]

The new scientific perspectives opened up by Meyer and Preyer gave the impetus for the founding, in 1896, of the *Deutsche graphologische Gesellschaft*. Among its members were Hans H. Busse,[19] a criminologist, and Klages. To promote graphological theory and practice, the *Graphologische Monatshefte* were issued. Through the untimely deaths of Busse and Meyer, Klages, then known as a brilliant young philosopher, became the leader of German advance in graphology. He stamped his personality on every phase of the new science.

THE METAPHYSICAL APPROACH

The essential findings regarding the writing process, as linked with characterology by Preyer, Meyer, and D. Erlenmeyer,[35] were

7

combined by Klages into a single system representing a "science of expression." The array of his books includes, besides *Handschrift und Charakter,*[82] such works as *Die Probleme der Graphologie,*[77] *Grundlegung der Wissenschaft des Ausdrucks, Ausdrucksbewegung und Gestaltungskraft.*[78] He established "laws and principles" of graphology, characterology, and expressive movement, based largely upon his own metaphysical theory of personality.

The basic law of expression, Klages holds, is that each expressive bodily movement "actualizes" the tensions and drives of the personality. He points out that there is correspondence in the different realms of movement—speech, facial expression, and handwriting. They have a common "form level" (Klages' term is *Formniwo,* and the strange spelling is his own), which is adjudged according to the general "rhythm" of the individual's movement. Rhythm in Klages' sense is an "indefinable something" that can be understood only by "intuition." The form level of a script is the criterion of its qualities as a whole. It is a leading precept of Klages' that a handwriting pattern should be evaluated on the score of its form level before any scrutiny of its various features is undertaken.

The doctrine of form level, faithfully followed by the German graphologists, was rejected in other countries. At the present time, evaluation of handwriting primarily on the basis of the intangible phenomenon of rhythm is no longer an acceptable procedure; in the eyes of modern graphologists, it is "the evaluation of yesterday," as L. Kroeber-Keneth puts it.[85]

Klages' books were enthusiastically received in Germany. They were also highly rated abroad, though understood by few. Their pompous style and not invariably clear formulation of ideas confused and disaffected readers not attuned to the Teutonic romanticism of his philosophical speculation. His magnum opus is *Der Geist als Widersacher der Seele,*[80] in which he develops his "biocentric" doctrine. Here he advocates a kind of anti-intellectualism that became one of the cornerstones of the biological-mystical ideology

8

of the Nazi creed.* As Andras Angyal[4] points out, Klages' theory

exaggerates the conflict between what he calls *Geist* [conscious mental function, spirit] and *Seele* [feeling life, soul]. The two are, for him, antagonistic forces. The *Geist*, according to Klages, penetrates from the outside into life like a wedge, causing . . . a fundamental split. . . . Klages . . . regards the mind as a factor which disturbs living, as a *Lebensstörung*.

A whole generation of German graphologists grew up under the leadership of Klages and his *Zeitschrift für Menschenkunde*, with its supplement, the *Zentralblatt für Graphologie*. Through his personal influence Klages succeeded in curbing the graphological mercenaries who were legion in Germany at the time. He helped to give graphology a scientific standing; at the same time, he found ways of suppressing points of view and investigative trends that ran counter to his own.

At the beginning of the present century, much experimental work was devoted to the study of handwriting by Emil Kraepelin, a widely known German psychiatrist, and his co-workers.[68] Using the Kraepelin scale, they attempted to measure writing pressure and speed in normal[24] and mentally disturbed persons.[61] Klages, who was antagonistic to experimental psychology, claimed that graphology should be dealt with as a science apart, and studied by "psychologically minded" persons. Induction based on clinical observation, no less than the use of psychometric techniques, seemed to him an inadequate approach. He enjoined other graphologists not to participate in clinical and experimental work. The result was that co-operation between graphology and medicine ceased for a considerable time, and graphology was surrendered to metaphysics and armchair speculation.

---

*This development is traced by Lessing in his autobiography, *Einmal und nie wieder*.[89]

9

Fortunately for graphology, however, progressive forces were at work giving new impetus to experimental investigation and clinical procedure. Rudolf Pophal, a neurologist, undertook to study the physiology of the writing movement on the basis of findings made earlier by Kurt Wachholder[158] and Anton Rieger.[131] The purely somatic aspect had up to that time not been included in the field of inquiry. Pophal published several books on the subject of motor-physiological graphology,[120] dealing particularly with tension phenomena in handwriting.[121] After the second world war, when he was appointed professor of neurology at the University of Hamburg, he published a treatise entitled *Die Handschrift als Gehirnschrift*.[122]

Pophal established a typological system, classifying personality types on the basis of essential differences in types of motor behavior as reflected in the motor patterns of handwriting. He differentiates two essential types: the one is found in persons whose motor processes show a functional dominance of the phylogenetically younger part of the brain, i.e., the cortex or pyramidal area, while the other denotes persons whose motor activity is mediated predominantly by older parts of the brain, i.e., the extrapyramidal area.

Despite the depression conditions of the postwar period, the study and application of graphology has continued to gain impetus in Germany. Handwriting analysis is regarded as a branch of applied psychology, and graphologists are frequently consulted in the vocational and medical diagnostic fields. Courses in graphology are an integral part of academic curricula in psychology and are also pursued by many students of medicine. Robert Heiss,[65] W. H. Mueller in collaboration with Alice Enskat,[110] and Bernhard Wittlich,[164] have published manuals on graphological theory and the interpretation of handwriting for the use of medical students, psychologists, and criminologists.

ADVANCES IN SWITZERLAND

Since the middle twenties, Swiss graphologists have been making significant advances under the leadership of Max Pulver and his co-worker, Oskar Schlag. Pulver has elaborated his theory of the symbolic meaning of the writing space in a study entitled *Symbolik der Handschrift*,[128] in which large consideration is given to the concepts of depth psychology. Schlag has specialized in comparative studies of the findings of analytical psychology and graphology. Rejecting the form-level theory, Pulver has stressed the study of the biological self, which is ignored and desexualized by Klages' metaphysical precepts. Pulver has pointed to new possibilities in the interpretation of graphic features and done pioneering work in demonstrating how both conscious and unconscious drives are projected in the writing pattern.[129]

The high regard in which graphology is held in Switzerland, where it is used more frequently as a test procedure than the Rorschach and other projective techniques, is due to the thorough training provided for students of graphology in that country. Pulver has for many years been conducting courses and seminars in graphology at the Institute for Applied Psychology in Zurich, and has also been lecturing at the University of Zurich.

In 1939 three Czech graphologists, Otto Fanta,[36] Karl Menzel,[145] and Willy Schönfeld,[144] launched a journal called *Die Schrift*, which published the studies of graphologists in various countries who had been working independently of Klages or who had broken with his school. Although the journal quickly won recognition and was hailed as a significant undertaking, it was short-lived because of the political turmoil that soon engulfed all of Europe.

THE HUNGARIAN SCHOOL

In Hungary the study of graphology began about 1920. Although Hungarian investigators were familiar with both French and German graphological advances, their work followed an inde-

11

pendent path of development. It is significant that in Hungary psychologists in university positions as well as clinicians furthered the study of handwriting.[130] They used graphological analyses to supplement information obtained by clinical methods and by means of other psychological techniques.[49] Scientifically trained graphologists collaborated in clinical practice and in research.[54] Thus controlled observation facilitated the validation of graphological findings.[57]

In 1920 the Hungarian graphological association (*Magyar Irástanulmányi Társaság*) was founded, and subsequently an institute of handwriting research was set up in Budapest, under the auspices of the ministry of education. Efforts of individual graphologists were correlated and guided by the graphological association,[9] so that the results obtained had a collective significance.[63] The need of objectifying graphological procedure, and of dealing with investigative data in terms of measurement, led the present author to construct a device known as the graphodyne[50]; this apparatus has been used in large-scale investigations,[53] especially in the study of writing development in school children. This led to establishment of standard values that can be used as indices of maturation and mental growth.[51] The practical value of these standards was demonstrated in testing abnormal children, whose writing performances were found to deviate from the norm in proportion to the degree of their abnormality.

Dezsö Balázs and Richard Hajnal[7] introduced psychoanalytical concepts into Hungarian graphology and published several treatises and a textbook on the subject. Chief Justice Peter Németh used handwriting analysis for the better understanding of juvenile delinquents.[112] In a biographical study of Hungarian classical poets, Erzsébet Goldziher[59] matched graphological findings with available biographical data. The present author participated in a research project concerning the handwriting of twins, carried out at the medical school of the University of Budapest.[55] The results of this work were published in papers and textbooks, shortly before the outbreak of the second world war. Political events have put an end, for the time being, to graphological endeavor in the countries behind the "iron curtain."

AMERICAN DEVELOPMENTS

Investigation of handwriting in America received most of its impetus from advances made in France and Germany, at a time when graphology in these countries had already established its own traditions and schools of thought. One of the first American experimenters with handwriting analysis was June Downey of the University of Iowa. She became fascinated by the challenge of handwriting as an aspect of expressive movement, at a time when "trait psychology" predominated, and concentration on measurements of single traits—intelligence, for example—tended to preclude a broader outlook. Downey realized the difficulties inherent in observation of expressive movements, especially in the absence of any standard criteria. She approached the problem using the matching method, comparing judgments based on writing with findings based on gait, gesture, carriage, etc. In 1919, in *Graphology and the Psychology of Handwriting*,[27] she published the results of her investigation of the "assertion frequently made, that graphic individuality is but a specific example of a pattern that is impressed upon all the expressive movements of a given person."

An investigation closely resembling Downey's was conducted by Gordon Allport and Philip E. Vernon in 1930 and 1931 at the Harvard Psychological Clinic.[3] These authors based their investigation upon three assumptions: (*a*) personality is consistent; (*b*) movement is expressive of personality; (*c*) the gestures and other expressive movements of an individual are consistent with one another. These assumptions constitute a foundation for all practical attempts to diagnose personality on the basis of external movements.

Allport and Vernon made use of experimentation and statistical tools, but did not overlook the fact that "consistency of expressive activity lies not only in the correlation of measures, but in their

13

meaningful interrelation as well." They utilized comprehensive experimental records pertaining to speed, size of script, and pressure of movement; many of their experiments were carried out with the subject using both the right and the left arm and also both legs. Most of them were repeated, so that several hundred measurements were obtained. The results led to two major conclusions: first, a considerable degree of uniformity appears in a repetitive performance, just as manifestations of habit or repeated gestures are consistent; second, there is an internal consistency in all of the movements of an individual—that is, an identical quality marks the performance of several tasks with different limbs or muscle groups. If an individual is inclined to a rigid, inhibited pattern of behavior, it will be as evident in his manner of walking as it is in his writing, and no less in the way he holds his head, and in the facial expressions and the gestures that accompany his speech. It is interesting to note here that Rudolf Arnheim's[5] as well as Werner Wolff's earlier and more recent studies[169] have led to the same conclusions.

Allport and Vernon collaborated with professional graphologists such as Edwin Powers[125] and Robert Saudek in conducting handwriting experiments. At the time prejudice against graphology was at its height. Psychologists had been unfavorably influenced by inconclusive experiments based on copying exercises instead of spontaneous writings. The experimenters had measured in these scripts some of the elementary "signs" of older graphologists, and judged the subjects according to the supposed meanings of these indices. Finally, their judgments had been compared with personality ratings made by students untrained in either personality research or graphology. Allport and Vernon and their collaborators tried to explain that an isolated trait as such has no fixed meaning, and that the resulting evaluations were as invalid as the criteria and conditions of the experiments in question.

Saudek realized that in order to overcome the adverse attitude of academic psychologists, he would have to replace the speculative trend of European graphology with objectivity, and rely more heavily upon quantitative methods. Proceeding experimentally,[37] Saudek used microscope, pressure board,[139] and slow-motion pictures to examine handwriting movement.[138] He carried out experiments with the handwritings of persons of all nationalities and classes, analyzing the effects of different types of penmanship training; in this he was following a suggestion of A. S. Osborn's.[116] He compared the handwritings of disabled persons with those of normal individuals,[137] and studied the observable differences between the natural and the artificial handwriting of a subject—as when, for example, an individual who normally makes letters of minute size is asked to write in large letters.

Saudek's emphasis on the significance of speed as an index of personality led him to develop a table listing fourteen traits "related to the law of movement."[18] He also listed some ten general traits, any four of which, when occurring together in a script, were said to reveal dishonesty in the writer. Saudek founded *Character and Personality*, the first journal of graphology to appear in English. His publications aroused the interest of British psychologists and gained for graphology at least a limited recognition in the United States.[148] The impression in Germany was, however, that he was essaying problems beyond his scope, and overplaying experimentation in his attempts to measure and express intangibles in terms of ounces and split seconds.

After Saudek's death, and up until recently, there was a tapering off of interest in graphology in both Great Britain[100] and America, although a number of books[70] and papers[31] dealing with the subject appeared in this interval.[32] By and large they offered no new contributions, no original concepts, nor any innovations in technique. Endeavoring to explain and popularize the theories of modern European graphology,[71] these investigators tried to anchor their practical knowledge in the harbor of some accepted method of personality analysis,[101] such as psychoanalysis, projective techniques, Gestalt theory, clinical psychology in relation to pathological indices in handwriting,[75, 92] or the simple rationale of measurements and statistics. They even tried to combine several of these approaches and to impose upon them the speculative psychology of the German school.

A decisive step toward the introduction of a more objective method in graphology was taken in 1942 by Thea S. Lewinson in collaboration with Joseph Zubin.[91] These authors addressed themselves to "the problem of finding a common denominator for evaluating the quantitative and qualitative aspects" of handwriting. Their method, according to their own exposition,

> is based on the work of Klages in so far as it utilizes the concepts of contraction and release of the graphic factors and the concept of rhythmic balance as the norm. However, its point of departure from Klages' theory of rhythm rests on the premise that rhythm is the midpoint between contraction and release, i.e., rhythmic balance is the central point between the contracting and releasing tendencies. Every handwriting movement in the vertical, horizontal, or depth direction might be expanded or contracted. The balanced handwriting movement lies in the middle between contraction and release.

In accordance with this concept, the authors developed a system of scales, which they applied in a clinical manner to the handwritings of normal and abnormal individuals. The enormous labor entailed in establishing ratings and taking measurements with especially devised instruments does not permit of the use of more than a small part of a given handwriting specimen. It is a question whether single words can suffice to reveal the "differentiation pattern" of a handwriting.

Rose Wolfson, after participating in the Lewinson-Zubin experiment, applied the scales in an independent approach. In 1949, she published her *Study in Handwriting Analysis*,[170] which deals with handwritings of delinquents and nondelinquents. Wolfson analyzed four lines of each writing specimen, scaling movement tendencies as reflected in twenty-two factors. She found significant differences between the delinquent and the nondelinquent group.

The most important outcome has been that a possible "delinquent constellation" emerges from her work.

Among the most recent contributions is that of Wolff, one of the contemporary authorities in the field of experimental graphology, whose *Diagrams of the Unconscious* is the result of twenty years of research and observation.[169] This author is endeavoring to found a so-called experimental depth psychology based on graphological experiments. He has created a method of his own, based on intensive study of the signature. He measures the elements of the signature, seeking to demonstrate an inherent relationship in their length, position, and form, and proceeds to show that "graphic movements are not accidental, but a fundamental expression." He demonstrates that certain qualities in the signature persist throughout the life of the individual. Wolff's significant contribution lies in this postulation of the consistency of the graphic pattern. He has cleared much ground through both his theorizing and his experimentation. There is, however, some doubt as to how conclusive such measurements of the signature can be, and whether a signature in itself can actually yield a "diagram of the unconscious."

A still more recent publication is Ulrich Sonnemann's *Handwriting Analysis*.[150] This volume is a contribution to clinical psychology.

The foregoing brief review of the history of graphology has surveyed the successive efforts that have been made to utilize handwriting analysis as a key to personality. The distinctive nature of the handwriting function, together with the fact that every handwriting is unique and never duplicated by another, has led psychologists to concentrate observation upon it, sensing that it offers clues to the hidden regions of human nature. These are the regions of personality that intuition has so often recognized, but that psychological science—up to recent years—has noted so little.

From the nature of the material sought and the techniques and devices that have been developed so far, it is obvious that it is no easy matter to establish validity and reliability in handwriting interpretation. But similar difficulties beset all fields of personality research. Graphology took its start under the spur of "hunches" and naïve "common-sense" explanations. Then came various attempts to make it scientifically convincing through collection and organization of empirical data. The scientifically minded workers in the field have endeavored to base theory and method of interpretation upon evidence obtained through controlled observation. Their striving for satisfactory answers to the intricate problems of personality has led them constantly to re-examine and revise widely accepted hypotheses.

Two major challenges confront the graphologist of our day. The first is the need of verification of so-called laws and principles, which can be accepted as valid only after they have been checked and rechecked under the broadest possible control. The second is the need for development of new devices to further more adequate research along the lines of modern psychology.

The problems are before us. Many promising leads for future advances are at hand.

PART ONE

Developmental Stages
In Handwriting

(I)

SCRIBBLING

Children delight in scribbling. They enjoy wielding a pencil and marking up clean sheets of paper with a jumble of lines. Their random movements over the paper are the graphic equivalent of babbling—spontaneous motor play, engaged in for its own sake. In its swing and speed, in its release of force, the child experiences what French psychologists call *joie du mouvement*.

As the child goes on with this play, the random movements soon fall into a sequence; this sequence of movements is performed in the child's own individual way. One child may use loose, circling movements that produce whorls; another may propel the pencil with a tense and angular motion, producing zigzag strokes. In some children the movement is free and sweeping, in others it is restrained. Some make forceful strokes, others exert only slight pressure, covering the sheet with weak, diffuse strokes.

The given pattern, once found, will be repeated again and again. It is the child's own, his achievement and acquisition, and he is filled with pleasure at feeling himself the ruler of his own movements and master of his tools and thus of his environment. It gives him a new sense of self—and also a new means of expressing self. Indeed, each of his moods and emotions can find its own expression within the relatively stable pattern of his scribble. Cheerfulness expands his line pattern, anxiety constricts it. Sadness reduces its size and gives the stroke a downward slope. Aggressive feeling shows itself in increased angularity, and rage in an outburst of vehement strokes. In figure #2, specimen *a* records the broad, springy curve of a good-humored scribbler, specimen *b* reflects a

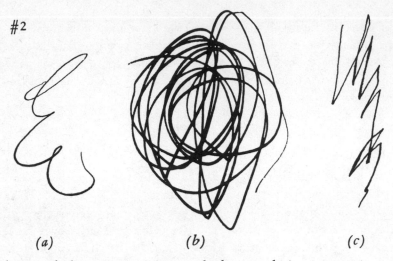

(a)   (b)   (c)

burst of dynamic activity, and the angularity of specimen *c* represents a release of aggressive feeling.

The by-product of this movement—the scribble itself—does not impress the child, who abandons it quickly. To the trained observer, however, it is a visible record of the child's self-expression —a manner of speaking for himself shaped prior to and independently of any teaching. Because of its individual execution, and because any given child makes all of its scribbles in the same way, the scribble of one child can readily be distinguished from that of another.

Repetition is characteristic of every kind of primitive pattern making. Performing a given movement over and over induces a pleasurable feeling, because it is a return to something familiar, which makes for a sense of security. The repetition moreover establishes a certain symmetry, which becomes apparent also in the scribble pattern. The sense of symmetry appears not only in humans but also in other primates. Paul Schiller, of the Yerkes laboratory, trained a female chimpanzee named Alpha to scribble with a pencil on sheets of paper. Alpha was fond of this activity and showed a remarkable sense of symmetry. When given a sheet of paper bearing a dot polygon with one dot missing, she would complete the figure. When she was handed a sheet with some figures already drawn on it, she preferred to scribble in the clear spaces on the paper. When dots were set in a cluster on one side, she would draw on the other side, producing a fairly well-defined symmetrical pattern.

Although psychologists both in the United States[11] and abroad[84] have studied scribbling, only graphologists have recognized that it expresses fundamental personality traits.[87] Free expression is curbed while the child is learning to write under school methods that force him to imitate copybook letters. But once he acquires ease in writing, there is a return to free expression, and thus the graphic individuality that marked his scribbles will reappear in his handwriting.

INTERPRETATION OF SCRIBBLES

The persistence of these early revealed traits was first observed some forty years ago by Minna Becker, a German schoolteacher. Her ingenious interpretations of scribbles were based upon graphological principles that have since been developed and broadened. Just as in the analysis of handwriting, the graphic features of scribbles are examined under the three aspects of movement, form, and arrangement (p. 124).

The characteristics of the movement are reflected in the stroke.[64] The latter is judged according to (*a*) size, i.e., whether the stroke is long or short; (*b*) direction, i.e., whether it is drawn from left to right, from top to bottom, or vice versa; and (*c*) pressure, i.e., whether it is forceful or weak. In addition, there are other, more subtle qualities of the stroke that are likewise determined by the dynamics of the movement.[123] We may get a hint of these if we compare a writer tracing a stroke with a violinist drawing a bow across the strings of his instrument. Just as each violinist has his individual, unique way of bowing, which determines the essential quality and expression of his tone, so each individual has his unique manner of tracing a stroke. It may be heavy or light, smooth or

23

jerky, full or flat, rigid or flexible, sharp or fuzzy, dark or pale, tense or slack, etc., according to his specific bodily equipment, his emotional make-up, and various other attributes of his personality.[129]

In respect to form, we look to see (*a*) whether the strokes are integrated into a whole or into groups, or remain unrelated; (*b*) whether the pattern consists of whorls and loops or angles and zigzags; and (*c*) whether the pattern is well formed or shapeless, clear or vague.

In judging the arrangement, our attention focuses on the manner in which the child uses the available space—whether the pattern is (*a*) centered or scattered, (*b*) compact or spread out, (*c*) large or small, and (*d*) whether the page is filled up or barren.

To the criteria of movement, form, and arrangement we may add that of the over-all aspect, or the general appearance of the scribble—whether it is unified or amorphous, monotonous or

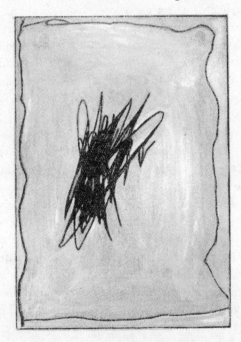

#3

varied, original or banal, neat or smeary. The qualities that play a part in the total impression are interpreted just like the corresponding qualities in handwriting.

Becker[10] described the scribble of a boy of four and a half years (fig. #3). He would begin by bordering the sheet with a neatly drawn wavy line. Then he would suddenly pounce on the paper, concentrating heavy lines in a patch. His energetic strokes cut deep into the paper; his movements were vigorous but controlled. Thus his first step was to outline or delimit his field of activity; then he would act impulsively, at the same time concentrating his energy. Becker relates that he manifested a similar action pattern when he became an adult. His sister, at the age of five and a half, would spread strokes all over the sheet (fig. #4). These scattered fine strokes were not combined into any definite pattern. This child grew up into a flighty girl with many talents and interests, which she was not able to integrate or to cultivate.

#4

5

Figures #5-8 present specimens from the author's own collection that point up striking similarities in the graphic expression of a child and her grandfather. Figure #5 shows the scribble of a girl of four and a half who belonged to a highly intellectual family. Figures #6 and #7 show doodles made by her sixty-year-old grandfather. It is quite unlikely that the child ever saw her grandfather's production; it was made absent-mindedly while he was engaged in a telephone conversation in his office, which the child never entered. The resemblance between the child's scribble and the adult's

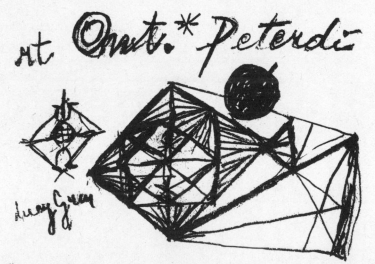

#6

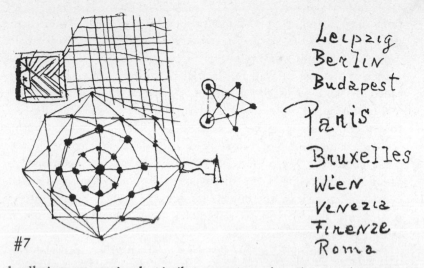

#7

Leipzig
Berlin
Budapest
Paris
Bruxelles
Wien
Venezia
Firenze
Roma

doodle is apparent in the similar grouping of strokes, in the analogous proportions of the large and the small patches, in the similar construction of the big patches by means of intersecting straight lines, and in the tendency of both subjects to use black dots.

That this resemblance is due neither to chance nor to imitation becomes clear in subsequent scribbles produced by the child (fig. #8). They consist of intersecting strokes (spec. *a*) eventually developed into triangles emphasized by dots (spec. *b*), or integrated into complicated, flower-like patterns (spec. *c*). These configura-

#8

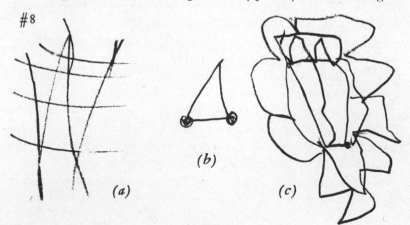

(a)

(b)

(c)

27

tions show a high degree of mental development in relation to the girl's age level, for, according to Arnold Gesell,[43] a child usually cannot even copy a triangle until it reaches the age of six. Hence ability at the age of four and a half to construct a triangle spontaneously and to mark its angles with dots represents an early manifestation of abstractive and logical capacity. This suggests that a child's scribbles may foreshadow special mental traits that will be characteristic of the fully developed personality.

At about the age of five, scribbling is generally abandoned in favor of drawing. Having discovered the world around him, the child begins to draw the objects he sees. He shows greatest interest in drawing a man, and, as Karen Machover[94] has pointed out, he assimilates his body image into his drawing.

In his scribbling and his drawing, the child creates and consistently uses his individual movement pattern. In learning to write, however, he must temporarily suppress his spontaneity. He is obliged to adapt himself to a symmetry and rhythm that are not his own. This means a repression, and the urge thus thwarted seeks another avenue of release. Without realizing why, the child will underline or adorn letters and words that are emotionally meaningful for him. This stressing is to be interpreted as a regression to an earlier mode of behavior. Breaking through the constraints of acquired, conventional symbols, primitive "signs" and images go down on the paper, or scrawls and curlicues serve to revive the function of scribbling as an outlet for emotion.

We know that habits of expression formed in early childhood may persist into adult life, revealing themselves in "symbolic gestures." This is evidence, as Allport has pointed out, that adult expression is not free of its early ties.[3] The finding applies also to graphic expression. We have all seen signatures characterized by odd line elaborations, especially notable because of the contrasting simplicity of the writer's ordinary script. Such signatures seem strikingly to recall the scribble patterns of childhood.

How the urge to playful movement that is expressed in scribbles may persist into adulthood, even in the case of very mature and highly cultivated individuals, is shown in the two signatures reproduced in figures #9 and #10. These are the autographs of two men of high professional standing. A more detailed discussion of the signature as such appears in chapter XVI.

#9

#10

THE RIDDLE OF THE DOODLE

It is not only in the flourish on a signature that the adult seeks unconscious release by reverting to the scribbling impulse of childhood (fig. #11). Another outlet of this kind is doodling—the scrawling of nonsense pictures by letting the pencil play while one's attention is elsewhere. However, doodles differ essentially from children's scribbles in that they are not a direct discharge of feeling into movement. Rather, they are symbols, like those of dreams, standing for latent emotional contents or disguised wishes. Doodles have been described by one psychoanalyst as "fugitives of the unconscious." In scribbles, the movement is the salient factor;

29

in doodles, the form is the essence. Doodles may be static constructions, such as dots, geometrical figures, simple line patterns, or they may contain animated forms, such as human faces, animal shapes, or enigmatic grotesques. Doodles, like dreams, are not easy to decipher, but it can be done with the help of the doodler himself. His associations must provide the clue to the emotional experiences that underlie the masked and fragmentary evidence of the doodle.

In discussing some specimens of doodles, we shall begin with those of the intellectual grandfather mentioned above (figs. #6, 7). His doodles were made while he was discussing some scientific project that had no relation whatsoever to an overseas plane trip he was planning. In figure #6, which is a later specimen, the pattern has evolved into a design suggesting an early model of a dirigible. In his childhood, this man had been deeply thrilled by the experience of riding in a Montgolfier balloon at a fair. In figure #7, a list of cities appears alongside the doodle pattern. The word "Paris," the name of the city he longed above all others to revisit, is formed and placed in such a way that it plainly takes on a special significance. His forthcoming trip was to take him to an opposite part of the world, but his long-repressed desire to see Paris again found its unconscious expression in the doodle. It is clear that without the help of relevant data from the subject's life history, the riddle of this doodle could hardly have been solved.

There are, however, certain common symbols whose meaning seems so obvious that they can be interpreted without the help of the subject's associations. Among such symbols are squares and other geometrical forms, which seem to indicate ability to handle complexities. Triangles are indicative of a rationalistic bent of mind; dots, of tension and concentration; spiderwebs, of expanding associations. Dots marking intersections are seen in the doodles of individuals who think precisely.

It is more difficult to ferret out the hidden meaning of such seemingly simple pictures as that in figure #12, which required the use of psychoanalytic method to reveal its significance. The sub-

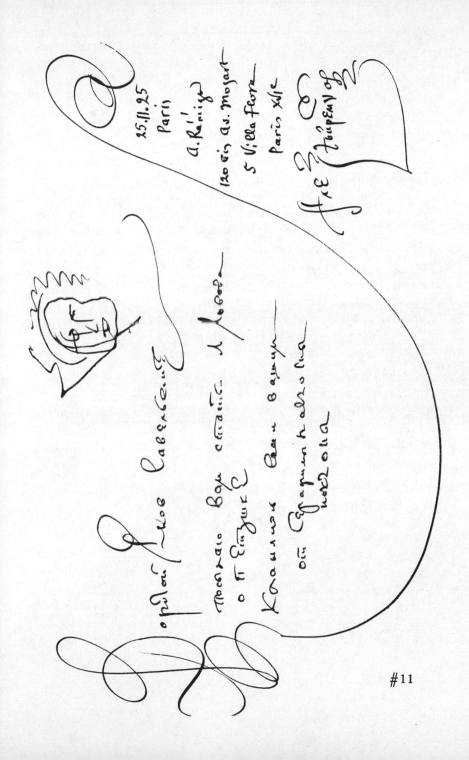

15.11.95
Paris

a. Remi...
120 бис, av. Mozart
5 Villa flora
Paris XVe

#11

ject, a woman, who had been drawing the same picture for thirty years, became aware of its emotional content through the process of free association, and having gained this insight, stopped repeating the doodle without even becoming aware of having dropped it. The drawing invariably consisted of one big treble clef followed by two small ones; by means of a few added strokes, these would be transformed into a big duck followed by two little ducks. Analysis uncovered associations pointing to the big duck as the subject's mother and to the two little ones as her sister and herself—the one nearer to the mother being the sister. The clef referred to an emotional experience of the woman's sixth year.

The designs in figures #13 and #14 cannot be fully elucidated, since the help of the subject has not been available. However, using symbol interpretations accepted in analysis of dreams and Rorschach responses, we can attempt a partial solution. We may safely deduce a compulsive tendency in figures #13 and #14, from the repetitive, meticulous application of the checker motif to fill out an imaginative form. This impression is supported by the fact that

#13

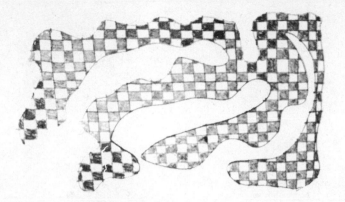

#14

the subject made six doodles of the same kind in the course of an hour. Similar evidence appears in a fence motif superimposed on handwriting (fig. #15). The doodles here discussed were shown to a large number of persons, who, with one exception, all said that the image in figure #13 looks like a male animal and that in figure #14 like a snake. A snake is most frequently interpreted as a phallic symbol. In other cases, as in the plastic creations produced by children in the course of play therapy, a snake may stand for overbearing parents or siblings.[171]

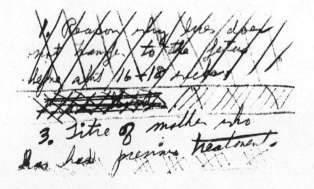

#15

Some years ago Henry Brandon[17] collected doodles made by some noted diplomats while attending an international conference. Eventually he asked Wolff to analyze these "diagrams of the unconscious." The motif in figure #16, Wolff says,

is the continuously repeated picture of a snake. . . . Although the snake is a traditional symbol of danger and aggression, the broad, resting posture of this snake is suggestive of a swan's curved neck. It reflects a desire to be friendly and relaxed. It is interesting to note that the author writes on the reverse side of his sheet the words "conciliatory" and "not retreat." He seems to be reminding himself to be conciliatory but not to back down.

Figure #17* shows a doodle made by a negotiator at a conference

*Courtesy of Joost A. M. Meerlow, M.D.

between representatives of an influential labor union and officials of a large manufacturing corporation. It was shown to a psychoanalyst, who, though unwilling to analyze the personality on the basis of such partial evidence, discussed a few obvious inferences. He felt that the doodle had been made by a man reacting "in the context of a changing situation." He pointed out that at times the doodler was quite unaware of what he was doing, while at others his full attention was concentrated on his drawing. He added that

#17

the subject was using the drawings as an outlet—"projecting his hostilities through his pencil, as it were." The man seemed to have "the feeling of being overpowered . . . caught in a maze. . . . His consciously drawn figures show aggression, suspicion, hostility, and menace. Normal reactions for a man who thinks himself lost in a labyrinth."*

---

* *Business Week*, Mar. 11, 1950.

Knowing little about the drawing in figure #18 except that it was made by a woman writer, we can nevertheless recognize that it has a highly emotional quality, while the structure of the book pile, precariously balanced on pin-point feet, plainly reveals instability.

#18

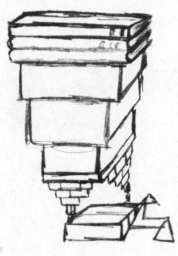

DOODLES AND PSYCHOTHERAPY

Some analytical psychologists, especially C. G. Jung and his followers, make extensive use of doodles as an aid to insight. Anja Mendelsohn has published a set of doodles that illustrate the successive stages of recovery in a case of compulsive neurosis.[102] The patient, a forty-year-old professor, was reluctant when first asked to produce doodles and drawings, but soon became accustomed to the idea and scribbled spontaneously. His first doodles were made at the very beginning of treatment. At this time he drew mainly straight lines bunched together, or single lines that he then crossed through, as if to nullify what he had done (fig. #19). This pattern

recalls the fence motif in figure #15. Mendelsohn concluded that the pattern expressed the patient's opposition to his environment and also his self-destructive feelings. At later stages in his treatment, the fence motif predominated, signifying the barrier of compulsive ideas that was imprisoning him. Subsequent drawings became more lively. Spirals whirled in the fence as the patient's thoughts spun around (fig. #20*a*). At a still later stage, the pattern expanded and the fence disappeared (spec. *b*). At this point the subject began to use colored pencils and shaped the individual spirals into flowers, hearts, etc. When asked what he was thinking about while drawing circles, he replied that he associated them with women's breasts.

 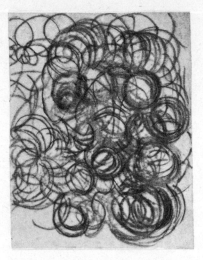

#20   (a)   (b)

The last of the numerous "psychograms" was drawn just before
treatment was terminated. It shows a quite different, well-conceived Gestalt (fig. #21). The circles have disappeared and the
familiar fence pattern is transformed into upswinging lines drawn
in red and blue that suggest a Gothic cathedral window. Mendelsohn applies the Jungian interpretation of colors here: red stands
for love of life, freedom from compulsions (as the feeling function is symbolized, according to Jung, by red); blue means libera-
tion of the mind from compulsion (blue standing for the thinking
function). The graphic production as a whole is interpreted as the
creative projection of an integrated personality.

To regard doodles as projections of repressed emotions and
thoughts, and to seek out their meaning through graphological
interpretation, seems reasonable. The procedure conforms with
other accepted analytical techniques. But the student of graphology must be cautioned that doodles have multidetermined meanings, and can be interpreted only in the light of the associative

38

content. As yet we do not have sufficient objective data to check the validity of our findings. In view of the need of accumulating an adequate body of observations, the study of scribbles and doodles might well be made a special angle of graphological research.

(II)

LEARNING TO WRITE

A child's scribble has no deliberate design. It is not intended to represent any specific thing. Hence there is no concern with position or direction, and the scribble as such can be viewed from any angle. In the scribbling movement, however, the child shows well-defined directional trends. The large majority of children trace their vertical strokes downward; they make horizontal strokes from left to right, and circular strokes in a clockwise direction. A mixed trend, or a tendency to work in the reverse directions, may serve as an early indication of left-handedness or of some other deviation in laterality and orientation.

As the child advances in age, scribbling is superseded by drawing. The product of the four- or five-year-old takes on form and intentional meaning. The child finds his greatest challenge in drawing a man. He makes the figure on the paper right side up; upside down or lateral representation is rare. Significantly enough, such drawings usually show no differentiation of details. A child of four or five years has "global" perception—i.e., he sees a thing as an over-all unity, a Gestalt, and he is as yet unable to fixate parts while maintaining his grasp of the whole.[74]

Educators like Montessori and Decroly realized that teaching methods must take into consideration the "enveloping" perception of the preschool child. They taught children of only four or five to write words as wholes before ever learning about letters. The child would copy the configuration of a word without knowing about its parts, the single letters.[76] He perceived the word as a unit pattern and drew it as a picture. Although this method proved effective, it won no followers.

40

Today, standard practice the world over is to postpone the teaching of writing until the child is at least six years old. Yet many children manifest interest in writing at an earlier age than this; they draw oscillating strokes, making believe that they are writing. The more alert ones try to print their names, copying the letters from book pages, display headlines, etc. Indeed, name writing marks a developmental stage. Gertrude Hildreth[67] found that if a child of six can write his name, he will be found also to have reached a level of mental maturity adequate for his age (figs. #22, #32, #26). Both of the specimens in figure #22 reflect such development; yet even at a glance we can see in the writing of young Franklin D. Roosevelt (spec. *a*) an accuracy of construction that is quite precocious. This child is remarkably clear about what he is doing, and the sample demonstrates his ability at an age between six and seven to recall a form and to reproduce it exactly. It is to be noted that in the precisely shaped *F*, the

(*a*)

(*b*)

#22

41

horizontal bars extending from the vertical letter stem form almost perfect right angles.

ASSOCIATION OF SPEAKING, READING, WRITING

When the child enters school, his fundamental understanding of language is essentially complete. He speaks in relatively correct sentences. However, this ability to communicate certain thoughts and denote states of being has been acquired in a rather haphazard way, while reading and writing demand more systematic learning —although both will be conditioned by the previously developed ability to use language. The basis of the entire process of reading and writing, as well as speaking, is nothing more than the associating of conditioned symbols. To the child, the sight of a particular round object means the anticipated pleasure of play. After further appropriate conditioning, the spoken word "ball" comes to have the same significance. This association is then extended to a specific sequence of four conventional symbols, the characters *b-a-l-l*. Thus associative conditioning is the route by which the child learns to speak, read, and write a language.

In the first year of learning, the two relatively new acquisitions of reading and writing are as a rule still not fully associated with the more familiar function of speech. Thus the first-grade child reads the printed word with no understanding, in a monotonous, dull voice. It is the same with his writing; he just traces letters, without taking in the sense of the word. It is a help to his understanding, however, to utter the word while writing it, because in this way he sees, hears, and writes it simultaneously.

EYE-HAND CONTROL

Everyone has noticed the unsteady or cramped movements of very young children as they propel the pencil over the paper in trying to copy a letter of the alphabet. Only gradually does a child acquire enough eye-hand control to trace the strokes properly and to copy a model accurately.[43] In this effort the swing earlier displayed in scribbling is lost. The child must now concentrate his attention on the letter form, following its outline with his eyes while tracing it with his hand. Often his whole head participates in following the contours. Through practice, he later becomes able to detach himself from the model at intervals, bringing his eyes back to the paper and focusing on the writing itself. When this eye-hand interdependence becomes less imperative, he does not look at each letter separately, but covers two or more letters in one fixation span, and ultimately a group of letters or a whole word.

The most pressing problem in teaching a child to write is to make the process simple and easy for him. Many an adult remembers his penmanship lessons as an ordeal of boredom and discomfort. He reveals the frustrations of his childhood in his embarrassment on having to allow his handwriting to be seen. He will take an apologetic attitude and try to explain why his writing at some moment or other is not as "nice" as he would like it to be —owing to the handicap of a poor pen, or of having written in a hurry, or in a subway train, etc.

The modern approach is to let the child begin writing with letter forms known as printscript. This "simple script" was introduced in Great Britain by Gladys Hardwick, although it is less used there than in the United States. It appeals to the child because of its simple forms, which are the same as those he deals with in reading. Each letter is pieced together stroke by stroke, most of the strokes being straight, and traced downward. This is helpful, since a downward stroke, which bends the fingers toward the body, is the easiest to make in writing. The upward stroke, made by stretching the fingers, imposes more strain. This significant distinction between the two kinds of finger movement arises from differences in the development of motor functions: in the human infant, the ability to contract the muscles for gripping or grasping appears long before the ability to extend the muscles in order to stretch the fingers.

When the child gains some facility in writing, the movements once set off proceed almost automatically. From that point on, it is possible for him to withdraw his attention in part from the motor act, centering it on the verbalization of his thoughts. At this stage of maturation, he is occupied with writing in terms of its social function, communication. The visual, auditory, and motor functions involved in speaking, reading, and writing are now fully co-ordinated and work intimately together. Gradually this association grows so close that reading, writing, and speaking become interchangeable, and a subvocal talking or "silent speech" develops. This process is identified by many behaviorists with thinking.

THE WRITING MODEL

It may be in place here to point out that although printscript is very useful in the initial stages of learning to read and write, no child should be taught to use this type of letter exclusively; at a later stage, a transition from print characters to cursive writing is desirable. Printscript is made up of detached letters built by means of choppy strokes. Because the writer is confined to a

I am learning

which are quite hard but

lot of fun and wish

were here to help me

#23

sequence of short, abrupt motions, he cannot drive the pen at full speed across the paper; the frequent interruptions, the stops and starts, waste both time and energy. Conversely, tracing letters in one sweep, slurring them together within the word, gives the movement continuous momentum and carries the pen from one letter to the next. Even a child who at the outset learns to write a printscript hand (fig. #23) tends, as his speed and skill increase, to transform it into a running or cursive hand (fig. #24). The word cursive is derived from the Latin *currere*, "to run," and was already in use (Latin *cursivus*) as early as the first century A.D., to denote the speedy and fluent hand used by Romans for routine purposes.

Printscript has recently been introduced into most of the private and some of the public schools in this country. For cursive writing many schools use the Palmer system, which makes for a version of the "business hand" developed in American commercial schools. Figure #25 reproduces a sample of Palmer copybook writing. This system advocates a "muscle moving" mode of writing, and the teaching method stresses drill by means of stereotyped exercises performed with the forearm. The student is directed to use only his arm and hand down to the wrist, and is rebuked if he uses the finger muscles. It is expected that the advantages of this kind

#24

Dear Dad —

Have a dinner date tonight so will probably be late. Europe seems to be catching up with me.

45

A B C D E F G H I
J K L M N O P Q R
S T U V W X Y Z
a b c d e f g h i j k
l m n o p q r s t u
v w x y z 1 2 3 4 5 6 7 8 9 0

#25

of penmanship are two. In the first place, as made with relaxed fingers, it avoids cramping. In the second place the rolling movement of the arm upon the muscle pad of the forearm produces firmness and evenness of tracing. But this system of teaching does not take into account that arm movement is a gross motor activity while handwriting is a highly developed skill and, as such, demands the modulation of general gross movements to specific fine movements. Therefore fluency and excellence of writing cannot be achieved without the adaptive use of our fingers.

Another particular feature of the Palmer script is its lack of shading, i.e., downstrokes and upstrokes are traced with equal pressure. Shading results from regular alternation of intensity in writing pressure, corresponding with changes in muscular tension and release during the act of writing. This interplay is the foundation of a natural, flowing writing movement that does not tire the writer.

Palmer writing is also slowed down by superfluous additions— pothooks, hangers, and certain initial and terminal adjustments.

Sudden changes of direction—as in the capital *I*—break the flow of the writing movement by a prescribed full stop. The ideal in cursive writing is continuity of movement and streamlined forms dispensing with those ornaments which hamper fluency and individual rhythm.

ANALYZING CHILDREN'S HANDWRITING

It is a popular notion that a child's handwriting cannot be analyzed, because it does not represent a free expression of personality. Nevertheless, analysis of child handwriting is possible, though not by the procedure employed in that of adults. We must take the school-model letters as a base, and the deviations from this standard as the criteria of evaluation. Ability to copy model letters is expected of the average child. Obviously, when he acquires some degree of skill, he will no longer slavishly follow these models. As his speed increases, conscious design and regularity begin to break down. In the course of trial and error, modifications are made; simplifications and elaborations, additions and omissions occur. The writing pattern of each child embodies a unique combination of such deviations from the standard letter forms, and this gives a clue as to the direction of development of his individual graphic expression.

The degree and quality of these deviations in any given case—whether they are above or below expectation—serve not only as an index of the developmental stage the child has reached in writing. They may also be informative in regard to his motor co-ordination, emotional balance, mental growth, language attainment, etc.

The deviations in a given handwriting specimen become much more revealing when studied comparatively. This means examining a child's handwriting side by side with specimens produced by other children of his group—his school classmates, for example. In such comparisons, differences in maturity and intelligence can readily be recognized.[129]

The letter forms reveal, in each case, what degree of visual form perception is present. Perceptive intelligence comprises many factors. One is the capacity for pattern vision, i.e., the child's ability, on looking at a thing, to get an over-all image of it. A second factor is visual acuity, i.e., the capacity to distinguish small objects or forms and the separations between them. In writing, this means the capacity to differentiate, in a block of letters, the single letter forms and the spaces between them. A further determinant is discrimination of brightness, the capacity by which the child recognizes the difference between figure and ground— i.e., filled-up and blank space—and the difference between light and dark strokes, and thin and thick strokes. An all-important element of perceptive intelligence is recall, which enables the child to recognize the letters and the pattern he sees, and also to bring them back to mind when they are not before him. Finally, there is the factor of capacity for attention, which focuses all the other capacities on the task, so that the child can perceive wholes and their details, discriminate between the qualities of these, and remember and reproduce the form he sees. He becomes able to copy letters, then words: he learns to write.

The samples of children's handwritings shown in figures #26-#30 all represent an exercise in copying one model, written on the blackboard in the first-grade classroom in a public school. Fred, the writer of the specimen shown in figure #26, manifests very

#26

48

clear perception. Putting dots between the words is his deviation from the model. It emphasizes his understanding of the separateness of the words and demonstrates his recognition in a definite way to others. This deviation indicates well-developed mental faculties and social maturity. The copy produced by Allan (fig. #27) reveals that the functions of eye and hand are not yet sufficiently co-ordinated; the child can see what the letter should look like, but cannot draw it accordingly (as indicated by the *n* in "Annex"). Nor does he always catch the word units (as seen in "W ewent").

#27

The handwriting of Sandra (fig. #28) is disorganized. The deviations are qualitatively below expectation. The child does not understand the structure of the letters and how the parts are fitted together (as revealed in the *x*); the letters are disproportionate in size and overlap between lines. The girl who pro-

#28

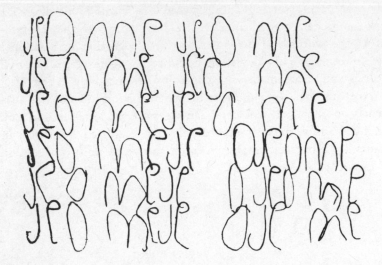

duced the bizarre pattern seen in figure #29 shows a manual skill beyond her age; at the same time, a severe aberration appears. Paying no attention to the model, the child presents an inappropriate, mannered pattern consisting of a few stereotypes that correspond in no wise with the common letter forms. In this performance there is a suggestion of schizophrenic behavior. The teacher, however, rejected this interpretation of the girl's handwriting, saying that she was a model child—always quiet, never talking or creating a disturbance.

Figure #30 shows another kind of variation. Here there is indication of perceptive intelligence but likewise of lack of organization and concentration (seen in the omission of "to the," the extra-large space between "we" and "went," and the running together of "Annex" and "1"). But the striking feature of this specimen is the pictorial supplementation. Apparently the child felt the inadequacy of his writing performance and tried to compensate with a picture illustrating the content of the graphic communication.

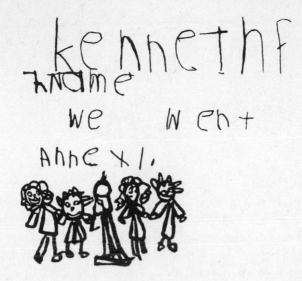

kennethf
hname
we went
Annex/.

#30

REVERSALS AND LEFT-HANDEDNESS

Other deviations pointed up by the comparative procedure may reveal difficulties in word recognition, even in children with rather good perception. Such children tend to change the order of letters or syllables in a word, or to reverse letter forms—e.g., to mix up their printscript *p*'s and *q*'s, or their *d*'s and *b*'s. Figure #31a illustrates such reversal in the case of an intelligent boy of eleven,

#31(a)

Taddle cloth

51

I AM FULL OF LUNCH. #31(b)

who had difficulties in reading and writing. Fig. #31b shows the
letter *u* upside down. Most investigators agree that this shows an
inclination to left-handedness,[66] or confusion in left-and-right[16]
or up-and-down orientation.[54] There may be a preferential use
not only of the left hand but also of the left eye[62, 109] and leg.[83] In
general, these children need outside help and special training in
reading and writing, in order to overcome their difficulties without suffering too much setback,[117] though some will of their own
initiative hit upon a way of adjusting to the conventional mode
of performance.

An illustrative instance is the following. The two best writers
among the second-grade pupils in a convent school were Veronica
and Dennis. Veronica (figure #32 *a*) was right-handed. Dennis
was left-handed—but he wrote with both hands, using two
pencils. He had found this two-handed movement useful even
when he was still only at the scribbling stage. In writing, he
worked on the left half of the page with his left hand, and on the
right half with his right hand. The slant of a letter shows which
hand was used in making it (fig. #32 *b*).

It is easy to understand that efficiency in writing depends to a
great extent also upon a special aptitude known as motor intelligence. There are children who attain the necessary degree of
ease and co-ordination later than others. Even teen-agers may
show inferior motor development. Such a child will contract and
move his tongue, head, and trunk as he traces a letter. The entire
body participates in what should be an exclusively manual per-

Veronica Opp

Veronica Opp

(a)

Dennis Bren

Dennis Bren

(b)   #32

formance. According to developmental standards, a child by the time he is eight years old should be using only those muscle groups which are especially trained for the skilled movement of writing.

A criterion of great value for detecting differences among children is the writing speed they acquire. Although writing speed increases with practice, the development of speed is determined and governed by the basic disposition of the writer, i.e., his personal pace (p. 240): the person who responds quickly by virtue of physiological speed, responds especially fast in the specific manual movements in which he has been trained. The author's experience in her study of identical twins confirms this assumption. In such pairs the two partners were found to have almost equal rates of speed in writing[57]—actually to within a fraction of a second—even though in many cases one of them was handicapped by left-handedness.[55] An individual's characteristic tempo, whether it is quick and decisive or slow and sluggish, is manifested early. The investigation brought out the fact that the child who

Mrs
I sit down for
and talk then
a game for a

shows superior speed in the first grade will be a fast writer as an adult.

Inferior motor development does not necessarily imply mental retardation. Figure #33 presents the handwriting of a very intelligent child with marked scholastic ambition. Although there is good performance in the structuring of letters and the forming of words, the tracing of the stroke (as in "talk") shows poor co-ordination. Any expression of motor inadequacy appearing in a child's handwriting should be followed up by observation over several years, since it may indicate an incipient disorder, or cast light on inadequately recognized difficulties arising from delayed or defective development of language function.

STUTTERING

The stutterer's handwriting reflects his defective somatic and psychic adaptability.[46] In such a child, almost any stressful situation will induce immediate heightening of tension, often followed by total blockage of the intended activity.[90] How this dysfunction manifests itself in handwriting, and how the graphological findings can be put to practical therapeutic use,[146] is explained in chapter XI.

KISSES

In figure #34, the straggling word shows the unco-ordinated, broken strokes of a seven-year-old stutterer of normal intelligence. His manual skill is quite adequate in other activities. Figure #35

Dear mother and Dadd It was nice that you came up today, We head to wright a letter home I norder to get our supper, I will wright a tetter to you Tusday Dont hate to finsh

#35

evidences the writing disorder of a twelve-year-old girl stutterer. The writing is not only ungainly and confused, it also reflects defective articulation (as in "tetter" for "letter," the omission of the *i* in "finish," etc.). Figure #36 presents the improved handwriting of this child after treatment for her speech defect; the script is neat and clear, and misspellings are fewer. That her coordination is still disturbed can be seen in the tremulous and broken connecting strokes between letters, indicating points at

#36

On February 22 we the Birthday of Gorge Washington. He was bor 1732 near Popes Creek Westmoreland County From the time he

which she was temporarily stuck (as between the *r* and *t* and the *h* and *d* in "Birthday," and between the *t* and *m* and the *e* and *l* in "Westmoreland").*

THE UNGAINLY HAND

Despite all educational effort, there is always a small percentage of children whose handwritings are untidy, deficient, ungainly by any judgment. Teachers and graphologists are basically in disagreement about this problem. Teachers, relying on the value of formal training, attempt to correct a displeasing hand by means of forced practice. Graphologists claim that coercive exercises never produce successful results and may even do harm.

Poor penmanship—and the ugly handwriting is merely an extreme instance of this—is not necessarily a serious economic handicap in our typewriter-minded world. But we must not overlook its possible symptomatic significance. It may indicate an emotional maladjustment, neurotic negativism, or a developmental disorder. A disturbed handwriting always calls for special attention, often for a study of the social background of the child, as well as physical and psychological examinations, supplemented by a graphological profile. In the author's own work, such procedures

---

* Specimens courtesy Deso Weiss, M.D.

have in many cases led to the uncovering of underlying emotional conflicts and thereby to improvement. The range of problems that may appear in such situations is suggested in the following outline histories.

A boy of ten, who showed good intelligence and remarkable skill in drawing, had a handwriting that was literally an offense to the eye. His letters were distorted and badly proportioned, the strokes were jerky and overran the lines; odd little pictures were scrawled in his margins. Despite suggestions offered as a means to improving his handwriting, he did not change. In school he also acted as the class clown and was a disciplinary problem.

We invited the boy to come to the handwriting research laboratory, asking him to help us with some drawings. He came gladly, and drew what we requested. Asked to label his drawing, he produced a rather attractive and ornate heading. We repeated the experiment, and while the boy was drawing we used a mirror to observe his behavior and facial expressions. Once we caught a look of great emotion. He had just finished one of his odd little pictures, a Mickey Mouse driving a car, when he suddenly stopped short, stared at the paper, and then wrote in tiny letters at the bottom of the page, "Why did I do it?" But he instantly pulled himself together and wrote his own answer, smacking of his usual clownishness: "Because the sky is green and the lawn is blue."

To get at just what that meant, we probed into the boy's family life, and at the same time analyzed his handwriting in its consecutive stages back through the years. We discovered that originally he had had a fairly pleasing hand, which changed suddenly for the worse. We learned that the boy was living with his father, but only making visits to his mother, who had separated from the father and remarried. Each parent would question the child about things occurring in the home of the other. Not wishing to turn informer, because of previous unpleasant experiences in conveying information, the boy began to act in a silly and clownish way. By this behavior he was trying to posture as too childish and irresponsible to be able to report or even notice anything. But once he slipped: he told something that was damaging to his mother. Ensuing repercussions made him feel guilty and unhappy. We established the fact that the change in his handwriting set in at that time.

It was clear that the situation called for a change of environment for the child. With the aid of the school medical advisor, we magnified the importance of a minor lung ailment and persuaded the parents to send the boy to Switzerland for his health. He stayed there for a year. As he regained his emotional balance, his handwriting improved.

A girl of eight had an ungainly hand that was steadily becoming worse. An indignant teacher made the child write a hundred times, "I will improve my handwriting." This did not help, of course; actually the chief trouble, lack of co-ordination, became more marked. The teacher misconstrued the girl's behavior as a form of aggression. When we examined the writing, we promptly suggested a neuropsychiatric examination. This resulted in a diagnosis of chorea, a serious nervous disorder, the unco-ordinated writing being one of its symptoms. The little patient

#37

the very cold
ns are the arctic
the antarctc.
er are near
e north pole and
south pole. Betw
tween the hot

underwent treatment and returned to school after six months of rest. Her handwriting became more normal, but the doctor advised the teacher not to overtax the child with writing.

Figure #37 shows the laborious writing of a boy who was clinically classified as schizophrenic. The characteristics of this monotonous, crowded handwriting, with its stereotypic letters, fall into what is called the schizophrenic pattern. In figure #29 we have a similar pattern produced by a first-grade child, and figures #59 and #326 show such writing patterns in an adolescent and in an adult.

HANDWRITING IN
PUBERTY AND ADOLESCENCE

Handwriting develops steadily during the primary-school period. The child generally acquires sufficient facility and precision to write a firm and controlled hand, at a pace that suits his ability and temperament. Individual differences in display of force and speed, in neatness, and in aesthetic organization of the pattern, become more and more apparent. An orderly and tidy-minded child strives to write as "nicely" as possible, and this slows his speed. But he feels compensated for the curb on his natural pace by the merit of his performance (fig. #38). Another child,

#38

being less careful, will write as fast as possible; he is unwilling to brake the rush of his ideas, though his hand cannot keep up with it. Thus he moves over the page with haste, producing somewhat distorted, clipped letter forms. The indolent or lazy or less able child will give a poorer performance, marked by inaccurate, sloppy, or incomplete letters even when he is writing at a slow pace (fig. #39).

The process of development toward graphic individuality varies in different children, though it must be recognized that, for all

60

their differences, all handwritings of children up to the age of puberty bear the common stamp of school-imposed forms. As development proceeds, the fairly well-balanced handwriting of the prepubescent undergoes marked changes. It is normal to find a picture of temporary confusion at about the twelfth year. The script becomes less pleasing and less regular. It grows labile both in slant and in shading, and shows extravagance and looseness in regard to loops and stems, which may encroach upon the writing line above or the one below. Some writings at this stage are splotched and smeary in spite of all of the teacher's emphasis on neatness.

These flaws foreshadow the developmental stage of puberty and also the personality changes brought about by this process. At puberty, when sex characteristics develop and the organism reaches a more adult stage, new needs arise. Erotic urges become more and more pronounced and often conflict with environmental restraints; this leads to emotional tension and aggressive impulses.

#39

GRAPHIC REFLECTION OF CONFLICTS

The conflicts arising from the child's attempts at adjustment are reflected in his handwriting. There are certain graphic peculiarities that are of symptomatic significance. Youngsters brimming over with vigor, and unable to control themselves, write with sudden bursts of pressure. We find preposterous exaggeration in size, as an attempt to compensate crushed self-esteem. There may

Dear Grandpa.

The Bike was
no good at all
spare parts not
possible.
no brakes or
tyres.

Peter

#40

be fluctuations in slant, or an extreme backward slant, concealing and at the same time revealing inner insecurity, exaggerated emotional responses, or defiance or withdrawal (chapter X).

Figure #40, showing the handwriting of an English boy at the height of the puberty crisis, presents a composite picture of all the disorders noted above. Strokes of great tension and aggressive expression, exaggeration in size, and a fluctuating slant, all add up to an expression of the writer's problem—the conflict between a growing sense of independence and the weight of parental

Dear Aunt Lolta.

Toni told me that you did not recieve my letter of thanks for my birthday present. I do not know how this happened because I distinctly remember posting it. However I will thank you again and I hope you will accept this apology.

yours sincerly

Peter.

#41

authority. The boy is in rebellion against family restraints. In the reduced size of the salutation ("Dear Grandpa") and the over-emphasis of his signature, he minimizes the standing of his grand-father and accentuates his own importance. This self-enlargement in order to overcome inferiority feelings is literally underlined in the slight, sparing stroke under the salutation and the sweeping, forceful line under "Peter."

The boy's handwriting at a later date attests the degree of emotional balance he had by then attained (fig. #41). It is easy to recognize the difference between the two scripts. The change lies

63

not only in the size and organization of the pattern and in the quality of the stroke; it appears above all in the emotional expression of the writing. The narcissistic attitude displayed in the earlier hand has disappeared; adjustment and some subdued frustration are apparent, while aggressiveness has given way to sensuous warmth (p. 265). Despite the differences, however, the two specimens have certain basic qualities in common. Both reflect superior intelligence, most obviously in the integrated and original formation of certain words (as the "not" in both scripts).

These specimens serve to show that the exaggerations and distortions found in the writing pattern of the pubescent are temporary manifestations. They must be regarded as expectable symptoms of normal processes of change.

EXPERIMENTAL AND STATISTICAL STUDIES

In order to obtain precise data as to how the changes of puberty and maturation affect writing development, the Institute for Handwriting Research of Budapest in 1931 instituted an eight-year research project, under government auspices.[51] More than two thousand normal school children, ranging in age from ten to eighteen years, were tested, the majority of them twice a year for eight years. Several hundred maladjusted children, such as left-handers, stutterers, and deaf-mutes, as well as children of known asocial behavior, were also studied for comparison.[53]

THE GRAPHODYNE

The tests were centered particularly on the factors of speed, pressure, and continuity, and the measurements were obtained by use of a newly devised instrument called the graphodyne.[50] This apparatus (fig. #42) is so constructed that it affords a mechanical transmission of writing pressure from a movable stylus to a recording device, by means of two tambours. The stylus consists of a metal tube, slightly heavier than a fountain pen, containing a lever. A pencil lead is affixed to the shorter end of the

lever, and one tambour is attached to the longer end. While the subject is writing, the variations in his writing pressure affect the air-filled tambour. These pressure changes are transmitted through an air hose and a second tambour to an ink writer arranged to inscribe a tracing on a paper tape moving at a uniform rate of speed. The tracing thus obtained shows the time consumed and the intensity of the pressure exerted in the writing movement. The time factor is represented by the horizontal co-ordinate (abscissa), whose length in millimeters, converted to seconds, shows the time consumed in the writing. The height of the vertical co-ordinate (ordinate) at any given point, converted to grams, shows the intensity of the writing pressure at that point (figs. #43, #44).

#43

65

Thus the tracings afford quantitative and qualitative measurements of the dynamic components of the writing movement, such as pressure and speed, interruptions of flow, and variations of emphasis, all of which are constituent parts of the supposedly intangible phenomenon labeled rhythm. The findings thus far obtained with the use of the graphodyne have quite justified Jean d'Udine's definition of rhythm as "the result of the relationship between the phenomenon of duration and the phenomenon of intensity."

#44

In the graphodyne tracing shown in figure #44, we can analyze the four units of the pattern that correspond to the four words of the phrase "United States of America" as follows: The first word was written without a break, the two final crests showing the pressure exerted and the time consumed in making the *i* dot and the *t* bar respectively. In the second unit the first broad crest is the result of the movement that produced the letter S; the points at which the curve falls to the base indicate the breaks in the flow of movement, and the tall crest at the end represents the coupled *t* bars. The "of" was produced by a single, uninterrupted movement. The fourth unit records the writing of the word "America," which was done with two major breaks in the movement, the last crest representing the *i* dot.

The data accumulated in this investigation were subjected to statistical analysis. This afforded a basis for the establishment of a scale for comparing any child's writing performance with the norms for its age and sex.

DEVELOPMENTAL SEX DIFFERENCES

In regard to sex differences, it was found that speed and pressure are respectively about equal in boys and girls around the age of eleven. With the termination of childhood, however, the average girl writes more quickly than the average boy. Qualitative differences in neatness and aesthetic aspect are pronounced, and girls were found to surpass boys of the same age in attaining a mature handwriting. This fully accords with the known fact that physiological maturation, with respect to both sexual and skeletal development, sets in and is completed earlier in girls than in boys. In general, girls mature about two years earlier than boys. It may be pointed out in passing that this fact is not sufficiently taken into account in co-educational school policies, though it

Writing Speed of Thirteen-year-old Boys and Girls

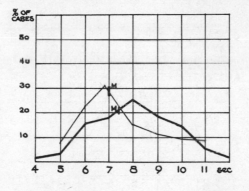

	Min.	Max.	Mean	St'd. Dev.
133 Boys ———	3.70 sec	11.30 sec	7.50 sec	1.66 sec
140 Girls ———	4.10 sec	10.90 sec	7.00 sec	1.05 sec

#45

is at the root of many of those difficulties arising in the course
of further development which are popularly laid at the door of
mother fixation, etc.

The investigation showed that sex differences in speed and
pressure are greatest at the time of onset of puberty, which generally occurs at thirteen in girls and at fourteen or later in boys
(fig. #45). The difference in handwriting development found at
this time reflects the difference in rate of sociosexual maturation
as between the sexes. As adolescence proceeds, the difference
gradually diminishes, and at about the age of eighteen there are
no longer any significant differences in speed and pressure between
the two groups (fig. #46).

Writing Speed of Eighteen-year-old Boys and Girls

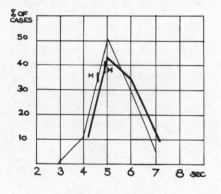

	Min.	Max.	Mean	St'd. Dev.
183 Boys ———	3.40 sec	6.74 sec	4.94 sec	0.90 sec
136 Girls ———	2.52 sec	6.40 sec	4.70 sec	0.98 sec

#46

(a) *June 15, 1946*

of blood, more than all
rbined. One other thing
down is that when
on does not wish that

(b) *Dec. 17, 1946.*

his thigh and leg. During this
& flying lesson. I was knocked
5 feet and landed on my side.
d my knee and arm which
the elbow. Boy when the #47

DIAGNOSTIC VALUE OF GRAPHIC INDICES

Educators and others concerned with the guidance of children ought to realize that the changes that appear in handwriting during pubescence are highly informative. They indicate whether the child is passing through the pubertal period smoothly or with some ups and downs, and whether the process is gradual or precipitate, normally timed or retarded.

Figure #47 presents two specimens of the writing of a normal boy, produced six months apart; the more fluent and integrated quality of specimen *b* reflects a normally timed maturation.

69

the graveyard of the little church rest the lovers in peace, perhaps in a better world than this which has treated them so cruelly

#48 (a)

Figure #48 shows the handwriting of a twelve-year-old boy with a medical diagnosis of obesity and retardation of genital development. After six weeks of glandular therapy, definite evidence of pubertal changes appeared. Handwriting specimens were obtained both prior to and after the first six weeks of medication. The pretreatment script (spec. *a*) is neat, slanted to the right, and fairly conformable to school norms. An observer trained to estimate writing speed will easily discern slowness in this performance. As evidence, the outlines of the *l* loops are tremulous; there are large gaps between words, indicating that there is no flow in the writing, and similarly no flow in the train of thought; the motion is particularly slow at the ends of words. The writing pressure is heavy, although within the standard limits for the boy's age level. All told, this is the hand of a school child, submissive, careful, concentrating on penmanship rather than on fluent communication of thought.

After the six weeks of treatment, the boy had lost seventeen pounds, pubic hair had appeared, and the genitals had developed to a fairly normal size. Specimen *b* was written after these changes had occurred. The most obvious changes in the writing may be pointed out as follows: The pen is now driven at full speed, with medium pressure; the rhythmic alternation of thick and thin strokes indicates smooth writing movement. The formerly tremulous outlines of the loops have become firm, and the letters, which

the street
If you take advantage of these
rules you will know that you
doing your share toward seeing

#48 (b)

formerly slanted rightward, are now upright. This uprightness
is an expression of control and independence (p. 192). In forming
his letters, the boy deviates from copybook standards—he omits
details, leaves loops unfinished, gives them exaggerated size: the
writing has become a casual, spontaneous, and expressive longhand.
Thus the boy's development in handwriting during the six-week
period of treatment kept pace with the precipitate maturation
of both his body and his personality.*

A contrast to this story of retarded pubescence is offered in
the plight of a fourteen-year-old school boy who experienced a
rather sudden pubertal development. One of the best students
in his class, with a high I.Q., he wrote clever compositions and
had a fast and fluent handwriting. Although his letters were
clearly formed and purposefully simplified, they were childlike
in quality. When after a three months' summer vacation he returned to school for the new term, his first homework composition
drew from his teacher the accusation that it had been written by
his father. Despite the boy's protestations, the teacher remained
incredulous, since the handwriting as well as the contents of the
paper were as mature as those of an adult. A test of the boy's
handwriting on the blackboard finally convinced the teacher that
a sudden change had indeed taken place both in the handwriting
and in the personality of the pupil.

---

* Case history and specimens, courtesy Max A. Goldzieher, M.D.

Disturbed handwritings may reflect functional disorders accompanying the process of maturation. The physiological process of pubescence depends primarily on the maturation and functioning of the endocrine glands. The interrelations of the glandular system are highly involved; hence a variety of factors contribute to the onset and completion of puberty. The response of the body as a whole, and especially of the central nervous system, to hormonal influences, must also be considered. In view of the enormous complexity of the processes involved, it is not surprising that physical, emotional, and intellectual maturation may not keep pace with one another.

Certain definite kinds of graphic irregularities and defects are specific indices of the imbalances of the pubertal period. Uneven pressure produces inappropriate swoops and swells (fig. #49).

#49

Lack of firm control causes the stroke to skid. When the movement deviates from its intended direction while shaping a letter, it creates jerky, tremulous, or broken forms, e.g., a crooked or

#50

twirled loop in an *l* (fig. #50), or a lopsided, twisted, or broken stem in a *t* (fig. #51). Changes in direction induced by inhibition block the nib of the pen as it moves over the paper; the writer's effort to overcome this blockage causes the pen to scratch and spatter ink. When the free flow of the movement is temporarily halted and the hand weighs heavily down on the pen point, a

72

black spot may result. Such spots, called nodules, appear as the graphic expression of emotional disturbance; they may also indicate circulatory, menstrual, or other disorders.

The bizarre handwriting shown in figure #50 is that of a sensitive, introspective girl whose menstrual periods began at the early age of ten and a half. Her emotional and mental growth lagged behind her precocious physiological development. She was harassed by feelings of obviously sexual origin, which she could neither understand nor fully control. She was attending a convent school, and tried to rise above the conflicts through religious devotion. The repression of her impulses led to inner tension, guilt feelings, and anxiety. Her handwriting shows elongated, overshooting, twirled loops (h, l, g), with the upstroke covering the downstroke. Where the bend of the stem forms the head of the

#51

loop, there is a nodule. These loop anomalies pantomime the constriction and inhibition of the girl's movements, arising from anxiety and defensive passivity. The graphic gesture reveals an attempt to conceal something of which the writer is ashamed.

It has been pointed out above that the various graphic peculiarities and defects associated with pubertal development are not abnormal. They are pathological symptoms only when they persist late into or beyond adolescence (figs. #127, #297).

WRITING PRESSURE IN ADOLESCENCE

The investigation referred to above yielded some rather important observations concerning the variability of writing pressure in adolescence. Pressure phenomena are difficult to judge by eye; hence it was necessary to develop a procedure that would afford a more accurate estimate. It was primarily to meet this need that the graphodyne was devised. Measurements made with the help of this instrument disclosed that as children advance in age, their writing pressure shows a progressive decline, which finally levels off with the onset of puberty. This level is maintained through the adolescent years, except for a short crisis period, in which a remarkable break suddenly occurs. Pressure drops to an unprecedented low; within less than a year, however, it jumps back to the writer's former level. This postpubertal phenomenon occurs abruptly in boys at some point around the seventeenth year. The graph in fig. #52 shows measurements of three adolescents. The disturbance is less pronounced in girls, and seems to set in earlier.

#52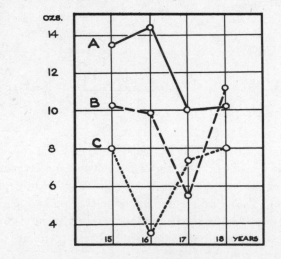

It is particularly to be noted that this extraordinary drop in the intensity of pressure is a unique phenomenon in the writing life of the normal individual. Such a low point is never again reached. It would seem that a lessening of tension occurs at about the time when a generally relaxed behavior pattern replaces the high-strung reactions of puberty.

It is logical here to ask what is going on in the writing subject during such a sudden breakdown of pressure. Does it mean a temporary slackening of vital energy, or only a reduction of tension owing to the fact that he has come to a less critical, more relaxed acceptance of life? Could statistical analyses perhaps furnish clues to a correlation between this temporary state and the incidence of nihilistic moods, accidents, or attempts at suicide?

Freedom, abandon, and release from tension appear in the script reproduced in figure #53. It is the handwriting of a healthy, extraverted adolescent, a highschool student, who still lacks the balance and control of a fully matured personality. The four handwritings shown in figures #54-#57 are those of other healthy

#53

Dear Jim,

We miss you very be back home with all we are wishing, we all Conflict would come to an

75

attempts to escape the tax or trickes by the famous "faux- were severely punished. The pla

#54

adolescents, in this case college students. The writer in figure #54 was an alert, clever boy, quick of temper and slightly lacking in maturity. The script of figure #55 was penned by an intellectually mature, soft-spoken, very cautious boy, who was totally uninterested in athletics. Figure #56 shows the writing of a girl of

therefore it would cause a demand

#55 *lead to inflation: Therefore, in employment, taxation is the best*

sixteen, brought up in a typical Southern milieu; she loves music, and her graphic expression reflects inner harmony and good adjustment to her environment. The script in figure #57 is that of a girl who was popular in her circle, and interested in boys; she settled conflicts by "smiling pretty."

#56

During the last century when they were the originators of many ideas and ways of

76

with colors blending in together
an indefinite atmosphere.
The main theme of his works

#57

GRAPHIC INDICES OF BEHAVIOR DISORDERS

Figures #58 and #59 present handwritings of emotionally disturbed adolescents. The script reproduced in figure #58 shows compulsive features. From the report of a clinical psychologist, it was learned that the subject had developed a system of defense manifested in contractive gestures; he was relinquishing his elbow-room. Anxiety was reducing his initiative, causing him to shrink within himself and to lose interest in the environment. These states of feeling are clearly reflected in his graphic expression. He confines his writing to one third of the page. He jams letters within the words, and his strokes overlie each other, particularly in the *n*'s. His capital *I*—the representative of the ego (p. 163)— approximates a closed circle. This formation suggests the universally known symbol of a magic circle used to ward off outward evil. Its repetitive-compulsive use stands for a ritualistic gesture

#58

I hope you will
be able to understand
these illustrations.
I like airplanes, to draw
comics, play chess, etc.
I think I know quite
a lot about aircraft.

77

(p. 327). In the same way, the space limitation the boy imposes upon himself reflects his introversive shrinking from the outer environment and even from his own inner self.*

Organic immaturity may also be a factor in adolescent behavior disorders. The boy of seventeen and a half who produced the specimen shown in figure #59 has registered infantilism and a

#59

bizarre mannerism designed to help him to save face and to resist anything that would assail his own routine. Although he was of average intelligence, his school record was poor. He was utterly lacking in ambition, his main concern being to find an easy way of getting along and to evade environmental demands. Persisting infantile self-love prevented empathy and emotional growth, deprived him of the competitiveness and initiative of the normal adolescent, and hindered him in developing normal heterosexual interests.

Figures #60-#62 present the handwritings of three juvenile delinquents.* The first boy (fig. #60) committed murder; the second (fig. #61) went to prison for petty larceny, and had also tried his hand at safecracking. The third (fig. #62), a weakling and male prostitute, had run the gamut of asocial behavior. These three specimens, obtained in the course of a penmanship drill in

---

* Courtesy Rose Wolfson, Ph.D.

78

#60

#61

#62

a reformatory school, show the inability of the writers to follow instructions and conform to norms. Their personal impulses and compulsive images intrude upon and break down the conventional symbols. It does not take too much ideographic imagination to see the ferocious gesture in the lower part of the capital S in figure #60, or the image of a jimmy in figure #61, or the contortions of a spineless body in figure #62.

(IV)

PERSONAL STYLE

Writing is a learned performance. For all its range of variability, its basic forms are imposed upon the writer. After he acquires a degree of manipulative skill, he refashions these forms in his own individual way. They begin to carry an expression of the style that characterizes everything he feels, says, and does. The style is the man, as the saying goes.

When can handwriting be deemed to have a style? And how much of this style, once developed, is the writer's own? How much of it is his uniquely contrived mode of expression, and how much of it has been taken over from a model? We know that the advent of puberty gives special impetus to individualization and brings with it a tendency to break away from standard forms. Writing style therefore develops in step with maturation and after adolescence tends to become personally distinctive.

In writing, there are fundamentally two ways of deviating from the common model[143]—by simplification, or by elaboration (fig. #63). Simplification favors economy of time and motion by dis-

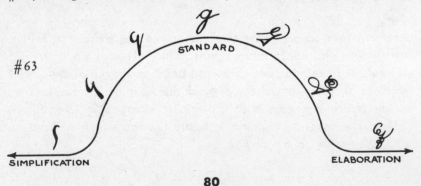

#63

SIMPLIFICATION   ELABORATION

80

I remembered a few
things which should
have gone on the

#64

carding of the unessential (fig. #64). It may go so far as to strip the letter to the skeleton, making it clear-cut and precise, or approaching an extreme of bareness or carelessness. Elaboration adds something to the plain form and garnishes it (fig. #65); the writing then takes on a rich and ample or too ornate or complicated character.[91]

Aside from these fundamental ways of varying the model, the writer may encompass a larger or smaller amount of space in shaping his letters; this results correspondingly in ample or in lean

#65

forms. The simple yet ample letters of Alexis Carrel (fig. #66) reflect the way in which this writer's literary style is designed to put in simple terms the difficult and abstruse subject matter with which he deals. Figure #67 reproduces the signature of Robert Koch, pioneer "microbe hunter." His handwriting is lean and almost stripped.

#66 *A Carrel*   #67 *R. Koch.*

THE LINEAR AND THE PICTORIAL PATTERN

In looking at handwritings, we can generally discern two types of pattern making—the linear or functional, and the pictorial or spatial. The linear pattern carries the movement of the writing with little concern for form. Straight lines and angles predominate; loops and ovals are extremely lean. The down- and upstrokes inscribe a simple pattern, sometimes almost like the tracing in a cardiogram (figs. #68, #284). The pictorial pattern,

#68

on the other hand, allows for the play of forms (figs. #69, #286). Generally, simplification and lean letters associate with the linear pattern, while elaborate and ample shapes consort with the pictorial pattern. This leads to the question as to which type of person produces the one or the other kind of writing pattern.

Studies of psychological types confirm the observation that the linear or graphlike pattern marks the motor-minded person, who

#69

is moved less by visual than by kinesthetic experiences. Such individuals react to the "inner rhythm" of structure and process. They tend to abstract thinking, and have a preference for non-objective modes of expression.

The pictorial pattern is associated with the visual-minded person, who perceives the world predominantly through the medium of form. His mental processes tend to produce concrete images supported by what is known as photographic memory. This type of individual is likely to be dependent upon the stimulation of visible form, and will surround himself with pictures and art

#70

objects. In his handwriting, there is definite emphasis on the design of letters, tending often to picture-like elaboration.

Another finding is that individuals who ornament their handwriting have a liking for the "trimmings" of life. They are attracted by embellishments, by showy, pretentious things. Some carry elaboration of details to such a point that the core of the letter form is smothered or lost (fig. #70). There are people for

83

whom there is no cake without icing: such a person will clutter his writing with adornments, and the superfluity of detail creates complexity and confusion (fig. #71).

— Nor must we think that this all other feeling. Rather this

#71

He who lives simply and purposefully writes a simple hand. Figure #72 reproduces part of a manuscript page of the autobiography of Alvin Johnson, president emeritus of the New School

#72

We expected to learn nothing in school, and we were not disappointed. The teachers tried hard to make us write according to the Spencerian copybook, to do simple arithmetic, to read aloud, to spell, to do the geography of New England. We always began with Maine

for Social Research. On the other hand, simplification down to the naked core reveals a dry, ascetic nature (fig. #64). Oversimplification, carried to the point of omitting essentials, shows a fanatic focusing of attention upon impersonal interests, to the exclusion of everything else. An example in point is the signature of Joseph Goebbels (fig. #73); here the letters *r, o, e,* and *s* are reduced to

#73

vertical strokes, and upper loops are entirely discarded—all this revealing extreme tension and stubbornness of conviction.

An illegible, heedless script may be the expression of a careless or sloppy person, or of one to whom life means nothing. Figure #74 shows the handwriting of a young man who, although endowed with a vigorous body and a good mind, gives little concern

#74

to his profession, and cares even less about his personal safety. He never becomes "serious" about girls. A reckless driver, he persistently flirts with death. This small, lax handwriting, with its half-completed forms, in association with the well-known devil-may-care attitudes of the writer, may be connected with a disintegration of personality and depressive moods.

Elaboration or simplification, ampleness or leanness, and linear or spatial patterning are basic criteria of graphic expression. It is necessary to ascertain whether the resort to the one or the other is genuine or artificial. There are no qualities so highly rated by graphologists as naturalness and unpretentiousness in writing.

THE SPONTANEOUS AND THE ARTIFICIAL HAND

A formally stylized hand, regardless of its possible artistic appeal, is deficient in those aspects of individual expression which for the graphologist supply the key to personality. An artificial style may stem either from a desire to devise an aesthetic or sophisticated form of self-representation, or from an effort to imitate the handwriting pattern of some person of importance. Thus it may stand simply for a pretense. It may be, on the other hand, a mask used to cover up the natural mode of expression. The use of some impersonal, socially sanctioned pattern may become so fixed that it is difficult to determine whether the lack of spontaneity is due to formalistic emulation or to an attempt at disguise.

We find artificial handwritings among victims of educational systems designed to conform personality to rigid molds: such scripts are impersonal and mechanical. A stilted formal style was developed and taught for many years in various church schools and military academies under the old Austro-Hungarian empire and in Germany (fig. #75). Crépieux-Jamin coined the term

#75

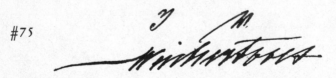

"*Sacré Coeur* handwriting"[22] to denote a certain mannered, angular style of feminine handwriting taught in French convent schools (fig. #76). A similar artificial style of writing taught in "ladies' seminaries" in this country was derived, according to Osborn,[116] from a pattern once favored in Great Britain and also used by many women in Canada. Although it was not taught in public schools in the United States, thousands of women imitated

#76

it, consciously or unconsciously, because it was considered fashionable. In Europe especially a style of this kind, labeled "aristocratic," has long been distinctively the "society hand." Apparently there are people all over the world who try to possess themselves of a writing pattern that is believed to be the hallmark of a social class higher than their own. But the attempt to acquire a style that is not one's own invariably results in a lifeless combination of outlines that lacks the distinctive élan of a natural hand. Such artifacts do not mislead the graphologist, for the real features of the writer always show through the mask (fig. #77).

#77

There are few personalities strong enough to maintain a style of life peculiar to themselves alone. Most persons feel secure only when they are following a general trend in attitudes and manners, and wearing the styles of hats and neckties that all others wear. To break away from the pattern of one's group, to be somewhat different, to follow one's own bent, to write one's own hand—this calls for the courage of an independent mind and some creative potential, i.e., originality. At the same time, a personal style may grow out of an interplay of imitative and creative forces. These interact to build up special expressive attitudes that, taken together, we call personal style.

88

CONSISTENCY IN PERSONAL STYLE

It is a most impressive observation that the same personal style appears consistently in all the aspects of an individual's activity—the manner of expression that is seen in his handwriting is found likewise in his speech, his gestures and his gait, his thoughts and his creative work.[3] In a study entitled *Handschrift und Zeichnung*, Max Seeliger reproduces side by side the handwritings and the drawings of many of the great artists of all times, and shows how the art product and the script are in each case consistent in style of expression.[147] One of the most significant demonstrations of this phenomenon of consistency in personal style was carried out by Arnheim.[5] Specimens of the handwritings of Michelangelo, Leonardo da Vinci, and Raphael, bearing no identification, were submitted to a group of judges who knew the works of these artists but had never seen their script. The subjects were asked to match the handwritings to the personalities they belonged to. Their pairings turned out correct to the extent of about 84 per cent, as against the statistical expectancy of 33 per cent.

Plate I and II similarly demonstrate the relationship between script and art product. Plate I shows side by side a detail from the painting *Poplars at Giverny* by the French impressionist Claude Monet, and his writing. The technique of his unconnected, loose brushstrokes corresponds strikingly with his disjointed, "impressionistic" script. Plate II juxtaposes the handwriting of a contemporary sculptor, Jacques Lipchitz, with one of his characteristic sculptures. The same type of curves are evident in both, in striking fashion.

INFLUENCES OF TIME AND PLACE

It is a truism that no matter how independent or individualistic a man may be, he is marked by his epoch, by the collective culture of his time and place. As we turn from one historical period to

(Courtesy of Curt Valentin Gallery, New York)

91

another, we see how personal styles are conformed to prevailing cultural patterns. For instance, the contrast between the Romanesque and the Renaissance spirit is exemplified in the difference between the handwriting of the Emperor Frederick Barbarossa (fig. #78) and that of Ludovico Ariosto (fig. #79).

#78

In addition to the broad influence of the cultural epoch, there are other general factors that make for stylistic qualities. Just as a national flavor marks gait and voice, speech and gesture among the people of a given nation, so national characteristics appear also in writing style. The differences between the emotional expressiveness of Latins, the rigid, disciplined behavior of Germans, and the traditional restraint of Englishmen, are universally recognized. We find corroboration of these differences in examining the school copybooks of the respective nations or ethnic groups.

The systems of writing taught in France, Italy, and Spain, for example, as well as in Great Britain and the United States, are based upon rounded letter shapes and curved connections. Preference is given to rightward slant, sweeping strokes, and extended

#79

92

t bars, all of which are indicative of a free outflow of emotional expression. In Germany until quite recently an angular style prevailed in the teaching of writing. This style demands a strictly regulated way of writing, with rigid upstrokes and downstrokes meeting in angles (fig. #181). This necessitates an abrupt stop at the point of the angle, which requires precision and control. The difference between the two types of writing action is best appreciated in actually carrying out the movements of each. Thus we shall easily experience the contrast between the free sweep of the one and the goose-step motion of the other.

The difference is well illustrated in the handwritings of two men of similar occupation representing respectively the divergent national backgrounds here under discussion. Figure #80 represents the handwriting of Ferruccio Busoni, the pianist-composer, who

#80

93

Ich bitte dieses Stück nur rückwärts — also à la "Krebs" — zu spielen ;
es wird dann für "Dissonanzenräuber" u. "tonalitätslüsterne" Ohren

wesentlich erträglicher klingen.

Demich. Rückführung vorbehalten

#81

was of Italian extraction, and figure #81 that of his contemporary, Max Reger, a German-born composer and conductor; both specimens are written in German. Figure #82 shows the handwriting of the French dramatist and actor, Sacha Guitry. A contrast to

#83

these three specimens is offered in the handwriting of a British officer (fig. #83). This script mirrors self-assurance and the traditional Anglo-Saxon restraint; it shows unmistakably the socially ingrained control of gesture that is such an essential feature of the behavior pattern of an Englishman.

THE AMERICAN HAND

Although the people of the United States and of Great Britain communicate in the same language, it may be asked whether there is a difference between their respective handwritings. The answer is that the cultural patterns of the two countries are so unlike that they result in different styles of life and thereby also in different expressive patterns.[140]

The first observation that results from examination of a large number of American handwritings is that they show no consistent common style. Possibly this is due to the mixture of trends that frequently subsists in personal life in America. Margaret Mead[98] points out that in the lives of the majority of Americans two contrasting patterns are operative—the one to which they are bred at home, and the one they acquire at school and in the outside world. In some cases, the contrast springs from a juxtaposition of cultures—American ways side by side with Polish, Italian, Irish, or other racial or parochial mores. However, the explanation is to be sought not only in the effects of this composite cultural orientation, but in the influences of regional and socio-economic factors as well. Unevenness in handwriting style is especially marked when the writer has received his primary training in penmanship abroad, on the basis of a different language and a different type of schooling, or when he has been obliged, at an adult age, to adapt his hand to an American system such as Palmer writing or printscript.[116]

In European countries students are compelled to accept one standard way of writing. In the United States, however, a greater degree of freedom and diversity prevails, and various writing systems are in use. Americans, unlike Europeans, are even permitted to write with either hand. Yet, even though there are no rigid traditions compelling Americans to adopt a standard writing pattern, the motive of group emulation or imitation tends to make them write more or less alike. In the same way that conformist patterns operate in consumer, college, and political behavior, so do they put their seal on handwriting. Hence, while American writing is informal, it is not very individualistic. And Europeans, curiously enough, while they begin with uniform standards, tend in greater degree toward individualization.

The question as to what distinguishes American handwriting might be answered thus: We can discover what is truly American by studying what is English, French, Italian, German, etc. In this way we shall find out what is *not* American, and the differences will become apparent. We shall see that American handwritings do have distinctive characteristics, and shall be able to define certain features and an over-all pattern that anybody will recognize as American.

It is with great regret
our departure from Inter
It has been very pleasant
have enjoyed so much
your pleasant people.

#84

Figures #84 and #85 will serve excellently to illustrate the relevant points. To European eyes, these specimens would look like the scripts of young persons; actually, they were penned by men in their late thirties, each highly trained in his profession. These handwritings are free of the self-conscious checks and balances that characterize British scripts produced by individuals of comparable education. Here we have unrestrained movement and uninhibited use of space. This reflects a conspicuously American outlook—a sense of living in an unlimited environment, a world in which there is room to move freely and be oneself. The conventional letter shapes point to relative lack of sophistication.

od infimation. Well, I guess things. Needless to say, I possability of getting free to go in the next year. Neither an could get over here to keep out

#85

It is even more difficult to single out a salient type or types in the handwritings of American women. Among professional women of high achievement we find scripts that at first glance appear quite unassuming or conventional, though nearer inspection discloses the superior traits that give the clue to the success of the

Stone walls do not a p Nor iron bars a

#86

writers (fig. #86). Others seem to strive for a free, unrestrained, and individual hand, though the effect is often merely pretentious (fig. #87).

#87

Thank you for your nice note — I am glad to

of the originators of th
of consciousness tech
of writing and has
called an artistic tree
of this style, his ba
vague and almost #88

Figure #88 presents what might be called a type example of a "nice" feminine American hand. It is that of a very young college girl, an excellent student who likes to have her own way, and this way seems to be a very straight and efficient one. Although the letter shapes conform to the Palmer system, she has managed to strip away all the accessories that hamper speed and fluency. The slender, rounded forms, good spacing, and rhythmic articulation within the writing line, make for an impression of clarity and balance. On the other hand, closer scrutiny shows that although the spaces between the letters are large, the letter forms themselves are narrow: thus a contradiction appears, because the wide interspaces indicate free self-assertion, while the narrowness of the letters implies caution and restraint (p. 157). This very combination, however, highlights the make-up of that type of American girl who displays initiative and effectiveness in her outward activities, but is inhibited in emotional expression.

PROFESSIONAL AND VOCATIONAL PATTERNS

Another influence bearing upon handwritings is that of the patterns prevailing in professional and vocational groups. For instance, a bookkeeper's writing has to be especially neat, small, and distinct. The conditions of his profession impose a prescribed and

#89

very conscious mode of dealing with the shapes of letters and numerals. However, the equally precise and exceedingly small handwritings of mathematicians and physicists present an entirely different picture. Their scripts, though essentially simple, are usually highly individualized (fig. #89).

#90

Where the professional or vocational pursuit becomes a dominant life interest, this absorption may impress itself upon the graphic pattern of the devotee (p. 318). Figure #90 shows the handwriting of a professor of archaeology who spent fifty years of his life studying ancient inscriptions carved in stone. His script suggests an archaeological relic; it might have been produced with a chisel rather than with a fountain pen. Figure #91 reproduces the handwriting of an eminent scholar of Oriental languages. The homogeneous expression conceals the fact that this specimen is actually written in two languages and represents two different writing systems. The upper part is in German, though rounded letter forms are used; the lower part is in Arabic. It is the unifying personal style of the writer that at first glance holds our attention, so that the differences in character between the two passages are realized only upon closer inspection.

#91

поэтетъ, <u>черезъ</u> его

вернуть взятые

листки „Гульчинеш

„Quadro Flamenco").

(насколько помню,

не предполагали

нужъ ему лично:

Итакъ эиду отъ

что бы совьтьстио

съ этимъ дьлать

The extraordinary script shown in figure #92 is a supreme example of a handwriting in which all personal gesture is fused in the motifs of the art upon which the creative imagination of the writer is concentrated. It is the hand of a famous Russian choreographer. In this unique stylization, we have a writing movement that actually schematizes the pattern configurations of a ballet. The essence of this script is form. In contrast to this, figure #93 presents a dancer's handwriting that acts out the living movement of the ballet. This is the signature of Anna Pavlova, who brought fixed choreographic forms to life in an unforgettable personal expression. The same creative personal quality appears in the writing style. The intense concentration of the start, the bold attack, the perfect equilibrium of form and movement, and the artistic unity of the configuration, reveal the body dynamics that determined both the dancing style and the graphic projection. In this hand we have a notable example of consistency of personal style in the different expressive movements of an individual.

#93

PART TWO

Analysis
and Interpretation
of Handwriting

(V)

THE STUDENTSHIP

Up to this point we have been dealing with the phenomenon of handwriting in its successive developmental stages. Before entering upon a detailed survey of the various features of handwriting, it may be well to consider the endowment and training needed by the man or woman who undertakes to use the graphological technique in the study of personality.

The practice of graphology relies on principles and general experiences that are an integral part of psychology; it also avails itself of insights gained through clinical and psychoanalytic approaches and through biosocial studies. To appreciate the contributions in all these fields, and to integrate them in a discipline of his own, the graphologist must have, by way of general equipment, the gift of empathy—the capacity for identifying oneself with others—as well as a specific grounding in psychology. This implies something more than having read about psychodynamics and using the complex terminology of the advanced psychological sciences without real orientation and understanding. Hence a student should be encouraged to specialize in handwriting research only after he has had some years of graduate study in general and abnormal psychology, education, or social work.

The special scope of graphology also necessitates, as part of a balanced preparation, some knowledge of physiological psychology, particularly an adequate comprehension of the neuromuscular mechanisms underlying the act of writing. It must be stressed that writing is no subordinate, peripherally conditioned activity, but a complex integration of processes directed by the most highly developed brain centers.[117] In the words of Preyer, one of the pioneers of scientific graphology, "handwriting is brain writing."[126]

It is easy to understand that handwriting interpretation must rest upon knowledge of human individuals in both their biological and their psychological make-up, seen against the background of the social and cultural milieus in which they have their being. A qualified graphologist, therefore, is a well-rounded individual, acquainted with all strata of existence and aware of the full sweep of life. His educational orientation must be as broad as possible, to assure understanding of a wide range of people.

It is an unfortunate fact that graphology does not yet have in the United States the backing that it has in the European tradition, and that this country offers relatively little opportunity either for introductory study or for advanced work in this field. It is only within recent years that some progressive colleges have taken the pioneer step of including courses in graphology in their curricula. Until quite lately, besides, few standard books on the subject had been published in English. It is therefore not surprising that most of the practitioners of graphology in this country have been forced to acquire such training and experience as they have mostly through self-directed effort.

Nevertheless, many of these autodidacts feel quite confident of their ability to "read character from handwriting," for all their lack of formal graphological training and of the necessary preparation in psychology. They rely on two assets—intuition and "experience," i.e., certain broad assumptions built upon highly generalized precedents.

INTUITIVE PERCEPTION

By concentrating on handwritings, one can develop the natural faculty, possessed in some measure by every person, for understanding graphic expression. One can also refine intuitive sensitiveness to such a degree that one may hit upon disclosures that go beyond those to be obtained by psychometric and other rigidly controlled and standardized procedures. For some practitioners of graphology, this intuitive ability suffices for equipment. They feel no need of objective principles by which to check subjective perceptions and to clarify their vague and hit-or-miss impressions. At the best, gross blunders inevitably result.

To help to clear up some general misconceptions as to the role and value of intuition in graphology, it may be useful to describe a set of experiments conducted by Herbert Theiss at the Psychological Institute of the University of Berlin.[156] Groups of children, as well as of adolescents and adults, were shown an array of handwriting specimens. They were asked to give their impressions of the dominant character traits of the writers—whether they thought the writer in any given instance quick or slow, neat or sloppy, friendly or ill-tempered, etc. Seventy per cent of the judgments hit upon the actual characteristics of the respective writers. Moreover, it appeared that the children of about the age of ten were especially perceptive; in older groups, the judgments became less accurate. In the appraisals made by children of pubertal age there was a decided drop, as against the younger groups, and the poorest performance was that of the adults. The tentative conclusion was that genuine intuition comes most fully into play in that age period in which logical thinking and critical sense are still dormant. As soon as such intellectual functioning becomes more active—which occurs as a rule after puberty—the free acceptance of intuitive perception tends to be blocked.

This experiment also showed the limitations of intuitive response. The judgments were greatly influenced by fluctuations of mood, by feelings of liking or dislike. It became apparent that even the subjects who attained the highest scores in judging the handwritings had days when their empathy did not work, or when they had no luck in "feeling into" a particular handwriting, though they did have empathy in judging some other.

It follows from the facts just described that intuitive understanding of graphic expression is not an unusual but a rather common faculty. However, it is overestimated by most untrained graphologists, who allow it to play a too dominant role. Some of them exploit this ability as a means of impressing their friends; others commercialize their intuitive aptitude, winning reputations as clairvoyants, and securing a popular following among the gullible.

EMPIRICAL GENERALIZATIONS

The other asset on which the untrained graphologist relies is so-called experience—expediently used rough precedents, by aid of which he gropes for correspondences between the traits of broadly known personality types and the features of the handwritings they produce. Individual observation, together with the assumptions to be found in certain outdated books, can be used to put together a system of "signs." According to such a system, each isolated graphic trait, each single flourish or hook, is supposed to have a definite meaning, standing invariably for a certain character trait. This harks back to the piecemeal "sign reading" of the early days of graphology. Many of these assumed correspondences, as Downey points out, "appear to have little more basis than the sympathetic analogies of homeopathic magic." Modern graphology moreover has established the principle that only those empirical interpretations which accord with sound psychological principles merit recognition.

There are, nevertheless, practitioners of graphology whose work is based entirely on a kind of crude empiricism. The data they compile are organized as in an index system, which they use in a mechanical way. An extreme instance of this is when the client is handed a printed chart that bears some heading as: "Outstanding traits are checked according to YOUR handwriting." On such a chart, "clusters" of "signs" are numerically keyed to composite little thumbnail analyses designed to make each client feel that the information he is receiving applies uniquely to himself. The content of these ready-made character readings is about as precise as follows: "Your natural aggressiveness can be your greatest asset IF combined with tact."

So much then for the abuses of intuition and for the prop' of mechanized experience. Nevertheless, it is necessary to keep in mind that intuitive insight and keen observation, linked with a resultant accumulation of experience, have been the stepping stones of graphology.

THE SPECIMEN COLLECTION

To acquire preliminary experience, the student of graphology should begin by collecting handwritings. He should have a stock of specimens at hand, in order to be able readily to examine and compare different scripts. At the outset he may make use of all available letters, business documents, signatures, school notebooks, diaries, envelope addresses, etc. It is irrelevant whether the writer of a given specimen is well known to him or not, or whether the hand is that of a celebrity or an unknown.

As a collection grows, its specimens must be differentiated and grouped. The scripts should be classified in two ways. They should be ordered first according to the personal and social characteristics of the writers. There may be as many subdivisions here as the material warrants—as by age (differentiating the handwritings of children, adolescents, and adults), educational level, occupation. Other groupings might be made under such headings as vocational interests, special talents, marked behavior patterns, social or emotional maladjustments, states of health, etc. The second major classification of the specimens should be set up according to the graphic characteristics distinguishing one handwriting from another, such as size, slant, connective forms, conspicuous letter shapes, etc.

Handling and systematic classification of handwritings will, first of all, sharpen the uninitiated eye. Just as a student of biology on first using a microscope does not perceive in a specimen those differentiating features which he sees clearly after he has had a certain amount of training, so a beginner in graphology needs time to learn to perceive and distinguish significant details.

But even the most careful and thorough study will cover no more than a cross section of the vast array of possible varieties in handwriting. Each script presents something new, something not previously encountered. The question arises constantly: What produces all this variety? The answer is suggested by Osborn in the following commentary: "It is like the mysterious variation in human personality, which by a slight differentiation in features, proportions, size, individualizes the millions of the human family. Look at the vast crowd, similar and yet all different."[116]

As he gains in experience, the student will learn to distinguish the more common variables from others more rarely encountered. He must evaluate each for what it is, and avoid accepting such conventional differentiations as "normal" and "abnormal." Rather, he must try to find the answer to the question as to how such a feature developed, and why the given writer uses it more than another, so that it has become characterizing for him.

There are no absolute standards of normality. We find a wide range of variability in the individual features of handwriting, but the differences are only a matter of degree. Ultimately, any given graphic feature can be correctly judged only when viewed as part of the intricate architecture of the pattern to which it belongs.

(VI)

MATERIAL AND PROCEDURE

To get a good picture of the facts confronting him in a script, the graphologist must have an original specimen as the material of his analysis. Photostatic copies should never be used.

THE MATERIAL

It is desirable to have at least two full pages of the subject's writing, together with his signature. Additional samples produced under varying circumstances, as well as an envelope address, are useful, since scrutiny of different specimens of the same hand may safeguard against erroneous judgments arising from the fact that a given specimen may have been conditioned by an atypical writing situation. It is known that self-consciousness, or tension affecting a subject in a test situation, changes the expression and possibly also the mode of writing. Therefore a specimen written especially for the purpose of having it analyzed is not suitable.

Furthermore, personality is continually in process of change. Personality grows, matures, develops, and ages. It may also be subjected to experiences so catalytic or so traumatic that their effect is immediately reflected in the handwriting. Figure #94* shows two specimens of the handwriting of a German woman of seventy-two. Specimen *a* was written when she was admitted to a hospital suffering from hunger edema. Specimen *b* was produced after she had had medical treatment and—even more important—

---

* Courtesy Herbert Peter.

(handwriting sample)

(a)

(b)   #94

(handwriting sample)

after she had received a CARE package bringing her some adequate nourishment.

The content of a handwriting sample should not be dictated or copied, nor should it consist of any kind of memorized material, such as a slogan or a poem. It must be a spontaneous composition, a genuine expression of the writer's own thought and feeling. Of course there are persons who will pen some high-sounding stuff meant to impress or fool the graphologist, or who attempt to change their style of writing for no other reason than to try to find out whether the graphologist is astute enough to see through their maneuvers. But these tricks do no harm, since they are instantly detectable.

In order to rule out disturbing influences, the graphologist should train himself not to read, in his first scrutiny, the verbal communication of the writing. His interest should be completely concentrated on the graphic features and what they express, and on the emotional implications of the pattern. These convey things that are not expressed in the actual words and that are partly unknown to the writer himself. Not until after the main conclusions have been drawn should the text be read. Only then should the graphologist look for "stimulus words" recurring in the writing or made conspicuous through emphasis, misspelling, omission of letters or letter parts, etc. (figs. #130-#32). Such "slips of the pen," which are induced by unconscious motivations, can be analyzed and interpreted as "trivial errors of everyday life" in the Freudian sense[39] (pp. 162-63).

Ever since the crucial experiment of Crépieux-Jamin and Binet[14] demonstrated that the sex and age of a subject cannot in every case be ascertained from the handwriting, it has been established practice for the graphologist to obtain information on these points before proceeding to analysis (p. 5).

We often see handwritings of young persons that look like those of their elders, and vice versa. It will be seen in the course of our discussion later that there are youngsters whose handwritings quite early show mature features, and others whose writing, up to college age and even later, is immature or infantile. Slow physical development and maturation are frequently a manifestation of any one of a number of endocrine dysfunctions in children or adolescents. A stature shorter than the average for a given age may be associated with retarded skeletal hardening in a child suffering from a thyroid or pituitary disorder; tall stature, with incomplete ossification of the extremities, accompanies inadequate functioning of the sex glands. In both of these conditions, sexual maturation may be retarded, and the somatic infantilism may be associated with a rather infantile type of mentality and emotional behavior, all of which become apparent in the handwriting (fig. #59).

Conversely, senescence does not necessarily set in at any fixed age. Symptoms of advanced senescence may be noticed in persons in their late fifties or early sixties, whereas complete physical and mental vigor are not infrequently maintained even after the proverbial landmark of "threescore and ten" has been passed. Indeed, it is a general truth that discrepancies between chronological age and degree of biological and psychological maturity are found in a great number of individuals. There is an impression of youthfulness about the handwriting of Bernard Baruch at the age of

Thank you so much for sending
my "belongings"
It was nice seeing you
Sincerely
Bernard M Baruch

#95

eighty or more (fig. #95). Similarly, no one would guess that figure #96 represents the handwriting of a composer in his thirty-ninth year; this man's physical appearance also belies his actual age.

things which now most engage
of men, as polities and the
is true, vital functions of

#96

In connection with sex, the term masculine and feminine require further particularization. Medical research has shown that males may vary to a remarkable extent in degree of virility, in

*the proprionce is
closed. If you
any projecting*

#97

both the biological and the psychological sense. There are men who, though capable of procreation, and stamped with an over-all appearance of maleness, nevertheless have delicate body contours or behavior characteristics corresponding more nearly with feminine traits. Similarly, we find women with athletic muscular development (fig. #97), low-pitched voices or so-called masculine mental traits, whose biological functioning and sex behavior are those of the "normal" female (figs. #97-#99).

*A of most surely

the both of these*

#98

117

had a very good meeting of
of Allergists in London a few
members are making plans

#99

The graphologist will also find it useful to have information about the writer's nationality[116] and occupation, and, in certain cases, his medical history. It is further of help to know the purpose for which the graphological findings are to be used. In connection with personnel placement, for instance, it is important to give special attention to traits that are pertinent to the particular job. In the case of a man who seeks employment as a salesman, for instance, and who therefore is concerned with material success, it is well to establish whether he has the qualities needed to "sell himself"—assertiveness, persuasiveness, and gregariousness. In the case of an applicant for a receptionist's job, on the other hand, it is important to judge whether the subject possesses poise, tact, and good social form. Aspirants to teaching positions must not only have traits that make for effectiveness in interpersonal relationships, but must also be capable of stimulating intellectual curiosity. In other cases it will be necessary to center on the subject's emotional make-up and sexual adjustment. But regardless of the special focus or use of the analysis, the traits or abilities of a given individual must be viewed and judged in the frame of his total personality.

Graphological procedure consists of differentiation and interpretation of the features presented in the visible material—the graphic specimen—and involves the following steps:

A. Initial contemplation of the writing pattern as a whole, in order to grasp its essential expression.

B. Closer scrutiny of the pattern, for the purpose of breaking up the whole into its components, and differentiating the various constituent factors.

C. Ordering into groups those indicators, i.e., graphic characteristics, which commonly occur together in a syndrome, and in their interrelation predicate a certain kind of personality make-up.

D. Interpretation of the graphic characteristics as indicators of personality traits.

E. Synthesis, i.e., structuring from the components thus differentiated and defined an integrated portrait of the living personality.

A. The Over-All Impression

To obtain a first, tentative over-all impression, the handwriting specimen should be held at arm's length or even upside down, so that the content is not readable. In viewing a handwriting as we would a picture, certain sensory impressions arise, as of coarseness

#100

119

(fig. #100) or fineness (fig. #101), flatness (fig. #102) or fullness (fig. #103), weakness (fig. #102) or strength (fig. #104),
pallor (fig. #102) or color (fig. #104), coldness (fig. #101) or

#101

Cher ami

Verrez ans maries ven midi. Je mai

pour le campagne où je terminerai pendant un mois

#102

Meen one of the
ament French Politicians
ng the post World
II period. a a
'er in the socialist

#103

Kind thoughts. Friendship is a great
so nice to hear about you at Elisabeth
few lines for me to one of all your
me that you remember us. I can't go to
brother and one of my sisters lost _all_
And here, where ever you look around:

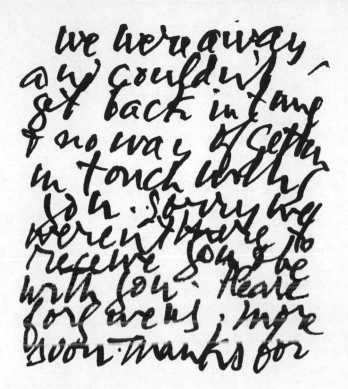

#104

warmth (fig. #104), etc. Simultaneously we are affected by whatever qualities of balance, rhythm, and harmony we may perceive in the pattern. There is a spontaneous reaction in the realm of feeling, where reason plays no essential part. As we all know, the relation of parts in a well-conceived or ill-conceived unity does not have to be understood in order to be experienced as rhythmic (fig. #105) or lacking in rhythm (figs. #94 *a*, #100). Such things can be as readily sensed in patterns of handwriting as in those of painting, music, or the dance.

Thus a handwriting conveys many things that cannot be put into words. It tells its story partly in the language of movement and partly in the language of imagery. Some of its meanings

#105

become clear in the light of the graphologist's immediate intuitive recognitions. In the close-woven line pattern, he perceives forms boldly in motion—stabbing daggers, whirling lassoes, striking harpoons, clawing fingers, clinging tendrils, spears erected, arrows in flight. To catch the meaning of these animated images, it is necessary to recall man's earliest modes of communication, and to imitate the gesture implied in a given image, so that the expressive forces behind it may work in and through one's own body. An easy way of doing this is to reproduce such an image by actually drawing it oneself, or, even better, by enacting in imagination the gesture it stands for. In this way, the meaning of the image can be experienced through empathy. In figure #106, we can clearly see how the writer acted out his mention of feelings of love by unwittingly drawing a heart, the universal symbol of love. Other instances of this kind appear in figures #136, #146, #339-#42, #362, #363.

Speaking of love & mass
had a baby girl.
lovely.

#106

But at the height of intuitive rapport, one must break off. Intuitive insight and response have a valid and fruitful function in graphological interpretation, though it must be unswervingly borne in mind that the essential requisite in handwriting analysis is observation controlled by accepted objective procedures.

Of course objectivity, in relation to both analysis and interpretation, requires that the graphologist apply controls not only with respect to the facts actually before him, but also with respect to his own subjective bias. He must realize how considerable a part his particular orientation and specialized interests tend to play in his evaluations to say nothing of the possible blind spots, rigidities, and defensive rejections that may limit his vision. Therefore the student of graphology should try to divest himself of or carefully to discount such influences. He must also be on guard against the fascination of popular theories and the allure of such oversimplifications as fixed categories of "personality types" and "trait clusters." As far as possible, interpretations should be built only on the evidence of the graphic material, and this evidence should be defined and analyzed clear of the influence of preconceptions or ready-made formulas. Prejudgments, even on the basis of such authoritative concepts as the form-level theory of Klages, or of psychoanalytic induction without reference to the subject's

123

personal associations or life history, prove to be main sources of error in graphological analysis.

B. DIFFERENTIATION OF GRAPHIC INDICES

The second step of our approach is the closer scrutiny of the pattern for inspection of its component parts. To discover the structural qualities of the separate graphic features, and ascertain what mechanical factors may have played a part in shaping them, they should be examined first with the naked eye and then with the aid of a magnifying glass.

The raw material of the graphic pattern is the stroke.[64] The stroke, or ductus, is the path traced by the pen on the paper.[123] We must note particularly whether the course of the stroke is continuous or broken, whether it is densely filled with ink or scantily covered. We must unravel the intricate network by which the stroke weaves the pattern: we must follow the trail in the rise and fall, the turning, the overlapping, and the crisscrossing that create the forms.[65] Just as we untwist a knot in order to see how it was made, we follow the path of the pen to ascertain precisely how the pattern came into being.[129] Let us observe, for example, in the specimens offered in figures #59, #98, #100, #102, #105, how an *o* is constructed—how it is "tied up" at the top, then linked to the next letter. There are innumerable variations in such simple details, each arising as a result of different body movements, which in turn are activated by different expressive impulses. As has been suggested above, part of a thorough and complete study of written forms consists in an actual retracing of them with one's own hand; one does not really see or understand a form until one has had the first-hand experience of drawing it.

In systematically analyzing a handwriting specimen, we must consider it in three aspects—(1) movement, i.e., the process, (2) form, i.e., the product, and (3) arrangement, i.e., the spatial disposition.[65]

1. Movement

Our basic premise is that the pen stroke or ductus is the visual record of the writing movement. Therefore in studying the qualities of the stroke, we examine the patterning with respect to:

a)   Expansion. We observe whether the movement is extended or limited in its range, with respect to both the vertical and the horizontal dimension.

b)   Co-ordination. We seek to ascertain whether the flow of movement is controlled or uncertain, smooth or jerky, continuous or interrupted.

c)   Speed. We determine whether the movement has been rapid or slow, and whether the pace has been steady or variable.

d)   Pressure. We note whether the pressure exerted in the movement has been heavy or light, and estimate the degree of tension indicated by the flexible or rigid character of the stroke.

e)   Direction. Each feature of a script must be examined with respect to leftward and rightward trend of the movement, and its upward and downward reach.

f)   Rhythm. The rhythmic quality of the movement derives from the fact that in the sequence of movements that weave the total pattern, certain similar phases recur at more or less regular intervals. Such periodicity is an expression of inner processes; it appears not only in writing but in all the movements of the living organism. The German graphologists refer to this basic phenomenon of movement as *Ablaufsrhythmus,* stressing the point that monotonous or unaccented regularity of movement has no rhythmic quality.

2. Form

In observing the forms built up by the strokes, we focus on the following features:

a)   Letters. We note whether the characters are structured predominantly of curved or rectilinear elements, whether they are simple or elaborate, ample or lean, uniformly or diversely shaped, fluid or rigid in form.

b) *Connections.* We note whether rounded (garland, arcade), angular, or threadlike joinings are used to form the letters and to link them within the words.

c) *Style.* Here judgment turns on whether the expressive picture is natural or stilted, individual or conventional, linear or pictorial in quality.

d) *Rhythm.* The criterion of "form rhythm" (*Formrhythmus*) is applied to the interrelations of the parts, according as they create balance and symmetry within the pattern. Here again, as in the domain of movement, unrelieved uniformity negates rhythm and produces only a stereotypic pattern, while extreme diversity or unevenness of form disintegrates rhythm.

3. Arrangement

Under this head we consider the distribution and the proportional relations of all the components of the pattern. This includes the relation of figure and ground, margins, alignment, and word spacing, the zonal proportions within the line (p. 137), and such features as slant of letters, direction of terminal strokes, placement of *t* bars, *i* dots, etc., in so far as these contribute to the organization of the whole.

The structuring of the total pattern produces what is called the "rhythm of distribution" (*Verteilungsrhythmus*). Klages regards rhythm as the most important of all the features of graphic expression, and differentiates three aspects of rhythm, found in the movement, the form, and the arrangement of the writing, as touched upon in the course of this exposition.

In carrying out an analysis as outlined under the three headings above, the graphologist may avail himself of an additional angle of insight if he bears in mind that of the three basic aspects of writing that we have been considering, movement has a salient importance in that it gives us the leading clue as to what kind of basic substance the personality is composed of. Movement represents an unmediated instant projection from the deepest strata of being; thus the stroke per se is least conditioned by any factor of training or even by conscious awareness (p. 23). The most volitional factor on the other hand is form. The shaping of forms requires conscious attention: it presupposes in the first place the capacity to reproduce a conventional symbol, and in the second place a more or less conscious effort to refashion it from an aesthetic or practical motive.[19, 123] Arrangement is the factor that serves to organize the other two. Therefore it shows us the writer's capacity for integrating inner promptings with outer reality.

We have thus far been considering these three aspects of writing in isolation from one another, for purposes of analysis. Actually of course they are inseparable and always interactive, and indeed to the layman's eye indistinguishable. Hence it requires specific training and experience to enable us to perceive any one of them apart from the others, to analyze its indications, and to reassemble the factors thus defined into a picture of the organic whole.

C. Ordering the Graphic Indices into Syndromes

Just as we cannot evaluate any of the major aspects of writing apart from one another, so no other single component or feature of handwriting can be interpreted without reference to all the others, even though for purposes of analysis we likewise set them apart, down to the smallest detail, and view each one technically by itself. No modern graphologist would claim that any one graphic feature has in itself any fixed meaning. We have by now left far behind us those followers of Michon who compiled a dictionary of isolated "signs" and their supposed meanings. We are aware that it is not enough merely to establish the presence or absence of certain features in a given writing pattern. While some implication of a given single feature may be a guidepost pointing to one possible interpretation or another, this single feature as such is significant only in relation to the group to which it belongs. Certain features may suggest meanings that reinforce the implications of others. Conversely, some features may suggest meanings that conflict with or weaken or neutralize the bearing of others. Therefore each feature must be weighed against all the rest, and against the general expression of the total pattern. We must remember that we are dealing first and last with a whole—a unity or system in which all the parts are subordinate and relative.

Obviously the analyst can make sure that his procedure is accurate at all points only if he systematically sets down his observations in detail. To facilitate such notation, the author has devised a worksheet (p. 129) on which all findings can be entered and organized at the same time, so that group relationships can be visualized as in a graph or chart. The broad divisions of this worksheet conform with the framework of procedure outlined above, i.e., the systematic scrutiny of the material under the aspects of movement, form, and arrangement.

Within each of these major divisions are placed the factors whose indications belong to the given aspect of the analysis. In the spaces allowed for each factor, the examiner may mark the essential qualities of ⁺he features pertaining to it. The spaces of the entry column further allow for appropriate differentiations. For instance, the examiner's rating can be so placed as to show whether the given quality appears in moderate or marked degree. A separate column at the right permits of noting the predominant feature or features of the script, and such other characteristics as appear relatively salient. Finally, under "Remarks," the analyst may enter additional observation meriting special note or contributing to or clarifying his interpretation. This sample worksheet is of course only a skeleton model; it provides for the essentials of any analysis, but cannot possibly cover the particulars of each and every possible handwriting. Every graphologist, as his experience broadens, will amplify such an elementary record form and develop a more particularized or more personally adapted sheet for his own routine.

Detailed descriptions of the various graphic features and of the qualities to be found in them, together with discussion of the

WORKSHEET

Name.. Age.......... Sex..........   Predominant features ✳

MOVEMENT		Marked	Moderate	Marked		Other salient features	Remarks
Expansion: in height	extensive				limited		
in width	extensive				limited		
Co-ordination	smooth				disturbed		
Speed	fast				slow		
Pressure	heavy				light		
stroke	sharp				pastose		
	shaded				unshaded		
Tension	high				low		
stroke	rigid				flexible		
Directional trend	rightward				leftward		
terminal strokes	long				short		
Rhythm	flowing				disturbed		
FORM							
Style	pictorial				linear		
	natural				stilted		
	individual				conventional		
Letter shapes	fluid				rigid		
	diverse				uniform		
	elaborate				simple		
	ample				lean		
	curved				rectilinear		
loops	standard				irregular		
Connective forms	garland				arcade		
	thread				angular		
Rhythm	balanced				uneven		
ARRANGEMENT							
Pattern, over all	organized				disorganized		
rhythm	good				poor		
Margins: top	broad				narrow		
left	broad				narrow		
right	broad				narrow		
Alignment: lines	parallel				divergent		
	straight				undulating		
	ascending				descending		
	well-spaced				overlapping		
Word interspaces	adequate				inadequate		
Zonal proportions✳	M < extensions				M > extensions		
	L < U				L > U		
	balanced				unbalanced		
Slant	rightward				leftward		
	upright				fluctuating		
i dots							
t bars							
SIGNATURE							
Congruence with text							
Emphasis on	given name				family name		
Placement							

✳   U —*upper zone*
M—*middle zone*
L —*lower zone*

The fact that a given quality is noted in the right- or the left-hand listing has no implication of positive or negative evaluation

possible meanings assignable to them, will be found in succeeding chapters. These expositions will supply the informational equipment that enables the graphologist to make his notations.

D. INTERPRETATION OF GRAPHIC INDICES

Having assembled and ordered his findings regarding the features of the script, the graphologist must interpret them as expressions of personality, i.e., he must correlate the graphic indicators he has found with the personality traits they stand for. The accompanying chart supplies a practical guide for this purpose. The parallel columns list on the one side the basic graphic indicators, and on the other the main component factors in the make-up of personality. The arrangement shows the student at a glance how to follow through in working out the meaningful correlations, feature for feature, between the graphic evidence before him and the various phases of functioning through which personality expresses itself in life situations.

Necessarily, an outline of this sort is chiefly orientational. It will serve to point up the interrelations discussed in detail below, chapter for chapter, and to show the application of basic graphological acceptances. The correlations it suggests are grounded upon a large body of empirical findings validated by experimental and statistical data, or supported by analogous experience in various fields of medical and psychological investigation. Beyond this, any mechanical use of such a tool leads to oversimplification. There can be no standard key for reading off personality traits; living features cannot be sorted out by formula and assigned to a type pattern on any one plane. It cannot be stressed often enough that every personality has its unique expression, and that the essential aim of graphology is to uncover and to describe, in the case of each given handwriting, precisely that unique quality of personal dynamic which arises from the particular constellation of features it presents.

GRAPHIC INDICATORS — PERSONALITY FACTORS

GRAPHIC INDICATORS	PERSONALITY FACTORS
Arrangement of pattern	Adaptation: outlook on the world
Rhythm and harmony	Functional integration
Style	Mode of self-expression
Structure of writing line *a) upper zone* *b) middle zone* *c) lower zone*	Personality structure *a) intellectual and spiritual range* *b) ego function* *c) biological demands*
Directional trend *a) rightward* *b) leftward*	Orientation *a) outward, toward the future: extroversive* *b) inward, toward the past: introversive*
Expansion *a) vertical dimension: height* *b) horizontal dimension: width*	Self-display *a) claim to status* *b) demand for elbow room*
Slant *a) rightward* *b) upright* *c) leftward*	Feeling response *a) compliant* *b) self-reliant* *c) defiant*
Connective form	Social behavior pattern
Connectedness and fluency	Associative processes, facility of expression
Speed	Tempo o. somatic and psychic functioning
Pressure	Vital energy, libido
Tension	Adjustment to strain and stress
Alignment	Sense of economy, goal orientation
Regularity	Emotional balance and control
Signature	Self image

PERSONALITY

E. SYNTHESIS

The final step is that of synthesizing the results—the task of constructing, from the separate psychological components, an integrated personality picture. In everyday practice, of course, what is called for in most cases is a simple description of the writer in question, appropriate to the purpose that the analysis is intended to serve. Such a description should be above all else clearly worded and free of ambiguities, and should never be weighted with diagnostic judgments. The graphologist should confine himself to the technicalities of his own science. If his report is sound and well presented, it will be directly usable in the context of any field of personality study—from educational or vocational testing or research to medical or psychiatric clinical work.

In any of these connections, diagnostic use of the graphological report is reserved to the specialist in the given field. Particularly where the analysis is to be used by a physician, the graphologist should resist the temptation to elaborate his findings in medical terminology; his co-operation will be more effective, and all the more appreciated, if he confines his report to an easily readable, accurate, and objective picture of the personal qualities and behavior pattern of the subject.

On occasion, the graphologist may be called upon to furnish an intensively detailed profile of the subject. This is a more exacting task, presupposing, in addition to the routine qualifications, an advanced interpretative skill, experienced psychological insight, and facility in written formulation. Indeed, in the sense that here the challenge is to portray a personality—to reconstruct the subject's inner and outer worlds and the role he plays in them —graphology, according to Allport and Vernon, is to be regarded as an art.[3]

THE ETHICS OF THE GRAPHOLOGIST

The graphologist, like the professional worker in any other field, conducts himself according to an established ethical code.

For obvious reasons, he must know to whom and for what purpose he is to submit the information derived from his analysis. When the report is intended for the use of a physician, psychiatrist, or guidance expert, the personality diagnosis may be frank and complete. It is understood in such relations that the report is submitted, received, and used in a confidential manner. When the graphologist is consulted by the subject directly, he must limit himself to constructive suggestions, giving no information that could lead to harm. It is advisable in such a case not to go beyond verbal discussion of the findings and to keep the report on the subject's own level of understanding.

If the graphologist is called upon to supply a person of nonprofessional standing with an analysis of the handwriting of another individual, he must make no revelations that could be misinterpreted or used to the injury of the writer. It is possible in any situation to be honest and informative without making inappropriate disclosures.

A graphologist furthermore regards as confidential all data in his possession concerning his clients or other individuals whose handwritings may be submitted to him for examination, just as a doctor refrains from disclosing information about his patients.

(VII)

SYMBOLISM
OF THE WRITING SPACE

The ordinary reader sees in handwriting a message deliberately communicated through the medium of written words. The graphologist sees this and more: to him, handwriting embodies also an unintended communication, projected in the graphic pattern through a release of the unconscious.

This nonverbal content is discovered by means of a symbolic concept of the writing field. This field is conceived as a spatial entity, having the three dimensions of height, width, and depth, and the directions of right and left, and up and down. The representation of the writing field as a space is not, as Pulver points out, merely an expedient intellectual construction; it springs directly from our inner perception. "This spatial notion is something we carry within us; perhaps it has its basis in the archetypal space image of which our outward tridimensionality is only a subsequent projection."[128] Hence it provides us with an elementary kind of symbolic or visualized order which becomes clear by following through the graphic phenomena, beginning with the simplest element, the dot.

When a writer puts the nib of his pen to the surface of the paper, he produces a dot. As his hand moves on, he produces a line—the record of the course that the pen has traced. The primary meaning of the word "trace" will help us to understand the writing space as symbolizing the field of life—the area of man's activity. For it takes us back to what probably was man's first experience of the line. Looking behind him, he perceived in the snow, or the sand, or the mud, the path he had traversed; looking ahead, his eye traveled toward the point he hoped to reach. If he was dragging something behind him as he went, he had a visible record of this experience—a line traced from his starting point to the point where he had stopped. If thereupon he shot an arrow or threw a stone from the spot where he then stood to his next point of venture, the course of his missile traced again a line—i.e., extended the original line—to that goal. With this line, man turned empty space into a field of action.

But there was further significance to this experience. It related space to time: the line going backward in space also went backward in time—it was the record of the past. To man the spot where he then stood was the present—the point of reference. From here he could look forward in the direction in which he proposed to move—i.e., into time to come. In other words, he was shooting his arrow into the future, into the coming field of action. In this way a line may denote both space and time, and relate awareness of space to experience of time. It can mean more: as the line of life it can represent the sequence of events; on another level, it may stand for the route of a train in motion. It may serve to define a margin or to bound an area; it can also be a divider, separating space into parts, or it may act as a bond or link between parts.

The line as such is physically one-dimensional, but it can be used to circumscribe part of a plane surface, and in this way to create two-dimensional forms such as the letters of the alphabet. In graphology we refer to the ink or pencil line that forms these letters as the stroke or ductus. Strokes in the vertical direction establish the height of the letters; those in the horizontal direction, their width.

As the course of writing proceeds from left to right, the rightward movement interacts with thrusts in the vertical direction (fig. #199), and in its steady progression links together the up-

and downstrokes. This interweaving of the horizontal and vertical elements results in a contrapuntal pattern that has an expression of its own, according to the emphasis the writer gives to the vertical or horizontal strokes. The interplay between the two directional impulses might be regarded as a symbolic expression of the continuous conflict between man's desire to hold his ground on the one hand, and of his urge to progress on the other.

The third dimension of the writing field is depth. The depth component is created by the pressure exerted upon the writing surface. This is indicated by furrows impressed in the paper or merely by dark lines whose shading gives the letter forms a bold relief. We tend to perceive letters as bodies having volume: three-dimensional configurations standing upright like a man standing on the ground. This ground is symbolized by the implied base line. For we speak of upright letters, in spite of the fact that they actually lie flat on the plane of the paper. This attests to something that projection theory has long recognized—man's tendency to project the self onto the object that meets his eye, and to invest this object with the tensions and emotional impulses actually operating in himself. In writing, this leads to an identification with the letter form, upon which the writer projects his psychic activity in the guise of images and symbolic gestures.[94, 141]

In order to make use of our symbolic concept, the writing field, we have first to consider the actual material factors. The sheet of paper on which the writing is produced represents, as we have seen, the writing space. Restricted only by the physical limits of the paper's size, the writer spreads out upon it the sequences of graphic movement. The pattern into which the sequences are integrated appears as a structure arising from the contrast of its dark forms against the light background of the paper space. This pattern, the body of handwriting, is made up of parallel rows consisting of words and intervening spaces, and the words in turn are composed of related letters. The basis of handwriting analysis is the line of writing, which may be further divided into three zones.

The working hypothesis dividing the writing line into three zones has been developed by Pulver and is generally used by most graphologists.[128] This zonal division serves to localize the unconscious projections of the writer's needs, drives, and cravings, and enables the graphologist to differentiate the meanings involved. The three zones of the writing line—or of any portion thereof, such as a word or letter—are established as follows (fig. #107):

MIDDLE ZONE

The letters resting on the base line and having no extensions constitute the middle zone. Formed completely within one zone (*a, n, o, w,* etc.), they may be called the unizonal letters. In the middle zone are to be found also the body portions of letters whose extensions reach into one or both of the other zones. Of these, the letters that occupy two zones (*b, d, g,* etc.) may be called bizonal, and those embracing three zones (the usual longhand *f* in English, and similar formations in older German script, or in certain obsolete styles), may be called trizonal.

Symbolically, or in terms of projection, the middle zone represents the sphere of actuality—that aspect of personality function which is concerned with conscious adaptation to reality, with social relationships, and with ego expression.

UPPER ZONE

The upper zone is defined by the stems and loops of such letters as *f, t, l,* etc.—i.e., the extensions that reach upward beyond the middle zone—and includes the *i* dots and *t* bars.

For the purposes of interpretation, this zone represents the sphere of abstraction—the realm in which man rises above immediate reality, in which interests and aspirations of mind and spirit come into play. Overextension here, i.e., when stems and loops are carried to extremes of height, so that they reach beyond the expectable boundary of the zone—into the stratosphere, so to

Leftward trend

← ─────────────────────────

	Stratosphere	= *sphere of imagination*	....
PASSIVITY	Upper Zone	= *sphere of mind and spirit*	....
FEMININITY	Middle Zone	= *sphere of actuality*	....
THE PAST	Lower Zone	= *sphere of biological demands*	....
INNER WORLD	Depth	= *sphere of the unconscious*	

anything base

ACTIVITY
MASCULINITY
THE FUTURE
OUTER WORLD

#107

speak—indicates a preponderance of those psychological processes which are not subject to rational control. This graphic trait reflects the functioning of intuition and imagination—betokening either creativity or preoccupation with dreams and illusions.

LOWER ZONE

The lower zone is occupied by the loops and stems of such letters as f, g, p, y, etc.—i.e., the extensions that reach downward below the base line. In this zone we find expression of the material demands relating to self-preservation, and of the sexual drive.

This area comprises the lower zone proper—representing the relatively more conscious sphere of the "biological imperatives"—and below it a sphere of overextension that relates to the lower zone as the stratosphere relates to the upper. In terms of projective expression, we may call this the depth. In this region we find expression of those powerful forces which function below the threshold of consciousness and seek outlet in sexual phantasies, regressive gestures, and antisocial acts.

The scheme of the three zones parallels the common idea of the universe as divided into three spheres—heaven above, earth in the middle, and the nether region below. The same threefold division is applied to the body image when the human form is regarded as composed of the head above, the thorax in the middle, and the abdomen below. Metaphysical thinking employs the three divisions of mind, soul, and body. This scheme of triplicity, inherent in man's thinking and imagining, is an ancient one and seems to function even in the unconscious. Freud, for example, was led to distinguish three aspects of the psyche—superego, ego, and id—in accordance with the same primordial symbolic disposition.

DIRECTION

In our topology of the writing space, another critical index is the expression of directional trends. Direction, like every other aspect of writing, is to be interpreted in relation to movement, form, and arrangement (p. 124). Direction is manifested in each individual feature of writing, as well as in the resultant whole. It is expressed in the rightward or leftward pull of the movement as it shapes the writing line, in the placement of the writing as a mass, in the slant of the letters, in the swing of the terminal strokes, in the widths of the individual letters, in the location of *i* dots and *t* bars, as well as in the placement of the signature on a letter sheet and of the address on an envelope. In other words, every feature of handwriting derives a particular meaning from its location and directional weighting. Thus the criteria of location and direction will have to be applied to every feature of writing in the detailed discussion given to each in turn in later chapters. However, in distinguishing leftward from rightward movement for purposes of analysis and interpretations, it must be borne in mind that writing requires movement in all directions. Certain letters such as the *c*, the loops of letters like the *l*, the ovals of letters like the *a*, are shaped by leftward as well as rightward movement. Thus, specific note should be made only of those strokes whose leftward extension exceeds the limits set by the common letter model. The same applies to the interpretation of rightward trend in the formation of letters.

Handwriting, as a function of communication, a tool of social expression, is in itself extraversive. It is as though the writer says: "*I* need to tell *you* about my feelings, thoughts, and plans. See, here I externalize them by writing." Yet this externalization is not simple to interpret. For in addition to the complex symbolization inherent in the three zones, there is a wealth of meaning in direction. The predominance of rightward or leftward trend is a main indicator of the relationship between the world within and the outer world. A predominance of rightward movement, and even more, a decrease of leftward movement, indicates a person predominantly responsive to stimulations from without, i.e., the type regarded as "extravert." Leftward emphasis suggests a person predominantly activated by promptings from within and less susceptible to stimulations coming from without, i.e., the type known as "introvert."

A preponderantly leftward trend in the middle zone is regarded as indicating selfishness. Rightward extensions into the upper zone represent alert mental activity, intellectual ambition, drive, and planning. A leftward trend expressed in the upper zone represents on the other hand an emphasis on the inner life, a tendency toward contemplation or introspection, a preoccupation with one's imaginings, or a brooding on memories. Viewed in its broader aspects, directional trend also provides evidence as to fixation: a leftward trend indicates withdrawal or regression, a yearning for the protection of the mother, for the shelter of the womb, while a rightward trend is a move toward the father's world, toward activity and adventure.[128]

PAST, PRESENT, AND FUTURE

Since direction is further interpreted in terms of time, the movement in each letter embodies past, present, and future. Hence we must scrutinize the beginning and the end of each letter in order to note whether the movement by which it was made was a continuous advance toward the right (fig. #108).

#108

A letter is part of a larger unit—the word—and the same test has to be applied to this entity. The word in turn is part of a sentence, and here too the continuity of advance—or the lack of it—gives indication as to whether the orientation of the writer is toward the past, the present, or the future. Further, the sentence is part of the continuity of the text as a whole. The line of writing might be regarded as a part of the totality of the page, while the sentence plays an analogous role in the totality of the document. In a letter, for example, this actual whole comprises all of the script mass from beginning to end, i.e., from salutation to signature. Here directional orientation is judged according to the placement of the larger elements as well as the arrangement of the total pattern on the page.

As a message, the writing pattern moves from the writer, the "sender," outward into the environment, i.e., away from the body. It may proceed toward the right or toward the left, the body of the writer standing as the median axis. However, writing usually starts at the left and moves toward the right, in the direction of the right-hander's outward reach.

Such a statement is often challenged by the question: What determines this convention? Why do Western writing and Sanskrit, which is considered Eastern, proceed from left to right, while Near Eastern writing, such as the Semitic, proceeds from right to left, and Far Eastern, such as the Chinese, from top to bottom?

DIRECTION IN ANCIENT WRITING

In the various writing systems, the direction of movement was primarily conditioned by the writing technique and the instruments used. We may accept the assumption that communication other than oral began with the use of knotted cords,[102] which was later displaced by the practice of notching, scoring, or scratching crude marks on wood or stone. These graven marks carry us forward to another stage of development, i.e., pictorial writing— the use of pictures to stand for actual things or combinations of things (p. 315). The hieroglyphic characters of the ancient Egyptians are carved pictures that could be read in either direction. The cartouche of Cleopatra on the Rosetta Stone, for instance, may be read either across or from top to bottom.[16]

143

In China, the first written records were scratched with a knife upon bamboo or wooden tablets. With cultural advance, the scratching technique gave way to the method of tracing characters with a wooden stick or quill and later of painting them with a brush upon a kind of paper. The introduction of a supple tool like the brush led to an evolution from characters formed by simple straight strokes to a pictorial style of writing that eventually produced the existing stock of ideograms (fig. #338). These wholly independent units are arranged in columns, beginning on the right-hand side of the page and running from top to bottom.

The characters of ancient Greek writing, adopted from the Phoenicians, were originally written from right to left, in the manner of Hebrew writing today. There followed a period of ambivalence, the lines progressing in alternation of direction, like furrows in plowing—one line reading from left to right, the next from right to left, and so on. It seems quite probable that the choice of direction was stabilized when man, instead of carving and scratching, began actually to "write," tracing characters with an implement conducive to fluency and swing. This rightward trend conforms with the orientation of the majority, the right-handed people, and thus became the convention for the Western world.

One observation that has thrown some light on the problematical origin of the reverse directional trend, the right-to-left writing, was made by Julius Sebestyén, a Hungarian anthropologist. In studying the ancient writings—carved on wood—of the Székely tribe, the earliest Hungarian-speaking inhabitants of Transylvania, he had the good fortune to run across an old shepherd who was one of the very few persons still using the primitive writing mode of his ancestors. Sebestyén observed how the man gripped the wood with his left hand, using his right hand to incise simple grooves arranged in columns running from top to bottom. When the writing was finished, the shepherd turned the wood clockwise, so that the vertical column of characters was placed horizontally, to be read from right to left.

Sebestyén felt that this explained why the ancient writing had to be read from right to left.

It is not unlikely that the leftward direction of Hebrew writing is a survival similarly connected with the practice of earliest times, i.e., the carving of characters in an up-and-down direction upon a solid object, which then for ease of reading came to be turned. The sacred nature of the early inscriptions discouraged change and acted to hold writing to the traditional direction.

THE MYTHOLOGY OF RIGHT AND LEFT

It is likely that the predominance of right-handedness among people accounts for the association of might with the right as the side of action. The somatic sensations of handedness are no doubt the source for the manifold symbolic meanings that have become attached to the duality of right and left, and that have found expression in all cultures and in all ages. They are reflected in law and ritual, in magic and superstition, in language and literature; and they are perpetuated not only in folkways but also in modern everyday usages.

In the cultural tradition of the Chinese, the mystical opposites yang and yin, which anciently meant merely light and dark, have ultimately come to embrace all the associational aspects of a fundamental polarity. Yang is the male principle, heaven, the creative, the active, the positive, the straight, the undivided, the favorable; yin is the female principle, earth, the receptive, the submissive, the negative, the crooked, the divided, the unfavorable.

In early Hindu and Egyptian religious cults, the right side of the body symbolized strength and aggressive action; the left side, feeling and receptivity. The goddess Isis was pictured with a sword in her right hand and a flower in the left. Extant primitive tribes interpret right and left in much the same animistic and symbolic terms: the body of man is conceived of as possessing male characteristics on the right side and female characteristics on the left. A Swiss cultural anthropologist, J. J. Bachofen, has described a most interesting reversal of this symbolism in certain matriarchal societies.

The antithesis of right and left extends beyond all physical implications into the domain of moral, social, and religious values as well. In the Old Testament story, King Solomon places his mother in the seat of honor at his right side; and early Christian theologians designated the right side in heaven as the superior sphere, while the left side was given a lower evaluation. The Gospel of Matthew, in explaining how the good are to be separated from the evil on the Day of Judgment, says, "And he shall set the sheep on his right hand, but the goats on the left."

It is not unnatural that right and left developed similar meanings on mundane levels as well, and that these have taken on an endless accretion in popular attitudes no less than in superstitions. To start off on the left foot brings bad luck; a buzzing in the right ear is a good omen, and a twitch of the right eye is believed to bring praise and money. Thus we find the "honorable" right and the "evil" left becoming the "lucky" right and the "unlucky" left.

Just why there has been this consistent disparagement of the left and how some of these connotations have influenced the interpretation of handedness is discussed in greater detail in the author's monograph on handedness.[54]

(VIII)

EXPANSION
OF THE WRITING PATTERN

The expansion of the graphic pattern is intimately bound up with the nature and quality of the writer's movements: it will depend upon whether these are expansive or restrained, released or contracted, and whether in the main his tendency in movement is to reach out or pull back. The norm is a movement that maintains a balance between release and contraction, producing due proportion and even distribution in the writing, with letter forms neither too widely spread nor too narrowly condensed.[91]

In examining the expansion of a handwriting, observation is focused on three factors: (*a*) the relation of the graphic pattern to the writing space; (*b*) the size of the individual letters; (*c*) the proportions of the letter parts.

In even a superficial scrutiny it becomes apparent that each writer has his own individual way of filling space with forms. One writer treats space with so much freedom that his entire page is scrawled over with a few words. Another treats space with so much economy that his page is crowded with a small, close, spare script.

To appraise size in written characters, it is first of all necessary to establish a standard. Thus we classify single letters in terms of height and width. When the unizonal letters, such as *e, i, n, s,* etc., are 3 millimeters high, they are regarded as of medium height. When they are 4 millimeters or more in height, they are regarded as tall. When they measure less than 3 millimeters in height, they are judged to be short.

In most copybooks the bizonal letter *b* is twice as high as a unizonal letter, and the same proportion holds for bizonal letters whose extensions fall below the middle zone, such as *g*. Some of the older writing systems make such looped letters four times as high as unizonal letters. The Spencerian system, for instance (fig. #161), is based on a scale of fifths: the letters occupy three spaces above the base line and two below, the *b* and the *m* having a ratio of 3 to 1 in height. In prewar German writing the letters are styled with longer extensions in the upper zone than in the lower.

The width of a letter is evaluated in terms of the ratio between its horizontal dimension and its height. When, in such letters as the *n*, for instance, the distance between the two downstrokes is approximately equal to their height, the letter is of medium width; when this distance is greater than the height of the downstrokes, the letter is broad, and when this distance is less than the height of these strokes, the letter is narrow.

The body parts of such letters as *a, g, o,* etc., which are usually oval, may be inflated or deflated. Enlarged loops and swelling curves result in fullness and width, flattened loops and curves result in leanness and narrowness. A loop or a capital letter is considered full when the amount of space it takes up is greater than the space given it in the school-model letter.

PROPORTIONS

The diagram in figure #109 shows how the letters of a word are positioned in the three zones of a writing line. The zonal division also points up the proportional relations of letters and letter parts, in correspondence with the zonal proportions, as follows:

(*a*) The height of the unizonal letters establishes the height of the middle zone; (*b*) The length of the upper extensions establishes the height of the upper zone; (*c*) The length of the lower extensions establishes the height of the lower zone.

In the frame of the three zones we can correctly appraise the

#109

relations within the individual letters—whether the letter parts are well placed and in balanced proportion to one another, or whether either the bodies or the extensions take up more or less than their proper share of space. In regard to the upper and the lower zone we must take into account not only the length of the loops and stems but likewise all the other elements appearing in these zones. For instance, *i* dots and *t* bars placed high accentuate the upper zone. The same may be said when letter parts belonging to the middle zone protrude into the upper zone. When *i* dots and *t* bars are placed low, or when letter parts and terminal strokes fall below their proper places, the writer is emphasizing the lower zone. Excessive height or extremely reduced height in one zone upsets the balance of the whole.

Experience supports the finding that persons of limited education and culture, as well as children, tend to enlarge the unizonal letters. When facility in writing is attained, the proportions change; the stems and loops become longer. With old age, however, they tend to shorten (fig. #110).

#110

149

The written character, considered as a geometrical form, is to a large extent measurable. The length of a stroke, the area circumscribed by straight or curved outlines, the proportional relations of letter parts, are all measurable elements of a script.

The author at one time undertook to measure the letters in the handwritings of several thousand school children, and found that by the time a child is twelve years old, the height of his unizonal letters is fairly well established. However, the ratio between upper and lower loops and stems is less stable, the length of lower loops being particularly subject to change. At the puberty stage, these loops increase in size. In certain later life periods, their size may decrease. It was observed, for example, that in the writing of young people under the strain of preparing for their most important examinations, the lower loops became shorter; after the examinations were over, these loops resumed their former lengths.

The school standard, by its very nature, is the soundest frame of reference for any evaluation of letter size, since its values belong to the accepted values of the social order. The degree of adherence to or deviation from this standard is a personal gesture that may give clues to the individual's inner attitude toward size and physical stature. Letter size is also an index of the writer's evaluation of his ego as against the environment. The same kind of expression appears in drawings.[94] An individual who considers himself superior to the people around him feels that he tops them in stature. A person who feels weak and dependent sees others as towering above him. These feelings are expressed in the individual's gestures, attitudes, and movements. Thus they are likewise expressed in his handwriting.

VERTICAL AND HORIZONTAL EXPANSION

The manner in which the writing is spread over the page indicates how much living space the writer demands. The vertical expansion (height of letters) reflects the degree to which he strives for stature and prestige. The horizontal expansion (width of letters) shows the amount of elbow room he requires (chart, p. 131).

A big, showy hand goes with a need for exhibiting oneself, thereby to impress the world and to win public recognition. The most obvious example of this personality type are theatrical people, politicians, and social celebrities. In the handwriting of Lily Pons (fig. #111), the vertical thrust indicates an awareness of being conspicuously placed, as on a pedestal, the focus of attention and admiration. Figure #112 presents the handwriting of an impressive public figure: natural brilliance, high aspirations, and dynamic

#111

#112

#113

The United States must guard itself against militarism; the civilian restraining force show vividly in the writing. Figure #113 reproduces the handwriting of this man's brother, a distinguished ecclesiastic, whose equally brilliant abilities are channeled into spiritual pursuits. The graphic pattern shows no conspicuous expansion nor dynamic accent.

A small handwriting indicates a person who is not concerned with what people think of him (fig. #114). He perceives the

#114

world as an infinitude in which he plays a finite, modest role. But his feeling of the validity of his part, small though it is, gives him an impersonal strength and a sense of worth. Pope Leo XIII

#115

had a small handwriting (fig. #115). However, the strokes beneath the signature supply the effect of a pediment, giving the name an elevation, as it were. This device may symbolize the hierarchic status of the writer; to some observers it also suggests an angel's wing.

#116

With much love

mkgandhi

Gandhi's handwriting (fig. #116) is very small. To the graphologist, its quality is quite impersonal. Its utter simplicity of structure and form, the absence of angles and aggressive strokes, are significant in connection with the writer's principle of "nonviolence"; such graphic qualities are in accord with the known character of this "fighter without a sword." It is interesting to compare his handwriting with that of Napoleon (figs. #274, #354, #355).

#117

These small handwritings contrast strikingly with the large script shown in figure #117. This writer has no over-all perspective of the world, but sees only the small segment of it that he can fill with his violent, clumsy, incoherent gestures. His letters, enormous to start with, grow even larger toward the end of a word, so that the space in which he is functioning—i.e., his environment—seems to shrink. It is the handwriting of Rasputin, the charlatan "holy man" who in his mad self-inflation used the closed circle of imperial court society in czarist Russia substitutionally for a world stage, dominated by himself as a fantastic puppeteer of fate.

There are handwritings in which an ascendant gradation in size appears—the terminal letter in each word being larger than the initial one (fig. #117). This occurs in the handwritings of children and childlike adults, or of persons who manifest a very limited understanding of others. The writing of mature adults as a rule shows a descendent gradation. The diminution may become so pronounced that the end of the word seems to taper to a threadlike finish, so fined down and pointed that it could be put through a needle's eye, as it were (p. 217). This, according to Pulver, is an index of acute psychological insight and capacity to function effectively in interpersonal situations.

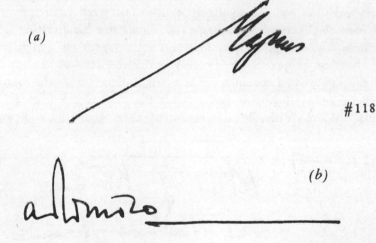

(a)

#118

(b)

A handwriting may be expanded in width by sideward strokes used in various ways. The writer may start his words with what might be called "springboard" strokes (fig. #118 *a*), or give his terminal strokes a rightward thrust (fig. #118 *b*). Strokes of this outgoing kind indicate mobility and strong activity drives, a need to keep moving toward a goal. Forceful, sharp sideward strokes betoken a desire for domination and conquest (fig. #119). If the sideward strokes appear in the upper zone, they reflect the presence of mental directives.[169] Figure #120 shows the handwriting of a woman who engages in planning and active work on a high level of altruistic endeavor. The type of horizontal stroke that appears in the lower zone to underline a word indicates a desire to construct a material support and a stable basis for living (figs. #111, #119, #352). It should also be noted that while the rightward

#120

156

-ses & telegrams
bit of springing
they were amusing

(b)

dream　　(a)

directed stroke stands for extraversion, the leftward turning stroke is self-oriented and signifies introversive (fig. #121 *a*) or egotistic tendencies (fig. #121 *b*).

The expansion of a handwriting is gauged not only in terms of the size of the individual letters. An equally important factor is the size of the spaces between letters and between words. Letters spaced generously in the writing field, and taking up more space horizontally than model letters, characterize generous, outgoing personalities (fig. #122). Excessive width is symptomatic of lavishness and extravagance (fig. #119). An example of letters prodigally outspread, to the point of abandon and sprawling release, is seen in the script of Ninon de Lenclos (fig. #123).

Inordinately broad letters mark the inconsiderate, immodest individual inclined to overextend himself—the man who in a bus or train sprawls over onto his neighbor's seat. Figure #124 reproduces the initial letter of the signature of a police officer who in a sudden rage killed his wife because, as he explained, she took too much of the quilt for herself when they were in bed.

Conversely, the narrow letter is the result of restrained and constricted movements. It indicates a self-conscious attitude.

157

Ah - there is life
it is mustling through
Great Music.
Your eyes are very Keen

#122

158

me semble qu'elle est trop
dans la solitude adieu
monsieur *Candos*

#123

#124

englishwoman but my father is a German
(a)

Maurice Benerbe

#125

May 19,
(b)

Monday in June.

159

Figure #125 *a* shows part of a sentence written by a very inhibited boy of fourteen, a stutterer, troubled by conflicts in his family situation. Narrow letters of more than usual height, with the first stroke jutting up markedly (fig. #125 *b*), can often be seen in the writing of very self-conscious persons who set their aspirations very high.

A handwriting that shows horizontal expansion in both letter forms and letter spacing is in general assumed to be the hallmark of a forthright personality, free and uninhibited in social contacts. However, there are handwritings showing an expansion that is merely an effect of wide spacing of narrow letters. This discrepancy points to conflict. It may indicate freedom in social contacts accompanied by inhibitions in the more intimate relations of life (figs. #88, #126). In a pretentious hand such spacing produces a pseudo expansion, because the desire to command space is contradicted by the retentiveness disclosed in the narrowness of the letter shapes.

#126

The older graphologists regarded the degree of expansion in a handwriting as a criterion of the subject's sense of economy. The narrow hand was adjudged to indicate a parsimonious disposition. This proves true in a general sense, in that the writer of a small, narrow hand is not only unconsciously conserving paper but is also inclined to hold back his available energy. In social relations this may take the form of passive behavior or reluctance to commit oneself to action or definite undertakings.

According to graphologists who apply psychoanalytic viewpoints, the narrow hand marked by smeariness is characteristic of the "anal type," i.e., the individual interested in his daily bowel movements and in anal humor. The retentive tendency may manifest itself by sublimation as stinginess or disposition to hoard.

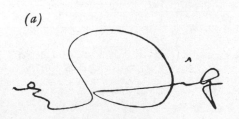

#127

A handwriting that illustrates both pseudo expansion and anal quality is that of Julius Streicher (fig. #127); the indices are the enormously oversized pattern and the narrow middle-zone letters, blotched by reason of their very constriction. The script is striking for its megalomaniac exaggeration in all other features. The rigid fidelity to copybook forms reflects infantilism and the writer's early background as a grammar-school teacher. The angularity that breaks even the loops into triangles, together with the intensity of pressure, expresses stubbornness and rigidity of mind, as well as the notorious sadism of the subject.

CAPITAL LETTERS

Capital letters are emphasized in most systems of penmanship, and considerable size is allotted to them. While the school-model capital is definitely larger than the other letters, this normal enlargement is sometimes even exaggerated. Vain people, bent on self-display and by the same token greatly impressed by wealth, success, and social prestige, tend to indulge in oversize capitals and elaborate ornamentation (p. 81). A narcissistic man will aggrandize his own initials (figs. #124, #128 *a, b*). In the script

#128

(a) *(b)*

161

Nemzetünk szolgálatában lehet halni, de elfáradni -

Szálasi Ferenc

#129

shown in figure #129—penned by the leading Hungarian quisling —the general features are typical of the hand of a lowly clerk. But the upshooting initial of the signature, a clear instance of what Crépieux-Jamin calls *surélévation,* betrays rampant ambition.

With quite different motivation, a writer may enlarge or otherwise emphasize the initial letter of the name of someone who stands high in his regard or affection (or the initial letter of a word standing for this person, e.g., a personal pronoun). Conversely, in relation to persons who have incurred the dislike or hate of the writer, such letters may unconsciously be dwarfed. Examples of this kind of emotional weighting are innumerable.

#130

quand Vous vous
Ghetto de new York

Figure #130 shows the handwriting of an ambassador stationed in a continental capital, who in a philandering note to a distinguished Polish beauty retouches the initial letter of the pronoun *vous* several times over, each time increasing its height. In

#131

figure #131, there is a double use of emphasis, in that the initial in the signature of the writer is large, while the first letter of the name of the addressee is not only smaller but deprived of its due capitalization. This specimen is from a letter written by a young man to a friend whom he at that moment hated as his rival for the hand of a girl. Similarly, deprecation may be expressed by dwarfing initial letters in such nominal expressions of sentiment as "Dear Sir," "Sincerely," etc., thus unconsciously canceling the literal content of the word.

#132

A salient example of deprecation by such means appears in figure #132. This specimen is from the hand of a rabid anti-Semite, who was advising a friend not to allow any "East End jews" to "push him around." The word "jew" not only lacks the prescribed capital; it is also smeary, blotchy, narrow, and almost illegible. Furthermore, half of the letter *w* is missing. The rest of the writing is contrastingly sharp, clear, and well expanded.

THE CAPITAL "I"

The English language differs from all others in the special function accorded to the capital *I* in its use as the pronoun of the first person—the representative of the ego. It constitutes a word

163

#133

in itself. The manner in which this *I* is shaped—its height and width, its proportional and stylistic relation to other letters, i.e., whether it is emphasized, neutral, or minimized, whether it is clear-cut or entangled in flourishes—all reveal the writer's sense of his own worth, the quality of his self-esteem, and in what sort of regard he wishes to be held by others (fig. #133).

#134

164

Figure #134 reproduces the handwriting of a young man who ran away from home at the age of thirteen, roaming about the country as a tramp. As an adult he worked only occasionally, and studied music when he had money to pay for lessons. At the time he wrote this specimen he was working as a handyman at a summer camp for artists. In the evenings he could be found in the parlor practicing on the piano. He also made sketches and drawings. He was a talented but confused person who regarded himself as worthless and useless. Throughout his script he uses a small *i* for the personal pronoun, to register his self-devaluation.

PROJECTION OF THE BODY IMAGE

A capital may symbolize a human figure. Clinical experience confirms the assumption that frequently the capital serves for a projection of the self. In this case it will reflect the writer's emotional conflicts and compensations in relation to his body image. Studies of personality projection in drawings of the human figure carried out by Machover[94] and others agree remarkably with graphological findings on this point. With the help of the individual's history or associations, this connection between the capital letter and the writer may be brought to light.

#135

The writer of the specimen shown in figure #135 was a woman spending her entire life in a wheelchair, with the lower part of her body covered by a blanket. She was very attractive and quite buxom; few people knew her pathetic secret. An injury in early youth had arrested growth in her lower extremities, and her legs remained like a tiny child's. The fact that she projects her body image as traumatized is apparent in the disproportion between the ample upper part and the shrunken lower part of the initial *E* in her given name, as well as in the striking detachment of the parts. In figure 136, we have the self-symbolization of a similarly afflicted woman; the script so strikingly illustrates this type of projection that it is presented here even though the expression appears in noncapitalized letters. The shriveled letter forms stand for the writer's atrophied body, and the skeleton stems of the *f*'s for legs that were "like broomsticks." The fact that this woman was emotionally concentrated on her disabilities arising from a bladder dysfunction quite obviously explains the idiosyncratic lower loops. An equally revealing projection of the body image appears in the initial letter of the signature shown in figure #363.

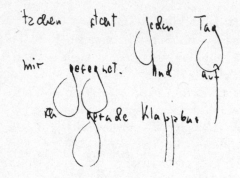

#136

ZONAL INTERPRETATION OF SIZE

As is plain from the foregoing discussion, the interpretative evaluation of size is conditioned by the implications of various factors. We must therefore examine size and proportion within the framework of the three zones and also in the light of the dominant directional trend. This will enable us to link the graphic features of a script with the inner motivations and attitudes of the writer (p. 137). It is constantly to be borne in mind, however, that while for purposes of analysis any one zone may be singled out for examination and description, none can be dealt with as registering any manifestation of personality functioning in dissociation from the other two.

166

The analysis of proportions in terms of zonal significance proceeds as follows:

MIDDLE ZONE

The middle zone has been described as reflecting the conscious needs of the ego in terms of everyday reality. When the elements located in this zone are of medium height in proportion to those of the other zones, we may assume that the writer has a wholesome self-confidence and good adjustment to life. An example of such proportion is found in the writing of Enrico Caruso (fig. #137). Gandhi's writing, though small, also shows good height

#137

in the middle zone (fig. #116). Extreme height in middle-zone elements betokens exaggerated self-assertiveness in the writer, a tendency to overrate his own importance and thereby to detach his interest from other persons. People who make great issues of their most trivial personal affairs tend to enlarge the middle zone at the expense of the upper zone. Pulver calls this an index of "biological egotism" (fig. #138*a, b*).

raese). Here the nobles rubbed ders with the intellectuals, drinking , intoxicating themselves with their

(a)

(b)

#138

she could stay over for a while because seems to dread so

A small middle zone indicates that the writer tends to underrate himself and is given to inferiority feelings or self-abasement (fig. #139). In such scripts we find the expression of an ego oppressed and depressed by the outside world.

In most handwritings the elements of the middle zone fluctuate in height, in width, and in slant. The degree of this fluctuation is an indicator of sensibility. A very responsive person will react

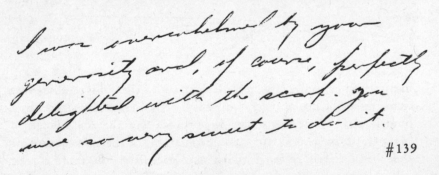

#139

to the environment with emotional lability. This gives us the problem of the sensitive individual: with richness of feeling and openness to experience there goes a corollary tendency to surrender wholly to emotional stimuli.

Parts of letters that jut out beyond their expectable limits where the middle zone is small, or unizonal letters that assume almost the proportions of capitals, may stand for compensative reactions, i.e., bursts of excessive self-assertion offsetting moments of self-devaluation (fig. #140). Figure #141 presents a striking example of diminution of the middle zone to such an extent that the individual letters appear truncated, or almost flattened out. This contrasts sharply with the *surélévation* of the first stroke in the initial letters of both names—the exaggeration moreover

#140

#141

carrying the stroke beyond the limits of both the upper and the lower zone. It is significant that the writer, after this first thrust of extreme self-assertion, draws in to an almost microscopic second downstroke, while the third shrinks almost to the vanishing point. The thrust and tension of the initial movement go with a large and aggressive claim on space. The kinetic propulsion comes from the depth, the movement taking its start from the left (the past), far from the stem (the present). Graphologically, this springboard stroke indicates extreme tension as well as aggressive feelings that have their source in past experiences.

169

Uniformity of height indicates unwavering self-confidence or overcontrol, to the exclusion of personal feelings. Monotonous regularity of height bespeaks the regimented, automaton type of individual (figs. #75, #76). The combination of a large middle zone and rigid letters of stereotyped regularity is one of the hallmarks of what may be called the schizoid pattern.

UPPER ZONE

The proportionate size of the stems, loops, and other elements in the upper zone gives a clue to the writer's intellectual and spiritual orientation—his cravings and aspirations that reach beyond the sphere of practical interests. Well-proportioned loops and stems, accompanied by high-placed *i* dots and *t* bars (p. 226), reflect mental alertness and liberal sentiments. An upper zone that predominates in height as against the other two suggests a disposition to the "holy curiosity of inquiry," as Einstein phrases

#142

it. This is illustrated in figure #142, which presents the handwriting of William Herschel, the eighteenth-century astronomer whose exploring spirit contributed notably to expanding man's horizon. A revealing feature in this sober writing is the extraordinary upper-zone configuration in the word "obed't."

#143

Oversized elements in the upper zone, easy swing, and pleasing design denote creative imagination. Abraham Lincoln's handwriting reflects imaginative power in the upswing of the initials and in the height of the upper zone (fig. #143). In Benjamin

#144

Disraeli's hand a complicated but organized design attests to rich imagination (fig. #144). Figure #145 reproduces the signature of an idealist in the romantic tradition, a religious philosopher and a revolutionary. The tall stems of his initials symbolize a

#145

lofty and liberal view of life. Their intertwining reflects a complex pattern of introversive and extraversive trends: the stem that arches leftward points to the world of introspection, the stem that springs rightward reaches toward the outer world and denotes a tendency to identify with the social goals of humanity.

A contrast to the foregoing picture is offered in the handwriting of Mihaly Zichy, a painter who became famous and infamous because of a series of pornographic drawings he executed for the czar of Russia. The fantastic configurations in the lower zone, carried beyond all bounds of measure, are matched by the vaulting upper loops and the high-floating *i* dots, indicating a phantasy working powerfully in both the higher and the lower psychic realm (fig. #146).

#147

A word of caution is needed, however, in regard to certain pitfalls attendant on the interpretation of the upper zone. Figure #147 presents a good case in point. Although the upper-zone elements appear to have height, this is an effect only, resulting from a mending, elongating, and retouching of the loops and stems—as in the second *t* of the word "situation," and the *h* in "happen." This writer is compulsively concerned with the gap between his achievement and his aspirations. He corrects and perfects his performance by enlarging and amplifying the upper-zone elements, in order to compensate his insecurity feelings.

Oversized, formless, or confused upper-zone elements imply a reaching into the realm of phantasy to substitute an imaginary world for reality. Blurred strokes and amorphous forms extending into the stratosphere betray merely an unconscious flight into dreams and illusions (fig. #148). A deliberate imbalance, ec-

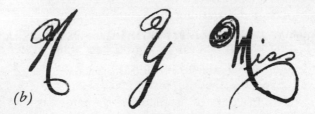

#148

centricity, or obfuscation of design in this zone reveals the fabricator who puts no bounds on his invention.

LOWER ZONE

The lower zone has been defined as carrying the expression of material demands, biological imperatives, and instinctual urges. In the upper portion of the lower zone are projected the tendencies relating to material interests. Pulver designates inflated lower loops as "money bags." Forcefully traced, full-bodied, long loops

173

in this zone denote strong sexual drive. In figure #149, specimen f is from the hand of a man to whom both these ascriptions applied. Specimen c is the script of a woman regarded by her friends as heartless; though she was driven by an insatiable sexual urge, she was never emotional in her erotic relationships.

In considering the clues to sex behavior that may appear in the elements of the lower zone, we must recall the limitation of graphology as regards the possibility of readily discerning the age and sex of a writer from his script (p. 115). It is true that the graphologist can perceive "masculine nature" or "feminine nature" in a handwriting—this referring, however, to the psychological rather than the physiological make-up of the subject. But since the functional roles respectively assigned to the sexes—those distinctive behavior patterns that have been "culturally over-elaborated" in the past, to use Mead's phrase—have of late become increasingly interchangeable, the reflection of the one pattern or the other in a handwriting no longer serves as a sufficiently certain index of the sex of the writer. It needs no more than to instance the female wrestlers in television productions and male "sitters," career women and dishwashing men—to mention only a few of the overlappings in modern life. Handwritings that might be those of either men or women appear in figures #64, #98, #149 h (these are actually female hands) and in figures #96, #149 a, #285 (male hands); the scripts are those of professional persons.

Thus the handwriting of a man or woman may deviate in some degree from the conventional masculine or feminine pattern without thereby necessarily pointing to homosexuality. This confirms the finding of Jacoby[69]— on the basis of a study of the scripts of thousands of sexually abnormal persons carried out at the Magnus Hirschfeld Clinic in Berlin—that homosexuality is not with certainty disclosed in handwriting.

However, considerable evidence has accumulated to indicate that handwriting yields information about sex behavior. For example, we have observed earlier (fig. #48) how the handwriting of a genitally underdeveloped boy changed during a period of

iting on a prescription
makes me feel light
& wonder what you
t tell from the
ting per se
previous
am *(a)*

strong
(b)

yet
(c)

get together,
(d)

system
systems
(e)

leaves jo

mess min
(f)

ting, but
we'll with
ng impression
posterity to
greatness
(g)

flat & r
a more m
was run
food & m
Jenny, f
for this
charge of
(h)

#150(a)

medical treatment that brought about the onset of sexual maturation. In figure #150,* we may note changes in graphic expression
corresponding with changes in the sex behavior of a male pervert
(a "fetishist") following on psychotherapeutic treatment.[119] In
the script shown in figure #156 a, the indications of lack of sexual
libido will become discernible in the light of the discussion below.
The pattern found in figure #59 reflects a twisted emotional attitude resulting from deficient sexual development. The script of
a male sex deviate reproduced in figure #151 shows effeminate
features.

#150(b)

---

* Courtesy of Herbert Peter.

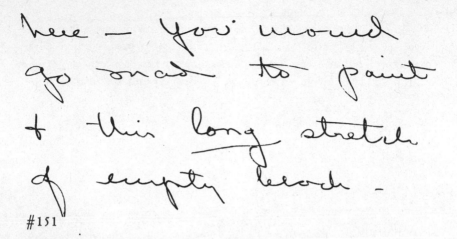

here — you would
go mad to paint
+ this long stretch
of empty beach —

#151

THE LOWER LOOPS

The question as to how a given individual comes to terms with sex can be approached graphologically through study of the lower loops in his script, though the final judgment must of course take into account the evidence of other features. It is important to bear in mind always that it is not merely the size nor the shape of the loop that tells us about the writer's erotic cravings (fig. #149 *a*), his tender feelings (fig. #149 *b*), or his brute lusts (fig. #149 *h, g*), his ability to establish relationship (fig. #149 *d, e*), or his tendency to repress (fig. #152) or suppress (fig. #156) desires connected with the gratification of erotic needs. As in all other aspects of interpretation, the over-all expression of the writing pattern is a basic criterion.

#152   *(b)*

(a)

177

In order to arrive at the true picture, it is necessary furthermore to know something about the physiological processes involved in tracing loops and stems. Our discussion of this point here permits of only a tentative explanation in oversimplified form.

#153

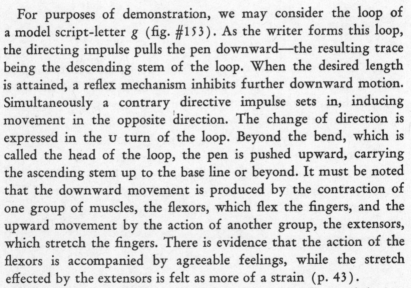

For purposes of demonstration, we may consider the loop of a model script-letter g (fig. #153). As the writer forms this loop, the directing impulse pulls the pen downward—the resulting trace being the descending stem of the loop. When the desired length is attained, a reflex mechanism inhibits further downward motion. Simultaneously a contrary directive impulse sets in, inducing movement in the opposite direction. The change of direction is expressed in the ∪ turn of the loop. Beyond the bend, which is called the head of the loop, the pen is pushed upward, carrying the ascending stem up to the base line or beyond. It must be noted that the downward movement is produced by the contraction of one group of muscles, the flexors, which flex the fingers, and the upward movement by the action of another group, the extensors, which stretch the fingers. There is evidence that the action of the flexors is accompanied by agreeable feelings, while the stretch effected by the extensors is felt as more of a strain (p. 43).

The pattern of motion in forming loops is well established as a result of practice and is carried through rather automatically. Though the mode of action is highly stereotyped, it is possible to turn on control at will. There are several possible ways of reacting. The writer may follow his motor pattern spontaneously and give free rein to the reflex mechanisms operating at the turning point, and thus produce a loop with a smoothly rounded head (figs. #131, #149). He may also modify his natural motion by elabora-

one of the charming evening
our lovely new home —
he is having — and was up
did — it certainly meant

(a) Lieut E. S.

(b)

(c)

(d)

Thank you ever and
so much. You truly are
darling to think of us.
We are looking forward
to having you out here
since the end of (e) (f)

(g)

May 19,

(h)

(i)

plaster
from

this means to you for your again

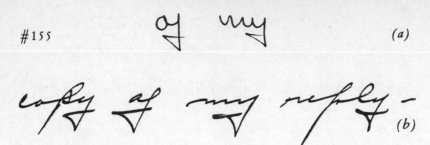

(b)

tion (fig. #154 *a-k*) or repress it (fig. #155 *a, b*). Or he may interrupt the motion and cut off at the turning point (fig. #156). Hence a variety of individual ways of self-regulation, or some inhibition or deficiency, may influence the length and form of the loop. A firm stroke together with a smooth curvature at

the destroyer Con

the sloop Amethy

attacked by Co

(a)

(b)   #156   *(c)*

(d)

(a)   *(b)*   *(c)*

(d)   #157   *(e)*

the turning point can be produced only by a writer whose movement is free and well co-ordinated; this suggests analogous freedom and co-ordination in all other bodily movements, such as
gait, gestures, and sexual functioning (fig. #149). Elaborated
loops betoken interference with the normal movement, and betray
self-consciousness, i.e., awareness of something that should be a
purely reflex occurrence (fig. #154). Jerky, tremulous, or broken
loops denote weakness (fig. #157) or disturbed co-ordination
(fig. #158), while a skeleton stem without loop formation points
to a rejection of sex (fig. #156). There may be other vagaries
projecting sexual phantasy (figs. #146, #154 *a, k*), or departures

(a)   *(b)*   *(c)*

#158

from normal patterning that disclose sexual evasiveness (figs. #121, #134, #152), aggressiveness (figs. #127, #155, #275), or perversion (figs. #151, #159, #279, #280); in figure #159 *a*, the treatment of the letter *p* strikingly attests the mental imagery of a male homosexual.

(a)

(b)   (c)

#159   (d)

It goes without saying that no activity proceeds without a certain measure of control. But there is a range of difference in degree, from the purely reflex level to overcontrol. It is well established that some diseases involving the central nervous system, and others impairing the motility of limbs or joints, may cause dysfunctions whose effects are recorded in odd formations of the loop. But there is also evidence that some peculiar loop formations testify merely to functional disorganization in an organically unaffected individual, in the sense that subconscious or only partially realized emotional factors, pleasant or unpleasant, interfere with the act of writing.

However, the different lower-loop formations, reflecting different modes of sexual functioning, do not refer to clearly defined, consistent types of sex behavior. In the writing of any given individual, the loops may change from one form to another, as a result of developmental changes, or of medication or psychotherapy; furthermore, any of a number of circumstances may activate inhibiting factors or influence the writer's mood and interest in sexual activity.

Various other graphic features such as slant, rightward or leftward trend in loops, clear-cut, pastose, or blotchy outlines, help to illuminate the particulars of the psychosexual make-up of the writer. These factors will be discussed in detail in later chapters. Only one further aspect of the indications regarding sex behavior to be found in loops and stems need be mentioned here—namely, how much regularity of size they show. The degree of irregularity, which may range from slight to extreme, reveals the degree of the writer's susceptibility to stimulation and his readiness for response. Beyond that it is also a gauge of emotional stability. Each individual has his own threshold of sexual excitability and his own measure of reactive control. Here again the general finding applies. Monotonous regularity in the size of loops bespeaks the dull temperament or overcontrol (fig. #138), whereas marked irregularity mirrors extreme excitability (figs. #146, #251) or lack of control (figs. #150 *a*, #255).

(IX)

S L A N T

The letters of a script are viewed as though they were standing on a base line. If the downstrokes tilt away from the true vertical by only a slight angle (5°), the writing is considered to be upright. When the downstroke is so inclined toward the right or the left that it slopes off no more than halfway from the vertical (45° angle), the slant is regarded as moderate. When the downstroke leans nearer than this toward the base line, in either the rightward or the leftward direction, the slant is rated as extreme (fig. #160).

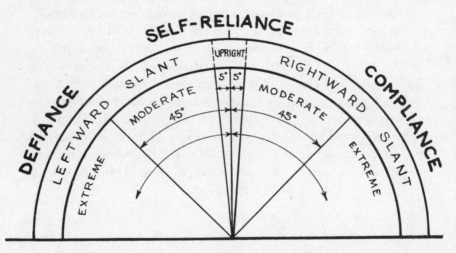

#160

In traditional graphology, a graphometer was used to obtain a precise measurement of the angle of slant. For interpretative purposes, however, such exactitude is unnecessary, although the graphometer is employed in scientific investigations and in examining documents suspected of being forgeries.

The rightward slanting hand represents the most natural way of writing and is the most frequently occurring one. It has more "go" than the upright hand. Particularly in speedy writing, the letters assume a rightward slant; that is, they lean forward in the direction of the writing movement. The graphic gesture can be visualized in terms of an image—the forward pitched body of a jockey as he gallops his horse down the home stretch.

In the United States, the earlier copybooks prescribed the rightward slant (fig. #161), but this is no longer the only accepted way of writing; indeed, the upright hand favored in many American schools is gaining ground (p. 45). A child at first necessarily follows the copybook model, but when individualization sets in,

#161

To Mrs. Klara G. Roman
With the compliments
of the author
New York
June 18, 1935.

Against the sect which impo

Against the empire proclaim

Against science when she

Against every principle

Against illness and again

#162

he generally chooses the slant that comes natural to him. He may adopt a rightward slant (fig. #162) or an upright hand (fig. #163), regardless of whether his school penmanship training favored the one or the other. He may, however, change to a left-ward slant (fig. #164), which is never taught in any school. Slant

Estimada amiga:

#163

Hoy tomaré a las diez de la mañana el tren para Boston. Espero que su docta amiga, miss Bixby no será demasiado ocupada, y podrá dedicar-me algunos momentos de su valioso tiem-

Thank you again for introducing us to Dr. ___ - we are grateful to both you and him - and he is such a lively person besides.

If you should find time we would love to know how the summer is materializing for you - anyhow you will hear from us again.

#164

is therefore ultimately a personal gesture. After the copybook stage, emotional motivations are its major determinants, as is indicated by graphological studies. As an outcome of direct experience, early graphologists believed rightward slant to indicate a dominance of feeling, while an upright hand was held to connote a dominance of reason. In the working hypothesis of modern graphologists, the three categories of slant—upright, rightward, and leftward—represent three basic attitudes, namely, self-reliance, compliance, and defiance (Chart).

The writing of spontaneous and sensitive young persons in general slants to the right, but there are youngsters who, in their eagerness to stand up straight, lean backward. With advancing years they become less impetuous, less emotional, and less defiant, so that the degree of slant in either direction decreases (figs. #40, #41, #337). An explicit example may be cited from the history of a woman whose writing has been known to the author from her earliest years. As a sensitive and emotional child, the subject wrote a rightward slanting hand. With the advent of puberty, she felt the strain of social, school, and parental restrictions, against which she tried to revolt. This was expressed in a negativistic and contrary behavior quite in contrast to her usual compliant conduct. In correspondence with this attitude, the girl's handwriting changed, taking on an extreme backward slant. However, thanks to a sympathetic and understanding environment, the rebellion lasted only a short while, and she soon achieved a fairly good emotional adjustment. In adolescence, her participation in the romanticism that prevailed among young people in the first decade of the present century in Europe was freely expressed in a rightward sloping hand. When the girl attained maturity, the slant gradually moderated and her script became nearly upright. This was especially marked in manuscript involving scientific formulations, whereas her personal and informal communications still showed a slight rightward slant.

Marked rightward slant is characteristic of persons who wear their hearts on their sleeves, or wallow in sentimentality. Excitable individuals whose reactions are enthusiastic or violent beyond average bounds, write with an extreme rightward slant. Excessive rightward slant goes with uncontrolled, irresponsible behavior and lack of resistance to internal and external stresses.

The handwritings of alcoholics frequently show such extreme rightward slant. The exaggerated slant is here generally only one of a cluster of telltale features: these include unsteady, tremulous strokes or a zigzag tracing that betrays gross tremor, and misshapen letters set irregularly in wavering downhill lines (fig. #165*). This group of features seems to indicate a type of in-

#165

I wish I was young enough to get married ag

---

* Courtesy James J. Smith, M.D.

188

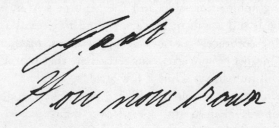

Although I don't drink
not 100% and after reading
reckon something went in
a deficiency somewhere in
system which went nero
down in 1941 and lost
pep and drive. My age

#166

dividual who is susceptible to alcohol not only because of lowered psychological resistance but also because of a metabolic imbalance. To those engaged in research on "problem drinking," it may be of interest to know that handwriting can disclose a disposition to drift into alcoholism.[149] It may also reveal in the course of treatment whether the patient is making an effort at control or is simply drifting. In the first instance, the handwriting will often show a change from rightward to leftward slant (fig. #166*); in the second, there may be no change of slant (fig. #167*).

Jack
How now brown

#167

---

* Courtesy James J. Smith, M.D.

An extreme rightward slant increasing in tilt within each succeeding word may indicate uncontrollable excitation or the overactivity of mania. The progressive incline may reach such a maximum that the final letter almost lies prone. This portrays a person who loses all footing, toppling over in his frenzy. An outstanding example of such a slant is supplied in the signature of Adolf Hitler (fig. #168).

#168

Figure #169 shows a script with a moderate rightward slant of utmost regularity. Its vigorous, rhythmic flow suggests a high degree of control. The pattern is impressive in its integrity of structure, arising from the even distribution of diverse and flexible forms, the steadiness of the shading, and the consistency of the slant. But as the movement proceeds, a striking irregularity appears in the word "Cordially": the enlarged C shows a deviation in slant, and the letter leans forward in a gracious enveloping gesture. There is obviously some welling up of spontaneous emotion here, so that the word is not written simply as a conventional *envoi*. The graphic expression and the genuine sentiment are one: there is a wish and a will to be cordial, and to extend a warm and encompassing embrace. The soaring upper loops, reaching into the sphere of idealistic concerns, suggest that the writer's warmth extends to all humanity. Thus a few strokes, pregnant with meaning, speak to the graphologist with a far richer eloquence than hundreds of verbal meanings spread over many pages. Here they give us in graphological epitome a profile of a noted American personality.

April 26/24

My Dear _?_

It was thoughtful of you to
enable me to send our greeting
to our greatly valued friend —

Recall you, also, for the report
of your work.

Cordially,

Louis D. Brandeis

#169

191

The upright hand with firm vertical downstrokes suggests the self-reliant writer who desires independence and is not prone to display his feelings. A completely upright hand is not found very frequently, since it demands the utmost control and will power (fig. #163). More often the upright letters are interspersed with slanting forms (fig. #170).

return — and whether or not

to close us out.

#170 *It is a completely stupid*

FLUCTUATIONS IN SLANT

A change of slant is the signal of a change in the direction of the emotional current. Figure #171 shows the handwriting of a young man of twenty-five who was thought to have an Oedipus

#171

and was absolutely astonish
was your Father. He wasn't lay
a matter of 3 or 4 blocks fra
nd me had a nice long cha
of England and the perils of D
roks much better And says
way. We're going to try to hav

complex. After the death of his mother he suffered considerable anxiety because of a fear of homosexual impulses. This state of mind is reflected in the writing, which at first is slanted rightward and forms a naturally flowing pattern. Suddenly, however, the writer, apparently gripped by anxiety, shifts to a leftward slant, and from the fifth line on produces such lower-zone anomalies as the p in the word "peril" and the y in the word "way." The abrupt change illustrates strikingly the immediate effect of a psychic occurrence on graphic movement.

In the writing of persons violently torn between love and hate, between fixation and protest, slant is quite unstable, often changing within a word (fig. #172 a) or even within a single pen stroke; in other words, the letter body and its extensions may slope in different directions (fig. #172 b). Fluctuations in slant bespeak a conscious effort at control that is disturbed by an ambivalent response to assailing influences; in the seesaw of inclinations of yielding and protest, the movement disintegrates and the pattern becomes an array of disparate elements.

#172   (a)

(b)

Extreme leftward slant points to conflicts whose sources lie in early life experiences. It is the mark of an individual who builds up defenses in the form of negativistic behavior, opposition to everything—persons, surroundings, whatever situation may arise (fig. #173). Mendel, in a study of such handwritings, made in-

#173

quiries into the early childhood histories of G. B. Shaw, W. M. Thackeray, Maxim Gorki, Hendrik Ibsen, and others. He found that each of them had had an unhappy childhood disturbed by an imbalance in the relations of his parents. Mendel maintains further that slant is "the indicator of the writer's position between father and mother, or, more specifically, between male and female leadership."[101] There is little basis for such an assumption. Graphologists are agreed merely on the general conclusion that slant, according to its direction and degree, is a gauge of the writer's acceptance of or resistance to environmental influences.

SLANT AND HANDEDNESS

Studies of the psychological significance of slant have frequently left out of account the possible correlation with the physiological factors underlying leftward or rightward orientation. The layman may be startled by the unequivocal assertion that rightward slant is linked with right-handedness, and leftward slant with left-handedness.[54] The fact becomes plain when an individual who has habitually used a rightward slant suffers some lesion that deprives him of the use of his right hand and has to learn to manipulate the pen with his left hand.[37] He may acquire sufficient skill to produce a script quite similar to his former hand-writing, but his slant will now be leftward. Saudek demonstrates this change by comparing specimens of the handwriting of Lord Nelson produced respectively before and after he lost his right arm at Trafalgar.[137]

The great majority of people are right-handed; they use the right hand as the master hand[16] in manipulating the objects of their environment, and employ the left hand only as an auxiliary. Moreover, a right-hander has greater strength and facility in all the members of the right side than in those of the left side; the converse holds true for the left-hander.[28]

A minority of persons are left-handed. The left is their master hand, with the right hand playing the adjuvant role. For these individuals, writing presents special problems[163] and difficulties,[117] since their natural way of writing is the reverse of the conventional right-handed procedure: this is called "mirror writing," i.e., it can be read like an ordinary script when reflected in a mirror. An excellent example of mirror writing has been left by Leonardo da Vinci, who, though equally adept with either hand, was left-handed. It is interesting to note that he employed a conventional right-handed writing for general communication, but resorted to mirror writing in his diary (fig. #174).

#174

The fact that mirror writing is the natural mode of the left-hander is well known, and has been experimentally demonstrated by the author.[55] For example, a number of students who were latently left-handed—though they were unaware of it and had always written with the right hand—were asked to write their

Elaine Blaukoum

I never tried to write mirror writing or upside-down writing before.

names with the left hand in mirror writing, and also upside down. They had never tried this before, yet they did it "right off the bat," and quite successfully (fig. #175). Genuinely right-handed students were unable to produce such writing.

But mirror writing is unsuited to the purposes of everyday life. Therefore the left-hander is obliged to produce a script in the expectable right-handed mode. He may do this with either hand. However, it can be shown that even retaining the privilege of using the left hand does not obviate the difficulties of the left-hander constraining himself to the right-handed operational pattern.[54] Therefore many a left-hander shifts to use of the right hand. Through practice he may achieve a more or less successful adaptation: he may appear to be ambidextrous, using either hand in various activities, or he may make an ostensible shift of handedness and function like a right-hander. But whatever he does, there is considerable evidence that his true orientation remains a latent influence.[62] And against the repressions that his shift entails, one of the ways of expressing his unconscious bent is to write with a leftward slant. There are left-handers who appear fully adjusted to the conventions of a right-handed world, even to the rightward slant in writing. In order to achieve this slant, they unconsciously hit upon the device of shifting the paper in a counterclockwise direction—a position markedly different from that used by the right-hander. But if the paper is placed straight in front of the subject instead of obliquely, he will be unable to produce a rightward slant, and his letters will definitely tilt to the left.

This was confirmed in the course of the author's study[57] of the handwritings of 283 pairs of identical twins. In most of the pairs, it was found, one of the partners wrote with a rightward and the other with a leftward slant. The investigation provided evidence that the dissimilarity in the handwritings of identical twins is due to a difference in lateral dominance (p. 234), since in most cases one twin proved to be right-handed and the other left-handed,[55] and this graphological finding was verified by clinical examination of the subjects. Prior to this research, no explanation of the dissimilarity in the handwritings of twins had been advanced,[114] although the question had been raised by Francis Galton, the founder of the science of human genetics, as far back as 1883.[40]

#176 (a)

(b)

Figure #176 shows specimens produced by two girls who were identical twins. The handwritings look almost exactly alike. However, in a second test the writing page was deliberately placed in the straight position before both of the girls. With this their scripts became quite dissimilar. One twin again wrote with her habitual rightward slant (fig. #177), while the other involuntarily produced an extreme backward slant (fig. #178). In the first test this girl had automatically compensated her leftward trend by turning the paper. When she saw her backward slanted script, she began to cry.

Since laterality is a salient factor in conditioning slant, it is obvious that its interpretation involves a variety of complex considerations. Not every graphologist has an opportunity of ascertaining whether a subject is right- or left-handed, but this remains largely a theoretical difficulty. In actual practice, the basic principles of graphological interpretation generally prove dependable. The usual reading of a backward slant as an indication of protest against or opposition to the environment (p. 62) applies to the left-hander in perhaps an additional sense: by sticking to his own bent he is protesting against the traditional action pattern imposed on him by the right-handed world.[16, 163] A recognition of this attitude is reflected in the terminology of political life. Groups or parties that tend toward the conservation of traditional values and of established ways form "the right"; the opposition—the dissidents, the nonconformists, the iconoclasts—constitute "the left." And the French phrase, *prendre l'affaire à gauche,* means to tackle a matter at the wrong end.

#177

#178

198

(X)

CONNECTIVE FORMS

In cursive writing, words are formed by joining letters to one another. The letters themselves are formed by linking together downstrokes and upstrokes. The tracings by which the joinings are effected are called connective forms. Graphologically, connective forms are classified into four types. These comprise the arcade, the garland, the angle, and the more or less anomalous joining that appears either as a mere thread or as a double curve (fig. #179).

#179

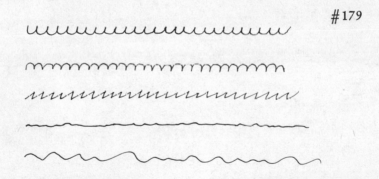

The arcade and the garland are rounded, the one being the inverse of the other. The arcade is shaped like an arch, the garland like an open bowl. Where downstrokes and upstrokes meet directly, we have the angular connective form. The fourth type appears where the linking of down- and upstroke is slurred to a threadlike tracing, or where rounded turns used at both top and bottom produce a double curve. These forms appear both in the shaping of letters and as ligatures between the letters within the word.

It is the mode of making joinings that gives the handwriting its distinctive character. The type of connective form chosen to join letters stamps the hand as rounded, angular, or of indefinite character. Used as letter parts, these forms respectively shape the letters: we may have for instance *m*'s and *n*'s of garland type, of arcade type, or of angular type. The fourth manner of connection produces a letter of indistinct shape (fig. #180). Thus the connective form, as a salient and basically characterizing feature of every handwriting, determines the essential expression of the writing pattern. From the standpoint of interpretation, it is a main indicator of the general make-up of the writer: it discloses both the pattern of his neuromuscular functioning (p. 278) and his psychosocial attitudes (chart, p. 131).

#180

In the writing of any adult, some one type of connective form will appear predominantly, and the same form will be found to predominate in his graphic expression throughout life. It might be supposed that every writer uses the mode of connection he learned at school. In mature handwritings, however, the manner of connection varies with the individual, regardless of what he learned in early youth. In Germany, the copybook model for the Gothic writing style taught up to very recently imposed the angular connective form (fig. #181), while in other Western countries the school standard prescribes rounded connections. Yet

#181

we find Germans adopting rounded connections because the angular style seems to go against the grain with them. This departure takes on striking implication when we compare the handwritings of two Germans of the old school who had, at least to a degree, a common conditioning—those of the yielding Hindenburg (fig. #182) and of the implacable Bismarck (fig. #183). Conversely, some individuals who have been taught to use a rounded hand change to an angular style later in life.

#182

#183

201

There are others, moreover, who use angles where none are called for—e.g., at the base or the top in oval letters such as *a* and *o* (fig. #184). Similarly, an *l* may be linked to a succeeding letter by means of an arcade, or *u* may be formed by arcades instead of having the expectable garland for its base (fig. #185);

#185

it is not at all unusual to find the converse—an *n* formed by garlands, so that it looks like a *u*. This makes the handwriting more difficult to decipher (fig. #186). Writers aware of the liability of confusion in such letter shapes try to correct their habit—usually without success. It seems that it is easier to change the size or slant of one's writing than the spontaneously employed connective form.

#186

In an experiment carried out by the author, in which a number of students were asked to make a casual continuous sequence of u's like garlands, and then continuous n's like arcades, each writer unwittingly revealed a marked leaning to the one or the other of the two forms, and this favored form was produced with greater facility and speed and with less tension and more regularity than the other.[58] This finding was derived from graphodyne recordings and measurements (p. 279). It seems to indicate that the tendency to use garlands rather than arcades, or vice versa, goes deeper than acquired habit and has its roots in the innate disposition of the individual.

If we analyze each of the connective forms in terms of the expression it projects, we shall understand why graphologists consider that the mode of connection used by a writer shows how he bridges the distance from the "I" to the "you," approaches his fellow men in general, and links himself or fails to attach himself to the environment. We must bear in mind constantly that the ductus is conceived as a path from the ego to the outer world. Hence the movement underlying the connective form is one of the writer's unconscious gestures contributing to the shaping of this individual path of his. That the manner of his gesture is a most revealing index of the quality of his personality, will become plain as we proceed to detailed analysis of each type of connective form.

THE GARLAND

The garland links the downstroke to the upstroke with a flowing curve swinging from left to right. It is a natural and effortless mode of connection. Its easy motion indicates adaptability; its shape suggests openness—in psychological terms, receptivity and responsiveness. This attitude goes with smooth functioning in the world, with instinctive avoidance of conflict and friction (fig. #187). However, the disposition to avoid conflict does not necessarily mark only the well-intentioned or the good-natured in-

alizing with myself and Groping to disprove it. You just don't know what you started! But then your more patient than all the rest combined.

dividual—the man who is careful to do no harm and to hurt no one's feelings. It is also found in the easygoing person who is inclined to take the path of least resistance (fig. #188), either from calculating self-interest or from weakness. Only the garland firmly and evenly traced can be evaluated positively (fig. #189).

for not having written to you sooner. but as you can see by where I am

#188

Rudyard Kipling   #189

Generous garlands flowing through the script with rhythmic freedom, their downstrokes producing a zestful accent like a recurring musical beat, express the energy of competent persons who give abundantly of themselves and yet do not yield nor lose their firmness (figs. #190, #273). Broad and imposing garlands

Dear Sir,

Thank you

letter of the

stand for extraversion and suggest a degree of exhibitionism (fig. #191). Shallow garlands running without modulation through the script betray the voluble individual given to empty talk (fig. #192). The flattened garland, traced weakly and flaccidly, indi-

Farewell

Summer

cates passive receptiveness, poor discrimination, or extreme susceptibility and lack of resistance (fig. #193).

to love circumstances

The underslung garland sprawled out so that it sags down on the base line indicates depression. Figure #194 shows such garlands in the script of a war veteran who had suffered a brain injury involving the frontal lobe; after the surgical wound was healed, he remained in a state of inertia and persistent depression. The pronated form that may be called a pseudo garland expresses adaptibility and amiability that are merely a veneer (fig. #195).

#195

Here furthermore the downstroke and upstroke are traced in such a way that they cover each other, and supply an illustration of the concealing stroke. This feature of tracing occurs rarely in broad garlands; it is found quite often in the pseudo garland and in the deep, narrow garland. This deep and narrow garland, for its part, is a contradiction of the true expression of the form (figs. #196, #368 *b*). Here the natural free flow of the movement

#196

vous mes remerciements compliments les plus

Marc Chagall

is under restraint, indicating that the genuinely extraversive disposition of the writer has been affected by environmental influences, and is veiled by shyness and reticence.

In the looped garland, when it is firmly traced, we have a form that appears fluid but actually arises from a taut movement. The springlike quality of the tracing is the outcome of tension mitigated by interpolation of a backward movement that necessarily produces the loop in the upper part of the letter—especially in *m*'s and *n*'s—from which the form is named (figs. #186, #197). Thus, just as the effort of inhaling is eased by the relaxation of exhaling, the strain of turning outward is relieved by turning inward, the alternation of tension and release serving to maintain a certain equilibrium.

THE ARCADE

Both the garland, which opens upward, and the arcade, which is closed at the top, bridge over the distance between the writer and the environment. Klages likens the contrast between these two forms to the contrast between the open and the grasping hand— the one receives freely, the other takes hold and covers. This image led graphologists to the generalization that the garland betokens a frank and liberal mind, while the arcade bespeaks the reserved and secretive personality.

#198

A glance at the handwritings of sculptors (fig. #198), architects and builders or planners in other fields (figs. #199,
#200), with their balanced arcades well integrated into the total
pattern, leads to a broader interpretation: the arcade implies a
structural sense. Its form suggests an arch, a bridge, a ceiling, a
hut on the ground. A corollary of this effect is the idea of en-
closure, covering, holding safe. By its nature the well-executed
arcade may have a pronounced architectural effect (fig. #212).
Not only persons working directly in the arts, but also those
concerned with aesthetic interpretation, such as art critics and
connoisseurs, etc., tend to produce arcades (figs. #199, #201).

#199

Germaine va toujours mal, ne
peut ni se lever ou s'asseoir, ni des-
cendre même l'escalier sans mon
aide.

Très amicalement à vous

#200

Thus the writer who uses arcades is concerned first and fore-most with structure, appearance, covering over or masking; a certain formalism checks spontaneity here. Pulver holds that this writer takes his stimuli in part from the visual and the aesthetic, in part from the deep sources of tradition and the collective ex-perience of his race and class. Thus while the garland expresses an easy and informal attitude, the arcade is associated with formality, control, and premeditation. The garland is the sign of availability for interpersonal relationships; the arcade closes the door, shuts out the world, shows only a façade. It is for this reason

Mrs. Klara G. Roman
121 Madison Avenue
New York 16
N.Y.

#201

Thank you both so much

for a lovely weekend in

that formalistic persons (fig. #202), as well as moral and social bigots (fig. #203) use the arcade. Where rhetoric and lip service take precedence over sincerity and genuine outgoingness, there the arcade will be found (fig. #204).

#203

and expense against your

an interview to determine

not I am correct in my

hints for saving time and money; any

one of them may be worth more to

#204

Hermine

Structurally unbalanced or shallow arcades call for a negative interpretation. A shallow arcade does not suggest a proud arch; rather, it shrinks to the image of a molehill (fig. #205). Top-heavy or ballooning arcades, interlaced in an irregular pattern, are often found in the writing of emotionally or mentally disturbed *ctrar Finance Commission organized to give assistance to banks, insurance companies and other*

#205

individuals; figure #206 shows the handwriting of a Lesbian, a cruel woman who was a troublesome and vicious schemer and a relentless liar. Figure #207 presents a handwriting in which commitment to the arcade is so strong that this form appears even where it conflicts with natural movement in the shaping of a letter, and the connection takes on an exaggerated or decidely conspicuous emphasis.

Since arcades result from controlled movements, they tend to be narrower than garlands. Markedly narrow arcades result from restricted movement, denoting inhibition. Arcades in which the downstroke and the upstroke are so close together that they

#206

#207

211

Now is forever
Then love is true —
So kiss me and hold me
There's no tomorrow
There's just tonight

partially conceal each other may reflect a reticent, timorous, or secretive nature, with a concomitant of insincerity (fig. #368 *c*). This form is often identified as the hypocrite's or sycophant's tracing; some early students of handwriting went so far as to regard it as the mark of the "wolf in sheep's clothing." Figures #208 and #209 both illustrate consistent use of arcades with concealing strokes. The first reproduces the script of a nurse who had had a very unhappy childhood. Her inhibitions led her to leave her husband after three days of marriage, and from then on to consume herself in overwork. She subsequently met another man whom she liked very much, but the only intimacy she permitted over a period of years was holding hands. Figure #209 shows the script of a nun whose only slightly concealed strokes suggest that the restrained behavior pattern they express was a social form, a part of her convent garb.

With remembrance in
9 days' prayer.

Sister Mary

*Édesapám festő volt és én
is vonzódtam a művészet felé.*

#210

The fact that the garland and the arcade are one the inverse of the other takes on special significance in connection with the handwritings of twins who differ in handedness. It has been observed that in such a pair the right-handed twin makes garlands, while the left-handed mate makes arcades. Figures #210 and #211 present the handwritings of twin brothers who were both architects—the first being the script of the right-hander, the second that of the left-hander. The latter, in tracing the wavy line requested of both subjects as part of the experiment, began by making garlands as his brother was doing, but found it uncomfortable and in the third trial resumed the connective form to which he was really conditioned.

This experiment demonstrates once more how the polarities of right and left, and up and down, help to explain disparate functioning in the handwritings of identical twins.[57] It has been shown

hirtelen választottuk az építészi pályát.

Édesapám szerette volna, hogy festők legyünk;

#211

213

how the opposite orientations of the right-hander and the left-hander express themselves in a rightward slanted script in the one and a leftward trend in the writing of the other. It should not be surprising therefore to come upon a parallel demonstration in their use of opposite form types in making connections—the one preferring the garland, and the other its inverse, the arcade.[58]

Where the arcade appears as the first element of the initial letter of a word, while elsewhere in the writing a different connective form is used, the variant tracing is regarded as standing for a formal gesture, a salutation or an obeisance (figs. #212, #221). Where the arcade appears as the ending of a word, it connotes inhibition, since it implies a movement of retreat replacing the natural outgoing spurt of a final stroke. This pantomine of holding in or withdrawal may be due to embarrassment or defensiveness; it may also, however, be evaluated as indicating a suppressive impulse arising from insincerity.

THE ANGULAR CONNECTIVE FORM

The garland and the arcade permit of a smooth, gliding movement with a forward impetus. The angular connective form, however, imposes a check on the continuity of movement—an abrupt stop and start at each turning point. The writer is obliged to brake the natural flow of his movement, since he can advance at satisfactory speed only by holding his pen firmly while joining the down- and upstrokes. This type of movement implies the same habituation to discipline reflected in the angular writing pattern as a whole (p. 93).

The angular formation is characteristic of strong-minded persons—those who welcome resistance and are disinclined to yield. This quality of personality is illustrated in the signature of a man who stood his ground in the Prussian ministry of state until he felt it imperative to resign in protest against the growing ascendancy of Nazi doctrine (fig. #212). The angular connection

#212

is found also in the handwriting of individuals who seek to impose their will upon the environment: it is an expression of the egotist (fig. #360), and of the "rugged individualist" or the nonconformist (fig. #213), and thus it may appear as the mark of the power urge; a classic example of such expression is the handwriting of Bismarck (fig. #183).

#213

The extremely regular angle, producing sharply cut, precise letters, is the choice of engineers and other technologists. This type of angularity can also be found in the scripts of persons occupied with the theoretical aspects of mathematics and the physical sciences. An outstanding example is the handwriting of Albert Einstein, which is notable on the one hand for its commonplace simplicity and on the other for the ingenious details in its upper zone (fig. #214).

#214

215

Irregularly formed angles bespeak a misguided attempt to display resolution, i.e., obstinacy or stubbornness (fig. #215).

THE THREADLIKE CONNECTIVE FORM

The connective form reduced to a threadlike stroke is the expression of an individual who is unsure about the world and most of all unsure about himself. He cannot make up his mind; he shuns the sharp corners of decision or vacillates between conflicting impulses. Klages interprets a thread formation appearing in the middle of a word as an index of the indecision that characterizes hysteria (fig. #216). On the other hand, the threadlike form may result merely from haste or excessive speed. When thought outruns the pen, the movement may be slurred in an effort to keep pace, at the sacrifice of form and articulation (fig. #217). A related form is the anomalous or amorphous tracing in which garland and arcade are combined, producing the double curve (fig. #218); this in rapid writing may appear flattened to a thread.

#216

is involved, and hence no problem

to cope with

formal economics, economic

I am enclosing

The protection of the ~~t~~ was a worker ot rather than a

Returning to ass during th last of th 19th century

A threadlike "dying out" of words has a specific meaning. It is the ultimate version of the tendency to decrease the letter size toward the end of a word (p. 155). It betokens an intuitive cast of mind—the individual who catches every thought of another, spoken or unspoken, who has the ability to "tune in," and also ability to wriggle out of difficult situations, to hit upon solutions. It is an index of the person who is not likely to commit himself to one course of action. In the illegible signature reproduced in figure #219, all of the middle zone is literally stretched out to a mere scrawled thread, except for the clear tracing of the initial of the given name. A striking feature is the phantom upper zone, in which the *t* bars and *i* dots are placed where they belong in relation to the letters that should appear. The signature is that of an urban district politician known for his sinuous dexterity in handling people. The inverse of this form is the threadlike ending *will the other the message*

#220

emphasized by sudden heavy pressure. This seems to be an expression of violence, a gesture of assault venting temper or discomfort (fig. #220).

THE MIXED CONNECTIVE FORM

In general, handwritings in which there is not some slight inconsistency in the use of connective forms are rare. Thus, many scripts will show a few angles interspersed among arcades; in others, isolated garlands appear amidst other types of connections. The interpretation of such variations depends, first, upon the manner and frequency of their occurrence, and, second, on whether they result in any weakening of the expressive effect of the predominant connective form. If the occurrence of variants is not frequent, and does not destroy the essential consistency of the writing pattern, it may be positively interpreted, as in figure #221. Here we have a changing movement recorded in a spontaneous writing pattern in which the variation of connective forms does not detract from the unity and clarity of the individual expression. A notable feature is that while the garland predominates, the beginning of a word or letter always takes the arcade form (as in the *m*), with the predilection for the garland thereupon immediately reasserting itself. The word or letter endings invariably show the garland formation.

This pattern of variation points to an interaction of conventional social motivation and heartiness of approach—the latter attitude taking the lead in interpersonal contacts. The impression is reinforced in the pattern as a whole by the rightward slant, the

My dear Mrs. Roman —

I am very kind of you,
to remember to send me
the copies of your articles.
I am so glad to have
them, and shall read
them with great interest.

It was such a pleas-
ure to meet you!

With cordial regards

Sincerely yours
Lillian M. Gilbreth.

#221

rightward tending terminal strokes, the generous spacing, and the
unpretentious design of capitals as well as other letters. In terms
of personality, such a consistently varied pattern indicates many-
sidedness, swift alternation of ideas, and a notable adaptability in
using—with speed and economy—the variety of . abilities and

ideas thus implied. Here we find the constellation of graphic and psychological features that characterizes the user of the garland in no wise impaired by the coincident appearance of the arcade.

A similarly definite constellation of features marks the script in which the arcade is dominant. The graphic traits include narrowness in the letters, upright or leftward sloping forms, controlled or restricted flow of movement, counterclockwise turns in circular formations, and abbreviated (fig. #305) or leftward tending terminal strokes (fig. #306). Occasional garlands appearing in this type of script soften the severity of the pattern and its expression of reserve and introversion. If, however, the variant forms are angles, the graphic picture becomes more severe, suggesting sharpness and ruggedness in the make-up of the writer.

Where we find relative uniformity in the use of connective forms, we may postulate a one-sided personality. Uniformity

new manner of reasoning and ing tradition. To be the patron-

it is a day-to-day account of happening by St. Simon. The story was not written

#222(*a*)

carried to an extreme produces stereotypy (fig. #222 *a*). Extreme regularity in forming angles is found in handwriting in which mechanical drill has destroyed the capacity for spontaneous expression (fig. #222 *b*).

annit magamini

#222(*b*)

220

(XI)

CONTINUITY AND FLUENCY

In cursive writing, the school model presents the word as a unit—a succession of letters joined to one another. However, no child is able to trace the form of a whole word in a single sweep of movement without once lifting the pen; indeed, very few adults are capable of doing this. In a flowing hand, several successive letters may be written in such a unitary movement (fig. #223). But individuals who write clumsily or laboriously find it necessary to raise the pen frequently for a fresh start. In some handwritings, there is a break after almost every letter; even a single letter may be traced with more than one stroke. These breaks, however, are not necessarily very noticeable. They may for instance be camouflaged in what is called the "soldered break," i.e., a retracing in which the writer attempts to fit together the parts of the broken stroke (fig. #224). However, no matter how well the joining is made, such adjustment always shows.

Otter Bein Co. manufacturers of special al stampings as Production Manager

#223

exporters might be worthy of If interested, kindly write, phone view at any time or place you

#224

221

The ability to connect a group of letters by means of a continuous movement is attained when writing becomes an automatic function. Walking, talking, using a typewriter, playing the piano, are all examples of routine skills acquired similarly by practice. Such functioning involves a complex co-ordination by which a sequence of motions performed always in a certain order unrolls with ease at any time.[159] When writing has reached this stage of development, the demands upon attention lessen: a single stimulation sets up a train of sequential motions covering a certain span. The larger the span, the greater the economy in time and energy.

An early study made by Rieger,[131] and more recent work carried through by Pophal,[120] have shown that there is a difference in the neural processes underlying the writing produced by separate motions as against that resulting from unbroken sequential movement. In the first, a separate innervation is required for the starting and another for the stopping of each motion. Sequential movement, on the other hand, arises from a single innervation, and thus consumes less energy than a group of separate motions. In the beginning, a child forms each letter separately. When he acquires skill, he carries out the writing movement almost without conscious attention, each part of a word automatically inducing the next.

The author's studies of writing performance in school children in Hungary showed that the average ten-year-old wrote the word

#225

10 YEARS
7 MONTHS

AVERAGE PRESSURE: 326 gm; TIME: 8.1 SEC

8 INTERRUPTIONS

11 YEARS
8 MONTHS

AVERAGE PRESSURE: 232 gm; TIME: 7.43 SEC

6 INTERRUPTIONS

12 YEARS
10 MONTHS

AVERAGE PRESSURE: 225 gm; TIME: 6.8 SEC

4 INTERRUPTIONS

"Budapest" with ten interruptions, chopping it up into eleven parts.[53] As the child grew older, the interruptions decreased to six or five. At the eighteen-year age level, the interruptions averaged three, not counting those that occur in dotting *i*'s or crossing *t*'s. The advance toward increasingly sequential movement is best demonstrated by graphodyne records showing the decrease of interruptions in movement in children's handwritings year by year. The graphodyne tracings in figure #225 show these changes in the handwriting of a boy of better than average skill, by a comparison of his writing performances at the ages of ten and a half, eleven and a half, and twelve and a half respectively.

The average adult writer interrupts his movement with each syllable in a word, besides stopping to dot *i*'s and cross *t*'s. This is normal practice and represents a medium degree of connectedness (fig. #226). When words are written by means of a continuous movement without any lifting of the pen, we have a high degree of connectedness (fig. #227). When the words appear markedly chopped up, we speak of disconnectedness (fig. #228).

#226

#227

#228

223

Connectedness is not to be judged solely on the basis of the continuity of the stroke, i.e., the trace of the pen upon the paper. Many writers do not interrupt their movement each time they raise the pen; thus the writing movement may be continuous even though the stroke is not. In other words, when the pen is lifted from the paper, an interruption of the stroke occurs, although the writing movement itself does not necessarily stop. The raising of the pen is merely a part of an unbroken curve of movement, just as a skier's jump produces a break in his trail on the snow but does not mark an interruption of his course.

Writing produced by a continuous movement of this kind is marked by flying finishes at the points where the pen was raised and new starts where it returned to the paper. If the ending point and the new starting point can be connected by an imaginary line that would coincide with the curve of continuity of the actual movement, the latter is assumed to have been unbroken. Conversely, when a shift of direction appears, the writing movement is regarded as having been discontinuous.

This test can be applied with striking proof in figure #229, which reproduces a letter from the pen of a French painter. It will be seen that the first seven words represent two unitary movements. *Cher Ami* in the first line and *Je* in the second are written in a single sweep: it is rather easy to perceive the continuity of movement taking in the *r* of *Cher* and the *A* of *Ami*. It is only a little less plain that the same sweep of movement, carrying on from the end of the *i* in *Ami* through the dot, vaults across the page to resume visibly again in the flying start of the *J*. Between *Je* and *suis*, however, there is a break. The long sweep across the page finally spends itself. A fresh impetus is needed to start on *suis*, as is evidenced by the adjustment between the two words—i.e., the initial hook of the *s* and the dying end stroke of the *e* in *Je* are on different levels. Going on with the imaginary reconstruction of the writing movement, we find the four words

Mardi.

Cher Ami

Je suis ici depuis
hier. Dites moi
où et quand je
puis vous voir.

Amitiés

Amanjean

suis ici depuis hier to have been produced by a unitary movement that came to a close attested by the period and the large blank space following it.

This specimen is striking for the sweep and unity of its pattern. The fluency and continuity of movement produce streamlined connections and build configurations in which every dot seems to be placed according to a creative plan. Such patterning makes a thematic unit of the written page. It comes naturally to men whose lives are integrated and who seek satisfaction in constructive work. A different type of continuity appears in the handwriting shown in figure #230; here the pattern of connectedness is expansive and complicated, reflecting a wealth of imaginative associations.

#230

The variety of individual habit in regard to raising or dragging the pen is especially reflected in the great number of ways contrived for dotting *i*'s and crossing *t*'s. One variant appears in the built-in *i* dot and another in the coupling *t* bar (fig. #231).

Thus far we have been discussing continuity and fluency as pertaining to cursive writing, which is based on flowing, con-

#231

tinuous movement. In regard to printscript, in so far as continuity appears at all, it must be considered in different terms. Here each letter is set down as a detached entity, and this requires constant interruption in movement. But most pen printing betrays joinings produced by impulses outside of the control of the mind and

APTER THE NATIONAL
DINNER MEETING &
ELECTIONS IN JANUARY.

#232

hand (fig. #232). Indeed, some scripts of this type, especially when the writing has been done at great speed, show a continuity of movement comparable to that found in cursive writing. Here too connectedness increases with speed and decreases when the forms are slowly and carefully traced.

DEGREES OF CONNECTEDNESS AND THEIR MEANING

Early graphologists held the presence or absence of connectedness to denote two opposite types of mentality—connectedness indicating a writer of logical bent, and disconnectedness an intuitive mind. The script of Henri Bergson, who analyzed the function of intuition in the thinking process, illustrates this point (fig. #233). Klages contended that connectedness, as reflecting a logical cast of mind, is a masculine trait, while disconnectedness, as associated with intuition, is a feminine characteristic. In support of his assumption he offered the following data. Out of 100 educated men, 80 had well-connected handwritings, 10 showed more than the average number of interruptions in connectedness, and another 10 followed no pattern; on the other hand, only 50 out of 100 women had well-connected handwritings. Modern graphologists waive such sweeping generalizations in favor of an objectivity that takes into account also the innumerable interrelated other factors.

The degree and quality of connectedness in a script constitute an amazingly individual feature, and it would take volumes to describe all the possible variations that may be encountered. At forme matérielle autre que celle qu'ils ont gardée depuis leur origine. J'ai refusé si souvent des offres si flatteuses d'éditions de luxe, ou de "Morceaux choisis," ou même, une ou deux fois, d'"Œuvres complètes", que je ne pourrais maintenant faire une exception sans froisser ceux auxquels j'ai répondu qu'il y avait là pour moi une règle. De toute manière je tiens à vous remercier, vous et la Librairie Gallimard, de votre aimable pensée, et je vous prie d'agréer, Monsieur, l'assurance de mes sentiments très distingués

H. Bergson

#233

best it is possible only to touch upon the main aspects of connectedness and their meanings.

Of primary import is the location of the joinings. In the middle zone, differing degrees of connectedness denote differing degrees

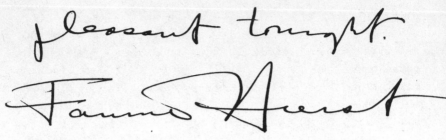

#234

#235

of ability (fig. #234) or inability (fig. #235) to connect experiences purposefully and to discern relationships on a common-sense basis—i.e., differing degrees of capacity for adaptive behavior.

The frequency and the quality of the joinings in the upper zone offer clues regarding the writer's associative processes—i.e., the manner in which his chain of thought builds up, and the extent to which emotional factors influence this structuring (figs. #106, #135). Disconnectedness in the upper zone, or between the upper and the middle zone, may signify lapse of attention or a weakening of the associative process (fig. #236). It may on the other hand represent an intuitive leap over those intermediate

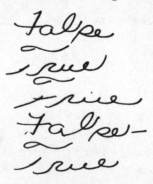

#236

steps of reasoning that go with logical thinking (figs. #105, #233).

The degree of connectedness found in the lower zone supplies indices regarding the extent of the writer's ability or inability to establish relationships. Absence of the ligatures prescribed by school standards in penmanship, particularly in the loops, manifests some form of refusal or incapacity to make a satisfactory socio-erotic adjustment (p. 177).

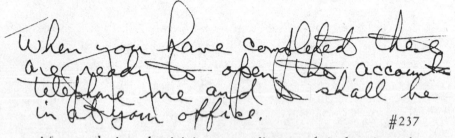

#237

After analyzing the joinings according to their location, the next step is to determine whether the ligatures are appropriate to the letter forms and to the general structure of the given script (fig. #229). Joinings should facilitate the flow of the movement and contribute to the integration of the pattern and its rhythmic expression, and should not complicate nor obstruct in these respects (fig. #237).

Overconnected configurations are produced by rhetoricians, verbose persons, time wasters, individuals who make much ado about nothing (fig. #238). Straggling ligatures making uncalled-for connections between words, although there may at the same

#238

231

*girls who are keen on art
equally dull. It is more
...ow people who are cultu...
minded are confined to
very small groups, with bal*

#239

time be interruptions of continuity within the word, betoken loose thinking (fig. #239), and suggest also a lack of discrimination. Unrelieved connectedness resulting in monotonous patterning may be an expression of perseveration, i.e., obsessive repetitiousness, since treadmill use of the same motion may mean simply a following of the path of least resistance, where attention is lowered by distraction or by mental or bodily fatigue. Superfluous joinings contrived by means of overextended strokes of immoderate sweep, or by means of swirling flourishes, are a sign of euphoric excitation, unbridled phantasy activity, or a tendency to delusional flights of ideas (fig. #148). These exaggerations eclipse the essentials of structure, shifting emphasis to secondary details and to arbitrary or supernumerary additions.

Some writers interrupt their movement on the stem of each *i* to dot it, and on the stem of each *t* to cross it. Others start a new sustained movement with the *i* dot, which may then be hooked with a peculiar antenna-like extension to the following letter or word (fig. #231). This kind of linking in some cases indicates a state of systemic fatigue. Duparchy-Jeannez, in a book entitled *Les maladies d'après l'écriture,* demonstrates such ligatures in the handwritings of individuals suffering from chronic nervous exhaustion.

#240

*...ing responsibility for
less than $750 a month,*

*oke, "Mass., fifty-
tall, weigh 165
and have one
from Worcester*

#241

In disjointed handwritings, connections are dropped. This refusal to join elements that should by nature cohere is the gesture
of an unco-operative mind; it shows lack of empathy, a need to
maintain psychic distance (fig. #240). In some disconnected
scripts, there is evidence of attempts to make normal joinings:
the writer is trying unsuccessfully to bridge a gap. He may be
doing it by retouching or mending, or by soldering, or by super-
imposing an arbitrary ligature on a finished letter to cover the
hiatus (figs. #147, #241).

In so-called fragmentary writing, the downstrokes are clear
but the upstrokes are partially or wholly missing; thus the letters
have only skeleton forms. Such scripts are produced by individuals
who, as Jacoby puts it, are trying to burn the bridges between
themselves and the world at large.[70] Such writing pictures what
Toynbee calls "schism in the soul" (fig. #242). Lines, words, or

#242

233

letters broken by gaps, or cracking to pieces, as it were, point to a peculiar disorganization, to incoherent and damaged expressive function. Such fragmentation may also be indicative of speech impairment: the subject may be found to have difficulty about speaking in coherent sentences, or in finding the right words for what he wants to say, or in articulating them normally.

FLUENCY IN SPEECH AND WRITING

Though the correlations between speech and writing are self-evident, their implications have not received appropriate attention on the part of either speech therapists or graphologists. It may be assumed that in the act of writing, silent speech is a preliminary to graphic exteriorization. However, there are individuals who can put their thoughts into writing without the mediation of silent speech—i.e., some visual-minded persons report that they have a vision of the written words prior to conscious verbalization. It may be that this group includes those professional writers whose easy and vivid style is in flagrant contradiction to their uneasy and clumsy speech. However, their speech difficulties will be apparent in their handwritings.

According to established scientific conceptions, one side of the brain only is involved in the speaking, reading, and writing functions; this side of the brain is called the dominant hemisphere. It is of great importance to realize that the hemisphere that dominates in control of these higher functions likewise determines handedness—i.e., the superior dexterity of the one hand as against the other. Paul Broca, who in 1860 discovered the specific functional organization of the brain, defined the phenomenon of handedness in these words: "We are right-handed because we are left-brained." The "we" indicates that Broca himself must have been right-handed, since it leaves out of account the individuals who are left-handed because they are right-brained.

In view of all this, there should be nothing startling in the postulation that handwriting mirrors speech, and vice versa. Good speakers generally write a fluent and articulated hand—i.e., the continuity and fluency of their writing matches the even flow of their speech. The person who spills out his thoughts in one breath presents a handwriting picture different from that of the individual who ejaculates his words with fumbling hesitation. A shallow, gliding script pattern may denote the filibusterer with his output of empty words, while slurred and dim writing, or fragmentary forms, may express the palsied feebleness of a slurring or defective speech.[37]

DISTURBANCES IN FLOW OF SPEECH AND WRITING

Interest in writing disturbances led the author to study the speaking and writing function in persons with speech disorders.[49] An examination of several hundred cases gave evidence that stuttering, faulty articulation, and severe defect or loss of speech are accurately reflected in handwriting. The many symptoms of speech defect, ranging from hesitation, or interruption and observable repetition, to spasmlike blockage or dead stops in the flow of speech, are mirrored in corresponding disturbances in the flow of writing[146] (figs. #243-48).

The anxiety and inhibitions that arise when the speech reflex is not securely established lead necessarily to feelings of social insecurity, emotional maladjustments, and even to neuroses and to psychosomatic disturbances of a secondary nature.[117] All of these personality difficulties accompanying speech disability can be read in the writing pattern of the individual so affected (fig. #35).

An even broader investigation of stutterers was undertaken by the author in 1929 in Berlin,[90] in association with Kurt Lewin. To uncover the congruence between verbal and nonverbal expression in such subjects, we studied the general motor behavior of stutterers in varying emotional situations. Our tests covered manual skill, speech, writing, gait, etc. Although we assembled a battery of new devices—for example, moving pictures and speech recordings taken simultaneously, which was quite an innovation at the time—it became evident that more adequate techniques were needed. This need was met by designing and constructing the special apparatus now known as the graphodyne (p. 64).

Figure #243 reproduces the graphodyne tracing of the given name *Pál* of a Hungarian schoolboy. Each crest of a wave shows the maximum pressure exerted by the writer in producing one stroke; the portion of the abscissa intersecting a wave indicates the time consumed in making the stroke. In his effort to overcome his difficulties in writing (articulating) a word, the boy expended 1220 grams of writing pressure instead of the 300 to 400 grams representing the average effort for his age. The time consumed in tracing the three-letter word (9.05 sec.) is excessive. The movement is interrupted by four blockages. Slowness of movement is evidenced by the stretched-out crests and the four dead stops recorded by the length of the intervals in which the tracing rests on the base line. After a year of psychotherapy and medication, the boy's speech and general motor behavior improved; this is demonstrated in his writing by decreased performance time (4.62 sec.) and reduced intensity of pressure (760 grams).[56]

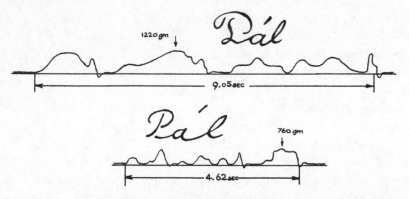

#243

Demonstration — n

 #244   #245

Figure #244* shows the script of a hemming stutterer who is obliged to make a long stop after the effort of the first letter. A commonly observed pattern of stoppage and break in the tracing of a letter appears in the *n* shown in enlargement in figure #245. The writer, unable to go on from the point of the break, doubles back and has to repeat the pattern of the blocked movement. Thus the letter looks disintegrated. Spastic movement of this kind may also lead to duplication of letter parts and entire letters (figs. #246*, #247*). These graphic gestures picture what occurs when the writer attempts to articulate a word.

#246

(a)

(b)

The Lincoln Reader, Edited Paul. M. Angle. (Rutgers Uni Press, #3.75). An inspirin of Lincoln culled from the writings about him. Sixty authors are represented,

---

* Courtesy Deso Weiss, M.D.

237

I was woken up at 8:00

Then I ate breakfast

#247

Many stutterers try to mask their writing difficulties, each developing his own style of camouflage. In the script shown in figure #248, the writer, in trying to control his defective movement, makes great pauses between words and syllables; the dots before the words register the probing movements he makes in getting a start. The shaping of the last word reflects a spastic moment that led to the marked fragmentation and distortion of the last word, *Soha*.

#248 *Nem, Nem Soha!*

June and I read all the books in

#249

In the handwriting of a thirteen-year-old boy reproduced in figure #249, we see evidence of lowered muscle tonus (p. 278); the indices are excessive slowness, slight pressure, feeble and tremulous strokes, and shaky loops. The defective writing in this case disclosed a general inadequacy of muscle tonus and of neuromuscular co-ordination, affecting not only writing movement but also speech articulation and other functions. In the light of accumulated experience, this pointed to an endocrine disorder. Upon the author's advice, a specialist in endocrinology was consulted. His diagnosis established the presence of a dysfunction of the adrenal glands. A course of treatment led to considerable improvement in the somatic condition, which was reflected in an improvement of speech and writing.

As a result of the author's research and experimental work with the graphodyne, handwriting analysis came to be widely employed in various countries of Europe as a tool in the diagnosis and therapy of speech disorders.[37, 38]

(XII)

SPEED AND PERSONAL PACE

Obviously speed in writing, like speed in any other motor function, increases with practice. By a natural and expectable development, the painstaking, slow, unsure tracing movements of the child evolve to the automatic, sure fluency of the adult. However, no amount of training can make a speed champion out of a sluggard. The tempo of all the complicated movements an individual learns to perform in a lifetime is set for him by his innate nervous organization. The rate of nerve conduction and the speed of associative processes as well as of motor responses—irrespective of how they are influenced by endocrine, nutritional, or other factors that determine the functional state of the nervous system—all contribute to personal pace.

Handwriting analysis offers a unique means for studying personal pace in all its complexities. Its technique enables us not only to distinguish between "quick" and "slow" individuals, but also to probe a little more deeply into the phenomenon of personal tempo. For example, it has helped us to learn something about the variability of the factor of personal speed, and the conditions or influences that may interfere with or modify it.

In graphological interpretation, quantitative accomplishment as such—referring to the number of letters or words written within a given space of time—is not important nor very revealing, though early psychologists[130] who were not graphologists spent hours in making laboratory measurements, under somewhat artificial conditions, of such things as the number of syllables written by a subject per minute, and the number of strokes produced in a

240

split second.[157] On the other hand, graphological study has shown that individual speed is variable and changes according to the writing situation. A man writes in one way when seated comfortably at his own desk and in another when standing at a bank counter. There is a difference in his speed when he is writing at dictation or copying a text and when he is writing spontaneously. An individual filling out a job application tends to write as neatly and legibly as he can, usually with conscious slowing down of his habitual pace. Conversely, when one is trying to finish a piece of writing in a hurry, precision and legibility may be sacrificed in favor of speed.

The reasons for fluctuations in individual writing speed are not always as simple as in the situations just indicated. One illustration of the way in which psychic factors may induce such fluctuations appears in the results of an experiment undertaken by the author for the purpose of testing writing speed by means of a Hipp chronometer.[10] In this test about one hundred staff employees and clients of a bank were asked to write a passage of neutral meaning dictated to them from a newspaper, and were instructed to sign their scripts. The time measurements obtained deviated from the anticipated outcome: it was found that the signatures had been written more slowly than the dictated material. Yet the test subjects, when questioned, did not doubt that they had written their signatures—i.e., familiar material—more rapidly than the dictated text, which was previously unknown material. But the chronometer records showed how erroneous these personal impressions were.

The same test was given to a group composed of high-school students and a number of men employed as attendants and simple clerks at the bank. The second experiment produced a different result: almost all of the subjects showed greater speed in writing their signatures than in writing the dictated text. The explanation is that in the first group, because it consisted of men conditioned by the attitudes of the financial and business world, consciousness of the importance of a signature inhibited spontaneity and put a brake on speed. The second group, not burdened by the impending factor of a feeling of responsibility, wrote their names quite casually and faster than they could write the unfamiliar dictated material.

THE DYNAMICS OF PACE

The subtler aspects of what constitutes personal pace may be grasped by analogy when we consider the phenomenon of personal modulation of tempo in music or the dance. The performer is always aware that in a given measure there are, for instance, eight measures, with four beats to a measure. But what he does within this time frame, and how he personally animates the given metrical pattern—i.e., his interpretative rhythm—determines the distinction and individuality of the rendering, and the ultimate

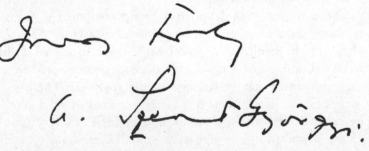

#250

meaning of the musical expression. Writing, like a musical performance, shows a certain flow of movement in which stops and starts, retardations and accelerations, fleeting pauses and actual standstills, occur with more or less periodicity. These are indices of pace: they show how the writer's use of time creates the rhythm of the movement and thus of the total writing pattern (figs. #250-52, #258, #259).

#251

#252

243

The graphologist must dig deep to isolate this basic factor of personal pace.[129] First, he must ascertain what the habitual tempo of the writer is, and whether under normal circumstances he would

#253

produce an accurate and legible script with adequate speed (fig. #253). Next, he must ascertain whether it is precision or speed that tends to be modified or lost when the writer is in a hurry,

#254

or unusually tense (fig. #254), or disturbed by interfering factors.[152] He must further determine the subject's capacity for resistance to interference.[44] In a well-adjusted person, control and concentration usually serve to maintain a steady pace in spite of the presence of possible distracting stimuli or feeling disturbances, whereas oversensitive persons will manifest a lesser resistance (fig. #255). Of course there may be interfering stimuli of such force as to affect the most balanced individual (fig. #94).

Another factor that may make for differences here is temperament, i.e., that fundamental factor in the individual's make-up which determines the speed and intensity of his emotional re-

of a New York Office
manufacturer.

Of course I am a college
other schooling. I am mar
any children at the mom
myself but I'll save the
and for the personal inte
write, phone, or wire me reg
solve your management problem.

#255

sponses. A person of lively temperament has to apply a greater measure of self-discipline to maintain an evenly flowing writing movement (fig. #250) than a person of phlegmatic disposition (fig. #256). Many writers develop habits of initial adjustment, resorting to a "warming-up" maneuver before launching on the

ding management engineering
sisted some of the country's
establishing policies and

#256

245

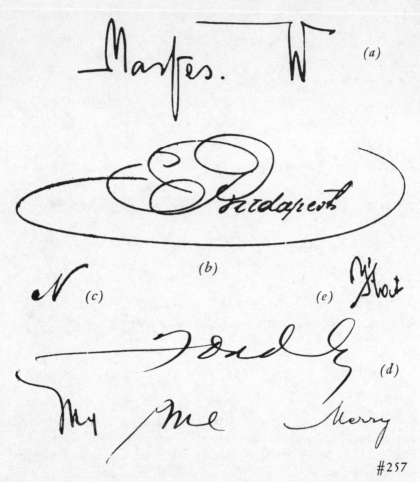

#257

actual writing (fig. #257). Some prolong (spec. *a*) or elaborate the start (spec. *b*). Others concentrate their starting effort in a dot (spec. *c*), or in a springboard stroke (spec. *d*). There are writers who hedge in making any kind of a beginning, whether on the whole writing or on a capital letter (spec. *e*) or a new line; but after the initial delay, such a writer usually picks up speed and maintains his pace until he reaches some ending point, where his speed naturally drops.

college, and hasten to reassure you that no apologies are needed for the omission of my name from the casting volume. Believe me, I was on the point of writing to suggest that it be omitted, but it seemed to me #258

Ordinarily the pen stops—registering a definite pause—at the completion of a thought or of a logical sequence within the larger whole. It is natural to find interruptions that are almost imperceptible—brief pauses to take breath. These are an organic part of the rhythm of the movement (fig. #258). However, their length and periodicity will vary according to the subject's physical condition when writing; the pause may become as prolonged as a sigh, as marked as an asthmatic gasp (p. 237).

GRAPHIC INDICES OF SPEED

One of the determinants of speed is the nature of the stroke. Freeman and Saudek[138] have shown experimentally that less time is needed to trace a long downstroke than a short one, and that it takes more time to form a very small or narrow letter than a large broad one. A straight stroke is by its very nature not only the shortest that can be used to join two points; it is also the most quickly traced. Thus a straight, unbroken tracing reflects a firm, quick movement. By the same token, a wavering or broken tracing is recognizable as a slowly executed one. Hence the shaping of angular letter forms, which necessitates an abrupt stop at each turning point (p. 33), is an impediment to speed. Conversely, the swinging motion used in forming curved strokes and rounded letters enables the writer to pick up speed as he proceeds. It is for this reason that the curved, swinging stroke has been made the basis of most systems of shorthand, with angular symbols reduced to a minimum.

The smoothness of the individual stroke gives the clue as to the spontaneity and speed with which it has been traced.[116] The more smoothly and easily a movement is carried out, the less consciousness accompanies it; thus the free, unhampered movements of spontaneous writing are relatively rapid, whereas self-conscious, controlled, and hesitant movements are relatively slow.[159]

#259

A spontaneous, speedy handwriting (fig. #259) usually slants toward the right; with haste or acceleration of pace for any reason, the slope grows more pronounced. Speed tends furthermore to reduce whatever leftward tending strokes the particular penmanship model may prescribe. It also distorts the *i* dots; instead of a neat point placed exactly above the letter stem, it may be pulled into the shape of a streak or comma and dragged forward by the momentum of the movement. In slow writing, the *i* dot is so placed that it appears to be lagging behind (fig. #231). The accompanying tabulation sets forth in contrasted groupings the salient indicators of speedy and of slow writing.

1 GENERAL APPEARANCE

General appearance spontaneous, natural

General appearance conventional, over-elaborate, or clumsy

2 PATTERN

Pattern animated, rhythmic

Pattern monotonously regular, or disorganized

3 STROKE

Stroke smooth, unbroken, sweeping; firm, swinging curvatures

Stroke controlled or hesitant, tremulous, broken or jerky, retouched or soldered; concealing strokes; jagged or broken curvatures

4 GENERAL DIRECTIONAL TREND

General directional trend rightward; rightward slant; clockwise circular strokes; rightward swinging end strokes; slight initial adjustments, or none; *i* dots streaklike, placed to right of stem or linked to next letter; *t* bars extended, placed to right of stem

General directional trend leftward; upright or leftward slant; counterclockwise circular strokes; abbreviated or leftward turning end strokes; elaborate initial adjustments; *i* dots round, placed just above stem or behind it; *t* bars short, crossing stem or placed behind it

5 CONNECTIVE FORMS

Connective forms predominantly garland or threadlike; good continuity within words

Connective forms predominantly arcade or angle; interruptions within words

6 LETTERS

Letters of medium size; letter shapes streamlined, slurred, or distorted; long stems; long, slim loops, with smoothly turned heads; ends of words decreasing in size, abbreviated, or illegible; neglect of detail

Letters very small or very large; letter shapes narrow or sprawled out; short stems; distended loops; ends of words increasing in size; attention to detail

7 PRESSURE

Pressure medium or slight; rhythmic alternation of thick and thin strokes; ovals clear; loops clear

Pressure insufficient or excessive; strokes unmodulated in width—thick or thin, pastose or smeary; ovals blotchy; loops blotchy at heads

8 ALIGNMENT

Alignment: lines ascending rightward; left margin widening downward

Alignment: lines steadily horizontal, or descending rightward, or undulating; left margin even or diminishing downward

249

It has been pointed out above that the writing situation, as well as inner states, greatly affect the speed of writing. A happy mood, or a state of elation, releases and accelerates the flow of the movement, whereas an anxious mood, inner tension, or depression slows down and restrains it. Excessive speed, resulting in a complicated, distorted, oversized tracing, without controlled course, is symptomatic of flight of ideas. It is that graphic manifestation to which the diagnosis of hypomania is ordinarily attached (fig. #260). Gross deviation from average speed in the sense of markedly slow pace goes with mental sluggishness Extreme slowness is the mark of the feebleminded.[53]

#260

Relatively constant, regular speed characterizes the well-organized person whose noticing, acting, feeling, and thinking proceed in an integrated fashion[152] and under the dominance of a relatively constant motive pattern—to use the words of Theodore Newcombe.[113] Such constancy does not preexclude the possibility of fluctuations or changes; these may occur whenever emotions arise. The writing speed becomes irregular when the movement is at the mercy of spontaneous feeling because of insufficient attempt to control and check such affects in the interest of the writing performance.[44] Fluctuations in pace due to emotional influences are revealed by such graphic indices as the following: occasional acceleration or slowing down, delays, or stops; headlong haste reflected in uncontrolled strokes overshooting their expectable limits, or a gesture of vacillation or a retreating step shown in leftward turning strokes; breaks, overt or disguised in soldered strokes (p. 221); scattered dots recognizable as the spoor of probing movements (fig. #248).

These are all very significant symptoms that must be noted and explored. They may lead to detection of emotional association or conflicts that distract, fatigue, or confuse the subject and force him to make inappropriate use of his natural endowment of pace. They may also point to the presence of deep-lying conflicts, or bring to light a fear or unwillingness to be frank and open. Thus delays, stops, marked pauses amounting to an unconscious gesture of emphasis, may work just like a lie detector: a word that is insignificant in its literal meaning may show itself to be a stimulus word in that it betrays eagerness, vacillation, or reluctance on the part of the subject in writing it down. The late Hungarian graphologist Dezsö Balázs had a notable ability in hunting out emotional conflicts on the basis of such indices.[7]

#261

Innumerable illustrations of such graphological detective work could be offered. In figure #261, we have a well-connected handwriting in which, however, notable gaps appear within two of the words. The pauses indicate that the writer was giving concentrated emphasis to these two words, which in themselves are key words in conveying the content of his communication. In the specimen reproduced in figure #262, the writer in referring to his "prob-

#262

251

lems" seems to have sought escape in the forward spurt of the *e* in this word, and then to have dragged himself back to the dilemma with sufficient control to finish the word. The easygoing, callow expression of the writing as a whole suggests an individual disinclined to face conflict or to solve a problem by himself. This helps to explain why the particular word induced a reaction of distaste.

#263

As the record of a situation of emotional crisis, the last signature of Ivar Kreuger (fig. #263), the Swedish financier who ruled the international match industry until his operations were found to be corrupt on a grand scale, is of peculiar interest. The signature is from his farewell note to his secretary. Knowing that within two days his tottering empire would crash, he committed suicide en route from the United States to Sweden.

Any graphologist will recognize in the features of this signature a genuinely speedy hand that on this occasion was impeded in its usually free sweep. The writer was almost unable to start instantly. The broken initial letter might give the impression that the pen was sticking for lack of ink. However, the nature of the break (its location in the configuration of the letter, and the probing dots), together with the well-inked tracing of the rest of the signature, refutes this assumption. All this indicates merely reluctance to go ahead—which becomes completely manifest in the weak and shortened connecting stroke between the initial and the following letter. The narrowness of the *a* is a further index of inhibition, while its blotchy execution is symptomatic of a failing of energy—a temporary inability to go on with the task. Similarly, the initial *K* of the family name—which in Kreuger's usual signature had a clear-cut form—is here blotted and retouched. For its broad, dark strokes result not from heavy writing pressure, but rather from an inertia that holds the writer fixed in one groove, avoiding in panic the imperative of moving on. Finally he shakes himself free of the emotional blockage, and completes in one sweep what must be done.

(X I I I)

WRITING PRESSURE

Writing pressure is a complex phenomenon. Careful observation and study are required to determine the effect of pressure upon the thickness, darkness, sharpness, and shading of the stroke.

At first thought it might appear that the qualities of the stroke depend merely upon the type of pen used—whether the nib is pointed or blunt, stiff or flexible, etc. However, writing pressure, like all other features of handwriting, is basically determined by the personality of the writer, and not by the tool he employs. The writer may produce his script with a pencil, or on different occasions with instruments of differing construction, ranging from a goosequill or stylus to a ballpoint pen. Except for superficial differences in the writing that identify the tool rather than the user, the writing is always recognizable as one individual's unique expression. We are accustomed to such recognitions in other fields: for instance, in looking at a drawing and an etching from the hand of Rembrandt, we should hardly take them to be the work of two different artists. Their secondary dissimilarities are due to the difference in the tools used in producing them; but they are clearly seen to be expressions of the same personality.

Nonetheless, it is necessary to study the various types of pens, and the kinds of manipulation required in using them. The pen is guided by the thumb and second finger in moving up and down and toward the left or the right. The index finger, resting upon the penholder, presses the point of the pen to the paper. The pen point, or nib, consists of two flanges lying close together. Pressure causes these flanges to separate, permitting of the flow of

254

ink. This flow of ink upon the paper, as the pen is moved along, results in the tracing or stroke, also called the ductus.

When the pen is guided over the paper with slight pressure, it produces a fine stroke of uniform width. If greater pressure is exerted, the nib splits more widely apart, causing a greater amount of ink to flow from the pen, and thus producing a broader and darker stroke (fig. #264). Some writers propel the pen over the

#264

paper with an easy, rhythmic motion; others move it with measured steadiness; still others shove the pen clumsily along in a heavy, halting way, and some send it forward feebly with a tremulous or shaky motion. The different kinds of movement leave their respective imprints, vividly evident in the variations in the firmness, smoothness, fluency, and other qualities of the stroke. The finger usually applies more pressure in making the downstroke than in making the upstroke (p. 43). This results in variations in line thickness: thick downstrokes alternate with thin upstrokes, while the curved outlines of rounded forms show gradations of thickening and thinning. This effect, which we know as shading, is one of the significant indices of writing pressure (figs. #161, #265, #266).

The general effect of heavy pressure is to increase the thickness and darkness of the stroke. When the pen is held firmly and close to the nib, so that it is almost perpendicular to the writing surface, it causes the nib to scratch the paper, leaving a sharp groove

#265

#266

on one or both sides of the stroke.[25] In the specimen shown in figure #267, we have heavy pressure resulting in firm strokes with sharp outlines. The nib marks are baldly visible in the extended *t* bar of the signature, where some failure of ink supply has left the breadth of the stroke unfilled. Slighter pressure, with a more oblique positioning of the pen, produces a stroke with less definite outlines.

It follows that when the pen is grasped farther from the nib and manipulated more loosely, somewhat like a paint brush, the downward pressure is no longer due entirely to the force exerted by the index finger, but mainly to the weight of the hand and the gross movements of the arm. The stroke produced under these conditions is designated as pastose; it is uniform in width, dense

Best wishes and Happiness to you

all

#267

#268

with ink, and its outlines are blurred. Examination under a magnifying glass shows the great difference between a stroke made with heavy pressure and one lightly traced: the former is clear-cut, with sharply incised outlines (figs. #266, #267); the latter is smooth, without incised edges (fig. #268) and commonly has ragged outlines, as in the specimen shown enlarged in figure #269.

In order to understand how these pairs of opposites—the thin and the thick stroke, the sharp and the pastose stroke—are produced physically, it is advisable to try out various types of pens,

#269

testing their effect and observing how they modify the quality of the stroke. This experiment will show that the character of the stroke depends not so much upon the pen as upon the writer, who has it in his power to mold his stroke according to his desire. It must be borne in mind that in writing the pen functions as an extension of the hand. We can, in-fact, think of the pen as a part of the body, hand and pen moving as a single member. The fingers transmit to the pen the directive impulses and the variations in muscular tension that, according to the nature of the

#270

258

writer's nervous organization, occur during the act of writing. Hence, as each writer has his own way of holding his hand, manipulating the pen, and exerting pressure, and his own rate of speed in moving the pen, the same pen in different hands will produce entirely different strokes (figs. #270, #271).

je tiens l'auto pour un Génie
ant qui, diminuant les distances, rend
... plus divers, plus riches et plus pleins,
plus grande, contribue à la prospérité
et travaille insensiblement à la
universelle.
    Je vous serre cordialement la main,
        Anatole France

#271

It goes without saying that each individual chooses the pen that suits his personal requirements, and in his use adapts it to his individual writing habits. As a result a writer often becomes so attached to his own fountain pen that he does not like to write with another, and is reluctant to lend his pen to anyone, knowing that it will be affected by the different manipulation of another hand. Moreover, the writer has an inner image (*Leitbild*) of the script he aims to create, and this predetermines his performance on the paper; obviously his choice of a pen will be greatly influenced by this ideal image. It may be remarked that the ballpoint pen obviates the significant qualities of the writing stroke, since

#272

it does not adapt itself to the subtle play of pressure. This is the reason why the sensitive writer feels frustrated in using it.

Furthermore, the individual choice of a paper must be taken into account. Some persons prefer a rough to a smooth paper. The resistance offered by a rough surface invites the finger to supply more force and to exert more pressure; such paper appeals to persons whose general tendency is to seek and overcome resistance. Individuals inclined to "take it easy" and to avoid unnecessary friction prefer a smooth-surfaced paper and a pen that "writes by itself," so to speak.

It is evident that both pen pressure and the resistance offered by the writing surface are factors influencing the writing speed. Pressure and speed counteract each other. A quickly gliding pen cannot transmit as much pressure as a slowly moving one; heavy pressure, on the other hand, slows down the rate of movement. Thus a person who writes both speedily and with heavy pressure displays considerable vital energy and propulsive power, whereas the combination of low speed and heavy pressure reveals insufficient application of energy in driving forward and overcoming resistances. In the script of a writer suffering from persistent depression, with loss of physical and mental efficiency (fig. #194), we may note "swallowtails" on the garlands; these are femme vous reposer une bonne journée ici ¿près de moi.

A vous deux mes pensées amicales et affectueuses

Wanda Landowska

#273

indices of heavy pressure and halting slowness at the turning points —reflecting the lassitude and apathy that prevented the writer from driving his pen with any speed across the page.[37]

Figure #272 shows a use of pressure that hampers speed and fluency. The all-out pressure on the downward stroke upsets equilibrium, so that the writer is forced to change the tilt of the pen, and some vagary in his manner of manipulating it produces both the swallowtails at the peaks of the scalloped tracing and the ragged outline at the base. The pressure pattern is further shown by the hairline stroke upon which the *o* is incongruously balanced. However the highly artistic configuration of the signature shows rhythm and balance, because of its aesthetic and original distribution of forms. A sharp contrast is offered in the controlled and forceful ductus of the script shown in figure #273.

PRESSURE AND MUSCULAR STRENGTH

Earlier graphologists equated writing pressure with volitional energy. Present-day investigators regard this as an oversimple explanation of the pressure phenomenon, applying only where steady pressure is exerted with vertical stress. Figures #266 and #273 present examples of such regularity, whereas in figure #265 the pronounced pressure in the vertical direction is neither regular nor genuinely a part of an integrated movement pattern.

The tendency to exert heavy pressure in writing is not attributable to possession of sheer muscular power. H. Jacoby[70] studied this possible relationship by examining the handwritings of several hundred shoe-factory hands whose work involved the use of pliers in a routine manipulation requiring great strength primarily. Yet Jacoby found that those workers who turned out more than the average number of pieces per hour, i.e., who had the greatest muscular strength, invariably wrote with no more than average pressure.

The present author investigated the pressure factor in the writing performances of 2145 Hungarian school children of both sexes and various ages.[51] The results showed that muscular strength has no bearing on the degree of pressure exerted in writing. Instead, they pointed to a significant correlation between writing pressure and inclination to purposeful activity, capacity for concentration, and endurance. These findings seem to be confirmed by an investigation of the writing of seventy-seven girls committed as juvenile delinquents to a reformatory, where they were put to work as farm hands. Poor writing pressure prevailed throughout the group. Indeed, 12 per cent of these girls displayed the minimal degree of pressure that could be noted by experimental measurement. This is all the more significant in view of the fact that tests of 1000 high-school girls yielded not a single case of similarly low pressure.

It was a seeming paradox that of the reformatory girls, those who rated lowest in writing pressure were the "toughest" in the group. They had been committed to the institution for sexual offenses or assault, and had to be segregated from the other inmates because of their aggressive behavior. The notable deficiency in writing pressure in these cases corresponded with the deficiencies underlying their type of psychosocial maladjustment—mental retardation, inertia, and flightiness. Medical examination showed them to lack the biological energies needed for environmental adaptation and for control of their frustration reactions. In tests concerned with the relation between handwriting and certain clusters of character traits, I. Pascal obtained results on the correlations between writing pressure on the one hand, and "energy," "impulsiveness," "dominance," and "determination" on the other,[118] that are comparable to the findings just outlined.

PRESSURE AND PSYCHIC ENERGY

Pulver conceives of writing pressure as a discharge of libido.[128] Here the concept of libido refers not merely to the psychosexual energy but rather to the total psychic energy as vested in all of the life activities of the individual. In this sense, libido accounts for all of the needs, drives, and cravings seeking either physical or psychic expression. Thus the well-energized, "vital" personality, endowed with a high energy potential, and thereby with some quantum of creative drive, writes with notable pressure. Pulver's general idea provides a working hypothesis that has proved fruitful. In a further development of it, however, he sets up the separate categories of "physical libido" and "psychic libido," and this attempt at clear-cut differentiation of complexly interrelated factors results in confusion. For example, "intensity" is listed as psychic, and "brutality" as physical. Obviously neither belongs wholly to the one or to the other classification.

An outstanding graphic expression of libido appears in the handwriting of Napoleon Bonaparte. In the signature shown in figure #274 a, the pressure is heavy and the strokes exceedingly sharp in outline, although in spots pastose and flooded with ink. There is a remarkable sweep and speed to the movement. This combination of qualities points to a superlative endowment of energy. The irregularity and the breaks in rhythm signify not only an absolute disregard for norms and conventions, but also

263

headlong ·ego urges, aggressive impulses, and a tendency to explosive fits of passion that disturb both psychic and somatic equilibrium. The terminal stroke of the signature—always an avenue for release of surplus energy—here serves for a remarkable exteriorization of an excessively powered libido. The tracing is sharp in outline, both in the slender part and in the extraordinary broad portion. Its swordlike form is a common symbol of war.

In a graphological study of Napoleon and his mother, J. Ninck[115] discusses the handwriting of Laetitia Bonaparte in her old age. Her script (fig. #274 *b*) parallels her son's, trait for trait: it shows the same heavy pressure, the same full, dark, sensuous pastosity, the same irregularity, the same disregard for conventional proportions and forms, the same breaks in rhythm, the same slant toward the right, and similar scrawled letter forms. The author of the study points out that of all the children of this remarkable woman—of her family of thirteen, eight survived to adulthood—none was as much like her as Napoleon.

It may prove illuminating to compare the bold and vivid script of Napoleon with the obviously "phony" hand reproduced in figure #275. The writer of the specimen was a very bizarre character whose eccentric propagation of varied causes won him a considerable discipleship. The ostentatious width of his strokes is produced by a trick of wielding the pen without pressure. These showy strokes, dark and broad, contrast with the rest of the ductus, which is thin and weak. This writing demonstrates in both its thin and its thick strokes the quality called pastosity.

#275

Pastose strokes, as pointed out above, are broad and dark, though produced without marked pressure. Such an ink-saturated, pastose ductus produces an effect of warmth and color, and has a sensuous appeal. This is borne out by an analogous reaction quite commonly obtained in the Rorschach test, when a dense black ink blot is seen as a bear rug with the furry side up. According to the precedents accumulated in the clinical use of this test, such a response may indicate sensitivity to tactile stimuli, a need for bodily contact. Graphological experience shows that pastosity is the expression of sensuous persons who manage to indulge their inclinations with little effort or strain. They manipulate the pen in a relaxed manner, and it has been observed that in such individuals a copious ejection of ink induces a pleasurable feeling with erotic overtones.[7] Figure #276 shows the handwriting of a

#276

265

young man of lusty appetites who pursued sensuous pleasures without inhibitions or anxiety. The pastose stroke is generally found in the handwriting of hearty, wholesome men and women who live close to nature, such as gardeners, farmers, horse breeders, etc. It appears also in the writing of hedonists and epicures, and is especially characteristic of artists who excel in the use of colors (fig. #277).

#277

Werner Wolff, discussing the symbolic meaning of writing pressure, regards the paper as the medium or "object" upon which the writer releases his "libidinous impulses."[158] The desire for bodily contact, or the impulse to caress or to hurt or be hurt, is vicariously realized on the paper. The writer may move over the paper with a light, sensuous touch, or strike down on it with suddenly erupting pressure. Wolff demonstrates this in the writing of "a German Nazi girl student who handled pen and paper as though she were slaying an enemy" (fig. #278).

The handwritings of three notable figures who have come to stand as types of libidinous personality supply further illustration, together with some significant contrasts. In the hand presented

#278

#279

in figure #279, we have pastosity, flooded loops and ovals, and
dagger-like terminal thrusts. These are the graphic features of the
Marquis de Sade, whose name is perpetuated in the term "sadism"
as the designation of a psychosexual aberration. A hand showing
strikingly sadistic features has been presented earlier in figure
#127. In figure #280 we have strokes curving forward—bowed
in a gesture of obeisance, as it were. The small, fuzzy letter shapes
are obscured by pastosity and smeariness. This is the handwriting

#280

#281

About New York,
my telling you how much
of you, the sound of your
gleam in your eyes, to a
in that seductive smile
When I write this (the fi
passed and I want to d
having great difficulty in
should I say the lady.

of Sacher Masoch, whose name is used in the word "masochism" to denote that type of libidinousness in which sexual desire is fused with the need for suffering. Figure #281 shows pastosity in the script of a male homosexual. Figure #282 reproduces the handwriting of Casanova, the "phallic man" par excellence. The graceful, forceful, upright strokes are enriched by a substantial pastosity that does not detract from the clarity and form quality of the script.

Ma tête en liberté Je
Prononce un voeu, Se
Perver tout haut! Grand

#282

One of the marks of lazy and irresponsible persons is pastosity appearing in a disorganized writing pattern. Such patterns bearing the further index of freakish, blotted letters are seen in the scripts of "shady" characters, drug addicts, and sexual delinquents. The rough and smeary pastosity of these writers is very

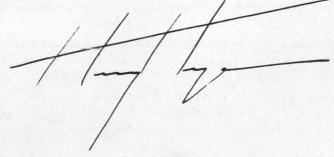

#283

different from the expressively modulated, colorful, and vigorous
pastosity of an artist's hand. Figure #283 reproduces the handwriting of a woman drug addict who claimed to have communication with various "spirits" that sent messages through her to
persons who paid for her services.

It has been instanced that thick strokes may be executed with
pressure, which produces clear-cut outlines, or without pressure,
which results in pastosity, i.e., blurred outlines. Similarly, thin
tracings may be sharply cut or blurred. The writing of Romain
Rolland (fig. #204) is light and fine, seemingly wafted over
the writing surface; nevertheless it is sharp and clear-cut. Sudden
spurts of pressure speak out in the extremely fine lines, especially
the needle-pointed end strokes. Their thrust into the stratosphere
shows that the writer's emotional tensions and aggressive impulses
are released in the intellectual domain.

Sharp thin strokes characterize the handwritings of persons of
incisive intellect and developed critical sense (fig. #102); such
strokes are an occupational badge of professional critics and of
surgeons. Extreme sharpness in thin, rigid strokes indicates cold
mentality (fig. #284); combined with pallor, this points to
frigidity, asceticism, or cruelty masked by seeming virtue. Thin

#284

269

joining the consulting firm, I
on my own in a consulting

#285

strokes that are blurred and weak, i.e., not sharp nor firm, appear in the handwritings of persons in whom the life force is easily swamped by fatigue or adversity (figs. #268, #285, #368 c).

DISPLACED PRESSURE

Ordinarily pressure is more or less evenly distributed, stressing each downstroke with a shading effect. The rhythm of emphasis thus produced parallels the interplay of muscular contraction and release that underlies the writing movement. However, pressure may be exerted in the horizontal instead of the vertical direction; this is called displacement or transference of pressure emphasis. The shift can be contrived deliberately. In order to apply pressure sideward, the writer may manipulate his pen in a special way (fig. #286). Artists who work at lettering use a special type of pen to obtain horizontal shadings; to achieve a highly stylized handwriting through similar effects, some writers use a pen with an extremely flexible nib. Such artificial shading is not regarded by graphologists as having any expressive value. The situation is otherwise when horizontal shading appears as a genuine displacement of pressure.

Pulver claims that true pressure displacement reveals a transference of sexual libido. The psychic energy is channeled away from the instinctual sphere and released in extraversive gestures in the direction of conscious goals. Such displacement may produce varying effects in the handwriting, which may be interpreted in various ways. Though the need of sexual expression is not really compensated by a draining off of the libido into the stream of other activities, the substitutional gratification gives a degree of satisfaction, and thus affords relief from tension. If the dis-

I am so glad I know you now & look forward with great pleasure to seeing you again.

#286

placement occurs without loss of force and rhythm, the script tells us about a successful redirection of psychosexual energy. This type of displacement is frequently observed in the hand-writings of active women. Figure #287 presents the hand of a professional woman who is in addition a painter and writer; she also had considerable skill in manual arts and greatly enjoyed outdoor activities. If the displacement of pressure is associated

Maestro Rocco Pandoleorio and his students Caputo Conservatory, 57th st bet. 6 and 7 ave N.Y.C

#287

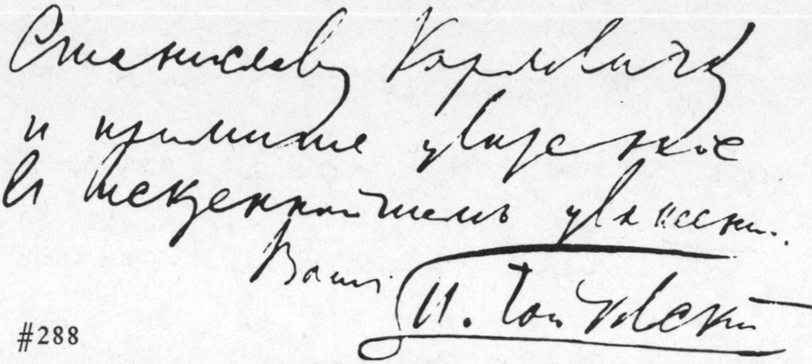

#288

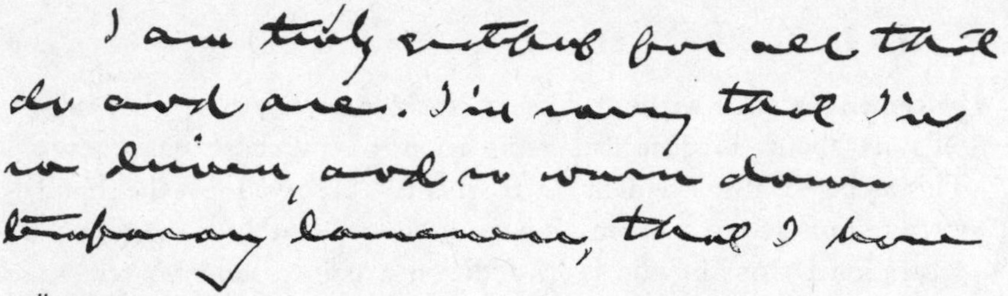

#289

with disturbance of rhythm, it betrays psychic frustration accompanied by increase of tension (figs. #240, #288, #289). The specimen reproduced in figure #290 manifests not only disturbed rhythm and marked tension, but also notable weakness in the

#290

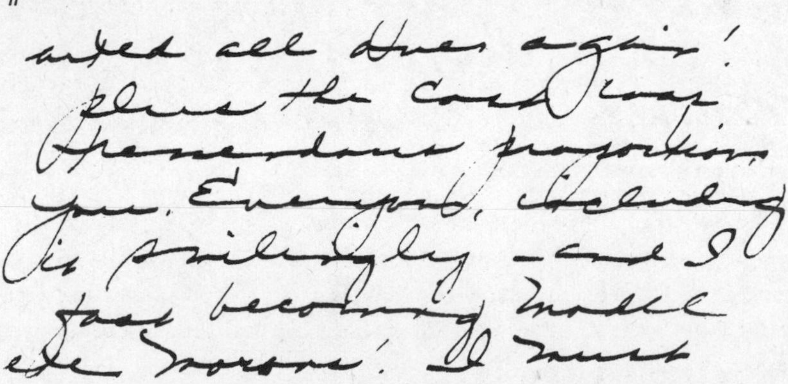

tracing of the overlarge lower loops. The writer was a young woman who, frustrated and blocked in the expression of her sexual drive, found a substitute outlet in sadistic behavior.

EMPHASIS REVEALED IN PRESSURE

A sporadic intensification of shading, as in a single stroke or letter, or a whole word or passage, means that an onset of strong feeling has been suddenly discharged in pressure, with more or

#291

less spread of emphasis. An instance of such pressure in upstrokes appears in figure #291. Such accentuations occur in oral as well as in written expression. The speaker's or the writer's meaning may be revealed more by the specific emphasis placed on a given word than by its literal content. Listening to speeches delivered by orators or actors, we cannot fail to realize that effective emphasis "speaks louder than words" and often eliminates or illuminates ambiguities.

In a written communication we conventionally emphasize by means of sentence structure, punctuation, underlining, or special spacing. This is a conscious emphasizing. But we also emphasize unconsciously and underline, so to speak, without being aware

of doing so. Such underlining—unintended italicizing, as it were—
varies the pressure accent and colors a script much as modulation
enriches speed. This kind of emphasis springs from the depths
of the inner life and communicates an emotional content (p.
162). This content is directly perceived even by those who because
of some preconception do not like to admit that so indirect and
ambiguous a gesture can be regarded as a communication. On the
other hand, the fact that pressure emphasis in writing is a key to
hidden emotional content has long been known and applied by
"mind readers." This recognition is the stock-in-trade of professional soothsayers and carnival "handwriting experts." Pressure

#292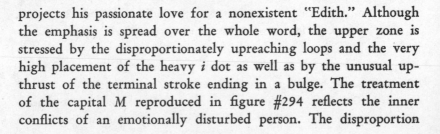

emphasis on a capital letter, for example (fig. #292), may enable
the "clairvoyant" to guess the initial of the given name of the
writer's sweetheart.

The location of pressure emphasis is as telling as the emphasis
itself. According to the zone in which emphasis is concentrated,
we can see from which sphere the emotional impetus is breaking
through. In figure #293, we see excessive pressure emphasis on
upper loops in the handwriting of a mentally sick poet, who thus

#293

projects his passionate love for a nonexistent "Edith." Although
the emphasis is spread over the whole word, the upper zone is
stressed by the disproportionately upreaching loops and the very
high placement of the heavy *i* dot as well as by the unusual up-
thrust of the terminal stroke ending in a bulge. The treatment
of the capital M reproduced in figure #294 reflects the inner
conflicts of an emotionally disturbed person. The disproportion

#294

between height and width betokens an imbalance between soaring ego pretensions and severe inhibitions in actual functioning. The exaggerated stress on the downstrokes expresses not force but merely strain. The slack, tremulous tracing of the upstroke and the thinning of the massive downstroke to a spearhead contradict the idea of force. Thus the stress is spread over the middle and the upper zone and fails in the lower zone. Graphologists hold that the kind of emphasis on a downstroke here exemplified stands for an attempt to exert force that fails because of lack of stamina. Emphasized downstrokes ending in spearheads appear in the script shown in figure #295.

#295

In figure #296, the pressure emphasis on the tips of the stems of the capital *K* takes added significance from the peculiar formation of the letter. The unusually high, backward twisted upper stems reach up like arms outstretched from a drastically minimized, practically nonexistent torso; they seem to lift the weighted

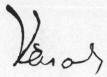

tips into the stratosphere. There is also an unusual, antenna-like accessory at the top of the *a*. The writer, according to his case record, was a professor of history who was institutionalized after reporting that he was hearing "voices" promising to reveal to him a way of saving the world from "annihilation."

Flooded ovals, and strokes marked with swoops, swellings, and nodules, have been discussed earlier as symptoms of emotional disturbance in puberty, arising from anxiety, shame, or guilt feelings (p. 72). A different evaluation is given to similar symptoms

#297

appearing in the handwriting of adults. Figure #297 reproduces the old-fashioned script of a nineteenth-century bride-to-be addressing her future husband. Here the indices belonging to the pubertal level of development appear in the expression of a physically and socially mature person. The nodules in the lower loops and the pressure swellings in the elaboration of the capital *B* indicate disturbances in the emotional sphere, particularly in relation to sex. This writer later was found to be schizophrenic, and her two sons and her grandchild were similarly deranged.

Figure #298 shows an abnormal and illegible handwriting. The middle zone predominates, as regards size and emphasis. Upper extensions are minimized, while the weak lower loops are not integral parts of the letter structures but are rather fitted on. The dominant form in the middle zone is an outspread ellipse filled with ink. According to the formula of earlier graphology, this formation might be interpreted as standing for the "black spot" in the life of the writer. Actually this emphasis betrays preoccupation with some secret that is choking the inner person. The case history reveals the writer as a homosexual with a background of excessive masturbation. He was constantly under the pressure of hidden entanglements and of the need of safeguarding himself against exposure by means of bribes.

(XIV)

TENSION AND RELEASE

The pressure phenomenon involves two components—first, the energy expended in the writing activity, and second, tension, representing a quantum of unexpended energy. Earlier graphologists distinguished, apart from tension, two kinds of pressure in writing—first, the pressure brought to bear by the point of the pen upon the writing surface, i.e., "point pressure," and second, the pressure exerted by the fingers in gripping and holding the pen, i.e., "grip pressure."[137, 139] However, the more recent studies and experiments of Pophal and the present author have produced evidence that grip pressure is a function of tension, significant only as a visible indicator of tension.[58, 122]

Every muscle of the body is in a certain state of permanent tension, even during rest. This persisting tension is called muscle tone, or tonus. Tension increases with physical or emotional stress, and diminishes with satiation and sleep. It may be reduced under hypnosis or narcosis, but it persists until death. This sustained muscular tension passes over readily into movement; it creates a state of permanent readiness, a potential available for future action. When stimulation induces the act of writing, several muscles become involved in a co-operative action. To bring about the series of movements called for, they contract in order to extend or flex the fingers. One group of muscles moves the fingers in one direction; another muscle group moves them in the opposite direction. Thus the muscles that extend the fingers are said to be "antagonistic" to those which flex them. The movements required in writing proceed smoothly if the two muscle groups are not contracted at the same time; that is, when one group responds to the stimulus by contracting, the other by relaxing correspondingly. The antagonism of the two groups gives rise to an interplay of tension and release. In any given individual, this interplay has a specific dynamic pattern that is unique as against the pattern of any other person.

What determines this pattern? A first determinant resides in the needs and desires of the individual. The stimulations arising from hunger, sexual desire, anxiety, ambition, etc., increase tension and direct the activities of the organism toward desired goals. Fulfillment of such needs induces a temporary release of tension. A second determinant is the kind of motor response that follows upon stimulation (p. 178). The response may take the form of a free and unhampered movement, with adequate release of tension. However, the response may be overcontrolled; in that case the release is not complete, and some tension persists. In this type of response the movement is inhibited, and the muscles remain taut. Increasing inhibition leads to sustained high tension, and motor activity may be completely obstructed. Any part of the body thus strait-jacketed is incapable of actual movement, and the blockage results in muscular rigidity or spasm.

GRAPHODYNE STUDY OF TENSION-RELEASE PATTERNS

The use of handwriting analysis for disclosing the most subtle variations of muscle activity is well established in clinical research, and is validated by both early and recent work.[37, 53, 60] The tension-release pattern peculiar to any given person can be made visible and measurable by means of a graphodyne recording of his writing movement. The crests and troughs of the resultant tracing show the increase and decrease of pressure and the pattern of alternation. Figure #299 presents a schematic drawing designed to demonstrate the points discussed above. The over-all height of the tracing (H) records the amount of energy applied to the writing (total writing pressure), comprising two components:

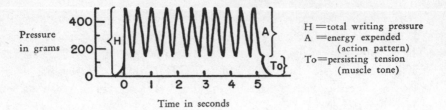

H = total writing pressure
A = energy expended
(action pattern)
To = persisting tension
(muscle tone)

Pressure in grams

Time in seconds

#299

(A) the energy expended in motor activity (action pattern); (To) the energy remaining unexpended and accounting for persisting tension (muscle tone). The ratio between the amount of the active energy (amplitude of oscillations) and that of the unexpended energy (blank area above base line) expresses the existing state of tension in the individual at the given time. The tension is considered normal if the tracing shows an output of energy at least twice as great as the amount of the retained energy. The tension is considered high when the amount of the retained energy is twice or more than twice the amount of the discharged energy.

Further essential factors are the frequency and regularity of the oscillations, which produce the wave form, i.e., the specific pattern (fig. #300). In previous studies, the author has repeatedly emphasized the significance of the individual tension-release pattern as a fundamental expression. A balanced tension-release pattern is indicative of a well-balanced psychosomatic state; conversely, an abnormal pattern is symptomatic of a state of imbalance. It is generally held at present that disturbances of muscular performance occur not only where disease interferes with neuromuscular activity, but also where emotional factors, such as anxiety, conflict, pent-up aggression, and mental strain, are present.[2] Thus the expressions "tense" and "relaxed," as referring to states or attitudes of personality, are obviously derived from their association with the muscular states they primarily describe. Kraepelin long ago demonstrated by means of his pressure scale how mental or emotional strain influences tension.[68] For

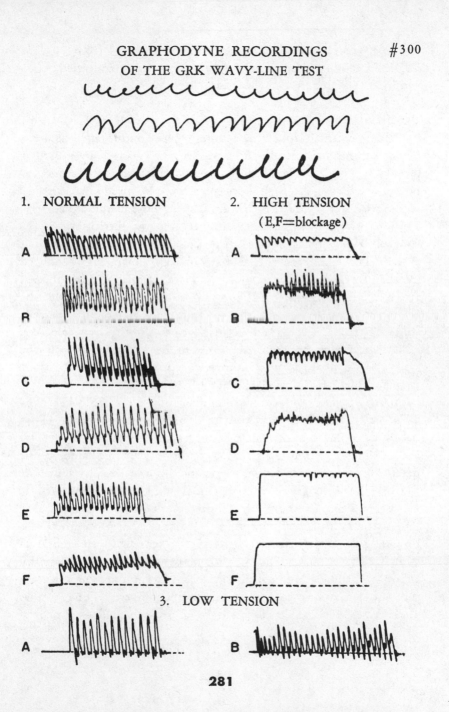

GRAPHODYNE RECORDINGS
OF THE GRK WAVY-LINE TEST

1. NORMAL TENSION

A

R

C

D

E

F

2. HIGH TENSION
(E,F=blockage)

A

B

C

D

E

F

3. LOW TENSION

A

B

example, subjects asked to write numerals in series from 10 to 1 displayed more tension in doing this than they manifested when writing the more familiar series from 1 to 10.[24]

PSYCHOSOMATIC ASPECTS

Among recent graphodyne studies, special importance attaches to the attempt to record and measure the changes in muscular tension in persons afflicted with rheumatoid arthritis and in certain nonarthritics such as hypertensives.[60] A preliminary study was carried out at the Institute for Psychosomatic and Psychiatric Training of the Michael Reese Hospital and the Institute for Psychoanalysis in Chicago, with the collaboration of the present author. The significant differences found in the tracings produced by the two groups of patients, as compared with those obtained from a control group of "normal" subjects, substantiated the assumption that a muscular dysfunction exists not only in persons suffering from rheumatoid arthritis but also in hypertensives. This dysfunction appears essentially to be a disturbance in the synergic use of the muscles, interfering with the interplay of tension and release during the act of writing.

Further studies are required to determine in what other conditions similar disturbances of the dynamic pattern occur. That neurotic conflicts and pent-up aggressive impulses, which are accompanied by increased inner tension, may be among the determinants of a state of persistent high muscular tonus or dyssynergy, is suggested by Alexander[2] and his collaborators. It can be assumed, on the basis of other psychosomatic studies, that long before the actual symptoms of arthritis develop, there are physiological antecedents, such as special sensitivity to emotional stimuli. These susceptibilities in themselves can be uncovered by means of handwriting analysis supported by graphodyne tracings. The use of graphological technique in such investigations justifies the outlook for the development of a distinct field of "medical graphology."[69]

An experiment initiated by the author dealt with the handwritings of young men and women students of architectural and industrial design and fine arts. This study was undertaken for the purpose of testing the assumption that adequate muscle tone and a well-balanced interplay of tension and release are usually associated with general well-being, emotional stability, and good vocational adjustment, whereas persistent raised tonus and a disturbed tension-release pattern accompany emotional instability, neurotic conflict, and poor adaptive capacity. On the other hand, individuals with low tension—their energy potential being reduced —would show less adequate equipment for sustained effort under stress and strain. In this test each subject was asked to draw a wavy line consisting of either garlands or arcades, according to his own preference, first with light and then with heavy pressure. In figure #300, the graphodyne recordings of the performances with heavy pressure are grouped according to the degree of tension revealed in each case. These investigations by means of graphological techniques afforded considerable insight regarding the personality patterns of the individuals studied. The findings accorded well with the information obtained from teachers and through medical examination of some of these students, and helped to explain their success or failure in school and life situations.

EXPRESSIVE SIGNIFICANCE OF TENSION AND RELEASE

The recognition of the importance of the tension-release pattern and of the factor of balance has become the cornerstone of various graphological hypotheses. One of Klages' main assumptions is that all features of graphic expression can be classified in two categories—as indices of either *Bindung* ("being bound") or *Lösung* ("being released"). He follows his own mystical concepts by assuming that these contrasted functions represent antagonistic forces within the human being, i.e., the mind and the soul. The former, as the controlling and regulating agent, inhibits and thus creates "binding" or tension. The soul, a "spiritual, cosmic life force," is responsible for the release of tension and the rhythmic recurrence of this process. The interplay of these two forces is reflected in the distinctive rhythm of movement found in writing.[80] Needless to say, present-day graphology has outgrown the stage of mythology and seeks objective data in the place of such assumptions.

The hypothesis that the alternation of tension and release may be regarded as a function of expressive movement was put to experimental test by Lewinson and Zubin[91] and by Wolfson.[170] They assumed that the degree of a writer's emotional control is expressed in his handwriting by corresponding graphic indices. These authors developed a scale for the analysis of writing by means of geometrical measurements and qualitative ratings.

In everyday graphological practice, however, it is not feasible to employ complicated scales or graphodyne tracings. Furthermore, Klages' lists and charts of indices pertaining to the tension-release phenomenon as he conceived it, are obsolete. On the other hand, we have learned through experience to recognize degrees of tension and release by means of certain graphic characteristics, and the reliance on such empirical criteria is supported by the fact that the findings tally with the results of medical and psychological experimental work and of psychometric procedures. As a rule movements tending downward, or downward and leftward, or simply leftward, symbolize retention, the attitude of taking and holding on; the concomitant muscular state is that of contraction without adequate release, i.e., tension. Movements tending upward, or upward and rightward, or simply rightward, symbolize an attitude of openness to the give and take of life, a free approach to persons and situations. The concomitant muscular state is that of release following on an interim of tension.

Writing in which there is a proper balance of tension and release is usually characterized by shading, i.e., an alternation of thick and thin strokes, or, in a very fluent hand, by slight, even pressure. Continuous flow, free handling of forms, predilection for curvatures and round *i* dots, and regularity in the sense of rhythmic periodicity—all these are indices of adequate release (figs. #65, #105).

284

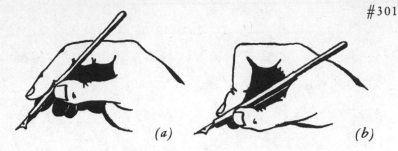

(a)　　　*(b)*

Effort, control, or repression increases tension. With increased muscle tone, the stroke becomes as taut and rigid as the fingers that produced it (fig. #301*b*); the outlines of round forms are broken, angularity predominates, ligatures become irregular or vanish. Word endings dart back sharply, taking the form of fishhooks or harpoons; *i* dots are distorted, stretched into streaks, or carried into the next letter.

In any appraisal of tension, angles and curves are particularly revealing. For example, a capital *E* formed with angles points to a considerable degree of tension. The same letter made with strokes rounded like two parentheses, run together in a little loop at the

#302

mid-point, reflects fairly released movement (fig. #302). In figure #303, the predominance of curves, and the total absence of angularity, make for an overly relaxed handwriting. An extreme degree of tension appears strikingly in figure #304. The skidding strokes betray spastic movement. The right, narrow letters (*m*, *n*), and the frequent leftward and downward impulsions, betoken

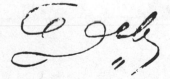

#303

#304

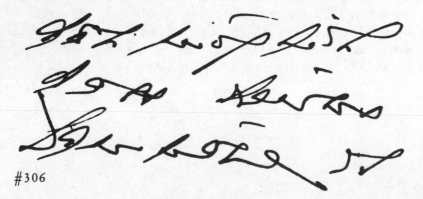

retention and retreat. The tangled pattern thus produced is eloquent of involvement, of a compulsive holding on, of a life process mired in its own complexities.

In figure #305 we see extreme narrowness, and a withholding, contracting motion in the last stroke of the *h*. The *m*'s and *n*'s are so narrow that the strokes overlie each other. This script was produced by an extremely inhibited left-handed boy. In figure #306, we can see how excessive tension affects an essentially

#305

#306

286

#307

sweeping hand, and breaks the flow and continuity of the movement. Forms are rigid and distorted, connections irregular or
lacking. The word endings dart back sharply, in fishhook or harpoon formations, and the *i* dots are stretched. The writing presented in figure #307 shows extreme tension, expressed in every
feature. The stroke is uniformly rigid, the connective forms are
acute angles, the lower loops are broken into triangles, and their
ascending stems are deflected into horizontal thrusts emphasized
by pressure displacement. Such manifestation of tension in lower
loops is found mainly in the handwriting of those women who
vent pent-up emotional tension in domestic tyranny.

Figure #308 is used by Pophal to illustrate high tension.[120] In
this hand, smoothness and fluency are hampered; tension inhibits

(a)

(b)

#308

287

free play of the fingers, so that the writer produces shorter letters than he would like to make. Similarly, his speed diminishes progressively. Fatigue and stiffening set in prematurely; this is reflected in the cramped loops and the antenna-like *i* dots (as in the first word of the second line). Another result of tension is the "fan phenomenon" (fig. #308*b*). Here the first and the last downstroke slant in different directions. Increasing irritability and fatigue impede momentum and divert the slant. In figure #309,

#309

the harpoon-like, snapped-back endings in the upper zone result from the tension that sets in when stretching movements are required.

High tension appears in the handwriting of Tschaikowsky (fig. #288). The strokes are rigid, the loops are extremely lean or transformed by an angular juncture of downstroke and upstroke. There is no regular emphasis on the downstrokes; the pressure shifts to a horizontal stress. The total picture is that of an irritable and erratic personality. The scripts of Romain Rolland (fig. #270) and Anatole France (fig. #271) exemplify two extremes: Rolland's pattern is one of utmost tension, with pressure shifted sideward, while the handwriting of France shows the free expenditure of energy characteristic for a forceful and sensuous personality.

(XV)

ARRANGEMENT

The term arrangement, as applied to the handwriting pattern, refers to the manner in which the writing as a unitary configuration is adapted to the writing space. In studying this spatial organization, we must take into account both movement and form. It is the rhythm of movement, and the balance of form it produces, that reveal the structure and dynamics of the given personality. Furthermore, the way in which the writer covers the page is an index not only of his aesthetic sense and his regard for economy but also of his integrative capacity.[129]

The writing as a whole presents a structured mass, by reason of the contrast produced by the dark line pattern against the light background. This line pattern makes up the body of the writing. It is usually set off by a more or less defined frame of blank space—the margins at top and bottom and at the sides. The graphologist notes whether the elements of the line pattern are crowded together or loosely distributed. As a corollary to this, he must judge whether the blank spaces that separate the writing lines from one another (interlinear spaces), and separate the words from one another (word interspaces), serve as clarifying and articulating factors (fig. #313) or disturb the integrity of the pattern (figs. #314, #326).

SPACING

A page that shows liberal spacing in all its features betokens a self-assured, expansive personality (fig. #310); a crowded page

#311

may imply a thrifty bent or a miserly disposition (fig. #311). An imbalance in the use of space—inconsistent spacing, crowding in spots and looseness at other points—shows conflict. This may stem from an opposition between the aesthetic and the economic motivation, or from an unconscious attempt to balance a niggardly trend with a gesture of liberality. Conversely, it may reflect a bountiful nature struggling against the limitations of time and space (fig. #312).

#312

ALIGNMENT

A child in learning to write uses ruled paper giving him a visible line as a guide upon which to base his letters. The practiced writer relates his letters to an imaginary base, hardly aware that he is doing so. In conformity with traditional usage in Western writing, the lines of his script run parallel, with some measure of space between each two. In a well-spaced script, the lower ex-

#313

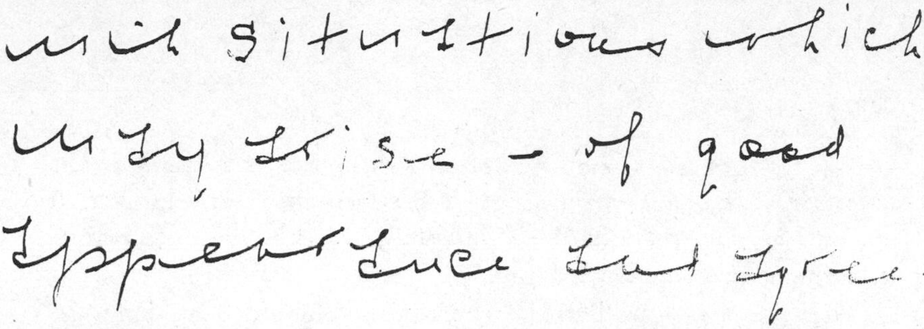

tensions of the letters of one line do not touch the upper extensions of those of the next. The writing line as a unit is understood to comprise the total configuration of the line—not only its compact middle zone, but the extensions above and below this zone as well, and also such accessories as *i* dots, *t* bars, punctuation marks, etc.

The spaces separating lines may be large, medium, or small. No school models set an explicit standard in this respect.

Good line spacing has its roots in a sense of order. This is an attribute of individuals who not only have the ability to organize their daily routine, but also the capacity to assimilate emotional experiences and maintain their essential integrity (fig. #315). Some scripts present lines in which the letters spill out beyond their allotted bounds; stems and loops jump the fence, so to speak. This is an expression of impulsiveness (fig. #312), inner unrest (fig. #311), or emotional confusion (fig. #304).

#315

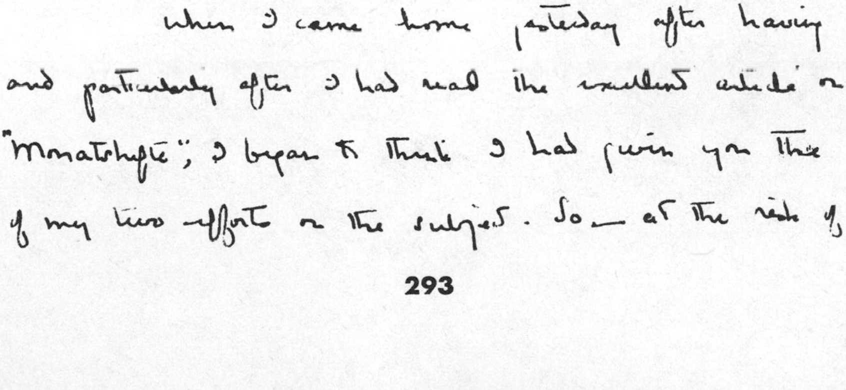

[handwritten script]

293

#316

Come up + see me some time
As ever

In regard to the alignment of the writing, i.e., the trend of the lines across the page, we distinguish between the steady horizontal or the sinuous, the uphill or downhill, the steplike or serrated, and the concave or convex line.

To shape a row of letters, keeping a straight course along the line of an assumed base, requires a sense of direction, firmness, and ability to maintain drive and move straight ahead to a goal (figs. #163, #316). Such abilities characterize the individual who persists in his aims and follows through in an undertaking, and who is not easily deflected by inner or outer interferences (fig. #314). There are writers who use ruled paper or underlay the writing sheet with a ruled guide, in order to keep their lines straight. This is betrayed, however, in the mechanically regular alignment that results. For others even this crutch is of no avail; their lines still totter (fig. #317). Still others deliberately sail above or below the ruled line, as though rejecting the help they have sought (fig. #318). All these are manifestly attempts to

#317

regular army, but since he married quite soon after entering the
the Shes rolls, St. Simon spent most of his time at Versailles or
not one of the writers who employ the first person singular pronoun
tell what kind of position he held at court, but it must have
judged all the notables there, both male and female, quite

#318

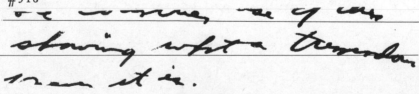

294

de sympathie exprimés dans votre lettre, je vous prie d'agréer mes respectueux compliments

Edvard Beneš

#319

compensate for an uncertain sense of direction, and a confession of deep-seated insecurity.

Lines that undulate, or waver in direction, express indecision or hesitancy—an inclination to hold back in order to avoid commitment. Such lines are related in form and expression to the threadlike connective form (p. 216). They signify a hedging attitude, a preference for compromise, or a crafty or diplomatic disposition. A commonly cited example of this type of line appears in the handwriting of Talleyrand, the French statesman who outwitted the Revolutionary Tribunal, Napoleon, and Metternich. The undulating line appears similarly in the script of Eduard Beneš, the Czech statesman, whose handwriting was judged by friendly graphologists to reveal a "diplomatic" mind, while hostile interpreters found in this feature the mark of insincerity (fig. #319). Broken lines staggering across the page may be a manifestation of incoherence in thought or action. The phenomenon may mean that the writer is a person who cannot "think straight," or who is going to pieces (fig. #320).

#320

with Mr Paul Whiteman, Faye Emer Beatrice Kraft & don & host of other celebrities

In lines that take an uphill or downhill course, the direction is largely determined by the condition of the individual while he writes. When the writer's arm slackens and tends to droop, the line slopes downward. This may indicate simply physical fatigue after a considerable period of continuous writing, or it may be due to a temporary state of low tension and its psychological equivalent, low spirits. It may express passing discouragement or sadness, or a fundamental pessimism. Downward tending lines may be regarded as symptomatic of a depressive state in the clinical sense, when found in association with small-sized letters, low pressure, slack connective strokes, leftward tending arrangement of the whole pattern, and a signature placed in the lower left-hand portion of the page. As A. H. Maslow says: "If a person is depressed, he is depressed all over."[96] Lines that run uphill

#321

I should like Theodore Brenson, an art has done some beautiful illustration. If he can anything for you I be be a good job. Yours

express some degree of excitement, prevailing at least during the act of writing (fig. #321). The excitement may be due to temperamental eagerness or hopeful anticipation, or to more acute excitation, reflecting a state of rage or exultation. However, in order to ascertain whether a rising or falling trend of the lines is indicative of a fundamentally optimistic or pessimistic outlook, or due merely to a temporary emotional state, it is necessary to weigh it against the evidence of all the other features of the script in question. Thus the writing of a hypersensitive and moody person will show extreme variability as regards alignment.

A different deviation in alignment appears in the writing of individuals who struggle against depression and seek to overcome fatigue and low spirits. The struggle may be expressed in a bowed line forming a concave arc (fig. #322). The downward trend at the start of the line reflects the sinking mood; the upcurve registers recovery of spirits. The same struggle may be expressed in a stopped or serrated line, in which the initial letter of each word stands higher than the succeeding ones, which sink down, so

#322

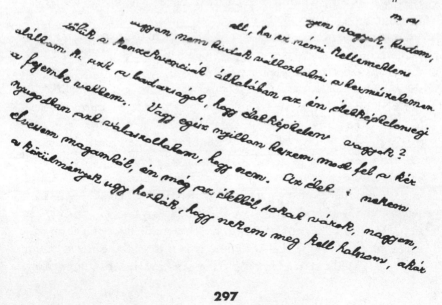

297

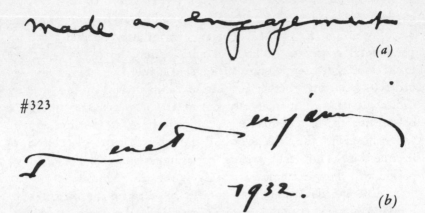

#323

(a)

(b)

that the whole word seems to droop (fig. #323 *a*). These stepped lines indicate that the fight against weariness is supported by a strong feeling of responsibility. The inverse of the concave line, the convexly bowed line, shows that the start was made with upflaring interest and eagerness that just as quickly gave out (fig. #324). The stepped or serrated line in which the start of each word stands lower than its end may be regarded as an attempt to put a brake on impulsiveness that nevertheless reasserts itself again and again (fig. #323 *b*).

Long study of the various ways in which handwritings maintain or depart from normal alignment makes it plain that the deviations are conditioned by significant emotional or somatic states. These in turn are closely related to functional variables —blood-sugar level, the dynamics of blood pressure, muscle tension. Therefore any generalizations—to assert, for instance, that uphill alignment betokens optimism, and downhill alignment indicates pessimism in the writer, are oversimple and undiscriminating and can have no claim to validity. The letter of André Gide reproduced in fig. #324 was written when he was past eighty, in the period of his last illness. He says to his friend, "It tires me to write, and I have only just enough strength to embrace you." Here the downhill line is manifestly the index of an enfeebled bodily state. However, the organization of the writing

... racotait pas, au contrair

s'endort; et quand je pense aux lointains

où vous êtes, je ressens de grands élans

vers et souffre de devoir les maintenir

tel mystique...

De mes "proches", nouvelles bonnes

sans intérêt. Yvonne Davet a cessé de

emplir près de moi les fonctions de secrétaire

j'avais besoin d'une tranquillité qui se

trouvait par trop compromise... Ça me

fatigue beaucoup d'écrire et je n'ai plus

de force que pour vous embrasser tous les

Affectueux messages de mon entourage

Fidèlement votre

André Gide

pattern, and the rhythmic flow of the movement, are proof that neither illness nor age have destroyed the integrity and spiritual force of the personality. The ascending line of the signature, exactly reproducing the tilt of Gide's earlier signatures, testifies to a resilient hold on life.

There is a kind of irregular alignment in which the lines begin with ample word and letter spacing and end in a tangle of pinched and distorted characters piled almost on top of one another, the last words curving precariously into the margin for lack of space. This line expresses improvidence and wasteful use of time and energy, and lack of organization and foresight. It typifies those individuals who dawdle in the morning and rush about helter-skelter by evening, or those who spend lavishly at the beginning of the month and live like misers at the end of it, or who consume the time and patience of others with preliminaries and are then obliged to rattle out desperately at the moment of leave-taking what they wanted to say when they came in (figs. #312, #325).

#325

WORD INTERSPACES

Words and the spaces separating them have an organic relation within the unity of the line. Hence the analysis must concern itself not less with the function of blank space than with the tangible graphic forms. The interpolations of blank space in

writing, like the pause in music or the dance, or the caesura in
verse, or the breath in speech, arise as the individual's innate
response to the demand for order and differentiation (fig. #229).
A prolonged pause may accent and give impressiveness to what
follows. Writing that moves forward without a pause betrays
something altogether different—a submission to the flow of free
associations with no time for selection and organization (figs.
#304, #311).

It goes without saying that the size of the interspace must be
considered in relation to the size and expansion of the letters of
the script. As regards proportions within the writing line, the
graphological criterion is that the spaces between words should
have approximately the width of one character of the script.

Overlarge interspaces interrupt the continuity of both pattern
and expression. The words appear to be isolated from one another, and this disturbs the normal impression of relatedness (fig.
#326*). Such interspaces indicate that the writer is isolated from

#326

* Courtesy Thea Lewinson Hall.

environmental relationships, either socially or psychologically. When the words in a line are set too close together, there is an impression of a disregard of the normal function of space—i.e., its function of maintaining a proper separation of things (fig. #327). The effect of inadequate interspaces is to destroy clarity, form articulation, measure and rhythm. In terms of personality expression, such spacing bespeaks the individual who does not keep his distance, who has no feeling for privacy and is always close at another's heels. It is an index of insecurity, of an unsure ego, and of a craving for contact. Where it appears in association with markedly narrow letters and extreme compaction within the words, it reflects anxiety, sometimes even obsession.

Most handwritings show a remarkable degree of consistency in regard to the size of their word interspaces. Irregularity of size in the word spacings indicates disturbance of the rhythm of the writing movement, and is interpreted as a sign of emotional instability (fig. #255). The appearance of a single inconsistently large space between two words means a break or gap in thought.

Such an occurrence must be interpreted within the context of the total pattern. It may be due merely to accident, a chance interruption from the outside, or to an interruption or dead stop in thought. The handwritings of mentally defective or feeble-minded persons may show a number of such gaps in the lines. In such cases the handwriting will contain a number of other features pointing to undeveloped or disturbed mental functioning. Gaps appearing not only between words but also within words may denote a certain seizure state—unconsciousness lasting only a few seconds (petit mal). Such seizures may recur with some frequency (fig. #328). Similar gaps have been observed in the handwritings of girls just before the onset of puberty. In these cases no signs of mental deterioration appeared later.

MARGINS

The arrangement of the writing lines on the page produces the margins. They reveal a number of things about the writer's outlook and organization in time and space, in relation to both the external world and the world within.

Maintaining a left-hand margin is a rule of writing fixed by convention and practice, and applied automatically by most writers. The width of this margin is set more or less consciously by the starting point of the first line. (It is understood that for the purposes of the exposition, paragraph indentations, etc., are left out of discussion). From this starting point the writing moves forward until it reaches the limit at which the writer terminates the line in order to return—with a leftward movement back across the page—to a point just under the beginning of the first line. In the same way each new line starts approximately under the first letter of the preceding one. Thus the left-hand margin as a whole is formed by the measure initially set. In contrast to this, the right-hand margin is less consistently set. Its formation depends upon the writer's actual impulses to end the line.

Nevertheless, in any spontaneous writing, the supposedly set measure of the left-hand margin is scarcely ever maintained. Carried away by the momentum of his movement toward a goal, the writer, in order to save time, tends with each succeeding line to shorten the span of the movement that takes him back to the beginning of the line. He starts each time a little farther from the left-hand edge of his page, i.e., a little more to the inside of the marginal limit he originally set himself; thus the left margin grows wider and wider as he proceeds down the page. Hence a left margin increasing in the downward direction is usually taken to indicate rapid and spontaneous writing (fig. #329).

Conversely, when the writer's spontaneity is checked, the propulsion of the movement toward the purposive goal slows down. The movement that takes him from the end of a line to the new starting point goes all the way to and even beyond the set marginal limit. The result is a narrowing of the margin and also a lengthening of the writing line, actually protracting the distance from the start to the goal and the time required to reach it. Hence a progressive decrease of the left-hand margin indicates slowness and reduced spontaneity (fig. #330).

Graphological observation has shown that the tendency to enlarge the left margin and to neglect the right-hand one goes with an extraversive nature. The writer is directing his gaze to the threshold of the outer world—here symbolized by the right-hand edge of the paper—which he is eager to reach. Enlarged right-hand margins point to self-consciousness and reserve. Where in addition there are irregular inlets of blank space indenting the pattern at the right, the graphological inference is that the writer is expressing a wish to stand aloof and to guard his privacy. Hori-

turned out to be t
happiest day of
doing a great de
too much to me
thinking of you
sure up until th
mostly of them
tell you, about
about certain etc
certain people
locked. But r
are other and
more personal.
I know, of cou
you are, and
our dear you u
be that from
want to we
a big lily
one that
but there a
one feels
tain ver
cause h
one of i

Hell

tell y
forward
I take i
have no
I hope h

Al
hard any
enjoy the
is very nice

I

a variety
report that it
will improve

f.
you when I a
Sept or sooner

jury — Have

or Tall — Tacho—

#331

zontal strokes extended through the right margin and reaching the right-hand edge of the paper (fig. #331) are interpreted as a ritual gesture—i.e., "touching wood," or a pantomime of warding off danger. A page without any margins at the sides, and lines bleeding off the paper, are interpreted as showing a disregard of one's fellow men (fig. #332). Figure #333 reproduces a portion of a letter from the hand of Robespierre, showing a small and diminishing left margin, with the writing running off the edge of the page at the right, and no margin under the signature.

The measure of the margin at the top of the page expresses the degree of esteem the writer professes toward the addressee. In Europe, the space left blank above the salutation of a letter varies in depth according to the status of the person addressed. A letter directed to a government ministry, for instance, will have a specifically enlarged top margin. The size of the margin at the

useful & I do appreciate it

It was a pity that

#332

Paris le 12 brumaire l'an I de la république

Mon ami, je n'ai pas oublié un instant ni l'armée du Rhin, ni nos deux commissions; j'ai pressé toutes les mesures nécessaires, et j'ai lieu de croire qu'aucune n'a été négligée. Le comité a adopté un plan qui me paraît très bien conçu, et dicté par le même esprit que celui qui a si bien réussi pour l'armée du nord ~~comme~~ ~~que~~ le plan est plus vaste et plus hardi, que celui qui consiste à défendre les différens points du territoire, avec ~~autant~~ autant d'armée. Il est ~~aussi~~ plus sage et atteint seul le but qu'on s'en a proposé. On ne vous a déjà écrit, pour vous le développer nous vous enverrons un collègue, dans peu de jours ~~...~~ pour ~~...~~ ~~...~~ expliquer nos idées, si vous ne les avez pas entièrement saisies. Nous comptons beaucoup sur l'énergie que vous avez communiquée à l'armée et sur l'activité que vous déployez. Pour moi, je ne doute pas du succès, je vous l'expliquerai, à l'exécution de notre plan ~~...~~ les ordres sont donnés, pour procurer à l'armée tous les renforts qui

sont à votre disposition. Adieu, je vous embrasse de tout mon cœur. Robespierre

#333

307

bottom of the page is nowhere governed by any convention, and seems to be of negligible importance as an expressive feature. However, the general principles that apply in all aspects of graphological interpretation yield certain conclusions here too. In the script of an individual in a state of depression, the whole body of the writing sags toward the bottom of the page, leaving no lower margin (fig. #364). In a manuscript from the hand of Paul Verlaine in which this symptom appears (fig. #346), we have the additional depression indices of letter forms becoming smaller and smaller, and lines and interlinear spaces becoming progressively narrower, with the pattern finally almost bleeding off the page. It is as though the writer and the writing were sinking down below the threshold of adequate functioning within the frame of life.

THE WRITING ON THE ENVELOPE

The writing on an envelope is appraised according to the criteria that apply in regard to any other unitary feature of handwriting.

Since it is important that this particular piece of writing be legible, and that letters and especially numerals be clearly traced, most people make a special effort to address an envelope carefully. Hence evidence of carelessness here means more than it does when found in the body of the script. Occasionally, in an otherwise legibly written address, a single word or name may be fuzzy or carelessly shaped. This possibly registers the unconscious effect of some ambivalent association with the word or name.

In general, smoothly written numerals indicate that the writer has a serious and sober attitude toward practical values, and a good understanding of monetary matters. Numerals may be emphasized by enlargement, decoration, or intensified pressure. Oversized numerals express an overconcern with the monetary values that numerals may symbolize, or with things that can be bought with money. According to Pulver, this manifestation has a peculiar ambivalence. It may be an expression either of the individual who is naive and impractical in money matters, or of the Midas personality. In both cases the expression springs from an unrealistic appraisal of the exchange value of money and goods.

Numerals of diminutive size, sharply and concisely traced, are characteristic of individuals who have a precise and matter-of-fact understanding of the function of numerical symbols—e.g., accountants, business executives, mathematicians, physicists, etc. Clumsily written numerals are supposed to be a mark of persons who are poor in mathematics. Touched-up numerals denote some neurotic reaction, possibly an anxiety turning on financial problems (fig. #334). Numerals transformed into decorative symbols indicate a fantasy excursus from the realistic aspect of material values.

#334

An envelope contains a message sent out into the world. If we apply our general graphological principles in examining the arrangement of the writing on the envelope, we shall obtain some clues regarding the attitude of the writer toward the world.

The envelope may be conceived of as divided into four parts, the upper right-hand quarter being the space reserved for the stamp, with the other three sections available for the writing. A writer who places the address so high on the envelope that it encroaches upon the space required for the stamp, can be said to be hasty or careless. Placing of the address markedly low betokens a pessimistic disposition or a depressive mood. Positioning of the address farther to the right of center than is usually done indicates outward directed interest, i.e., an extraversive personality trend. Setting of the address farther to the left than is customary reveals a writer whose interest is mainly directed to the world within, i.e., an introversive personality trend. The contrast between these two latter modes of expression, standing for contrasting personality types, is demonstrated in figure #335. The

309

addresses were written by two sisters. Specimen *a* expresses a
restless temperament given to pursuit of outward interests, while
the arrangement of the address in specimen *b* represents the attitude of a reserved and reflective person.

(a)

#335

(b)

(X V I)

THE SIGNATURE

The signature is the most distinctive of all the components of the handwriting. Ever since written personal marks have been used, the signature has been recognized as unique and fundamentally expressive; that it is a peculiarly revealing symbol of the self is common knowledge.

The usual signature in our culture consists of three or four parts—the given name, middle name, and family name, and, in most cases, a final appendage. This may be merely a simple dot or a terminal stroke; it may also be a complicated flourish or curlicue, or a characteristically formed jumble of lines. The signature may also as a whole present an undecipherable configuration of slurred letter forms and embellishing strokes that the writer habitually uses as his personal device.

THE DEVELOPMENT OF THE SELF

This kind of individual name writing develops at an early age, since even the very young child has need of such a visible representation of himself. He practices it on every bit of paper he happens to find. In contriving his particular form, he may try to imitate the signature of his father or of some other adult, because of a wish to identify with a personality ideal, or he may find an outlet for inventive imagination in fashioning an original configuration for his name, emphasizing or ornamenting the form according to his heart's desire. Thus the foundation for the ultimate pattern of the signature is laid in this formative period of life. This is outstandingly illustrated in figures #336 and #337;

311

the two pairs of autographs also show how the trend of personality development may be foreshadowed in early signatures.

#336

Figure #336 a presents a signature affixed by George Washington at the age of seventeen to the formal record of a land survey; specimen b of this figure shows a signature penned approximately six years later, in the course of his journey to Fort Pitt. The earlier pattern is still tentative and unsure. There is marked ego emphasis in the attempt to merge the given name with the family name in a unitary configuration of the initials, but the result is an awkward elaboration hampered by constraint; the simple forms of the rest of the signature are executed with greater ease. The second specimen, however, reflects a decided development of personality, and shows an amazing maturity for a writer of twenty-three. Here the G and W are joined in a clear and graceful design effected with a structural simplicity uncommon for the writer's age and for the period. Now the emphasis is only upon essentials; even the playful elaboration of the *t* bar is not out of relation, for it balances the strong loop of the *g* beneath it. It is also significant that Washington's signature changed little from this time onward, except for variations in the style of the *s*, which is consonant with the practice of his time.

Figure #337, showing the signature of Wilhelm II of Germany
as a boy of fourteen, side by side with his autograph as a man in
his fifties, in the prime of his power, provides a contrasting picture.
In this case the adult signature expresses no adequate personality
development: the definitive pattern was set in puberty and was
followed throughout life, just as persisting immaturity marked
the entire history of the writer.

It is a fairly common observation that certain handwriting
features, like other traits, may run in a family, aside from any
deliberate imitation. In the signatures of Joseph Chamberlain,
British statesman, and his two sons, who resembled him in their
career aspirations, there is resemblance both in general and in
certain features that would scarcely be noted by the layman; however, they stand out with telling effect to the eye of the

graphologist (fig. #338). For instance, there is in all three a characteristic formation of the letter *m*, in which the first of the three downstrokes is somewhat higher than the others. The graphological interpreter regards this as an indicator of personal ambition and of pride in accomplishment. The fact that here this basic character trait comes to expression only discreetly in an unconspicuous graphic element is in itself a clue to another trait marking the three writers in common—modesty in public demeanor.

IMAGINATIVE PROJECTION

It is a remarkable fact that the signature as a unitary pattern develops earlier and is stabilized sooner than the handwriting in general. Moreover, it does not always develop in step with the maturing of the handwriting as a whole. In the first stages of personality development, the individual apparently has a need to project an image of himself charged with his wishes and daydreams, his anxieties and frustrations; this projection finds a suitable vehicle in the signature. With maturation, however, most of us clothe our self-assertion in the rationalized forms of conventional penmanship. Yet it may be observed in the case of many an individual that, while the body of his script is in keeping with the maturity of his personality, the signature retains some qualities of infantile expression.

For the same reasons, the signature reflects more of free creative quality than the text writing. In the signature the fancy takes a freer course, and the constraints of conventional forms are somewhat less operative than in the rest of the writing. Thus in the signature, to a greater extent than in the general script, the way is open for imaginative projections.

Because the signature has a sphere of expression all its own, it is intensively scrutinized for the especially meaningful pattern it constitutes in itself. As in graphic pattern in general, we distinguish two major types of pattern in signatures, the pictorial and the linear (p. 82). It is understood of course that there is no such thing as exclusively pictorial or exclusively linear patterning. In signatures, however, pictorial configurations are more frequent, and may even undersign a predominantly linear body script. Such imagery as appears in the configuration of the signature may yield valuable information. In some cases the meaning is so manifest that it virtually hits the graphologist in the eye. The layman, however, may not at once perceive the meaningful motivations behind the configuration that he customarily sees only as an individual vagary of the handwriting.

THE ROOTS OF GRAPHIC IMAGERY

The fact that graphic forms may carry projections of unconscious imagery is understandable in the light of the development of the writing symbols. In the beginning of communication, the picture stood for the thing: there was an obvious identity between the form of the symbol and the form of the object it represented. In the course of time, the simple concrete character of these naive symbols changed; several meanings were compacted in one form —, i.e., one symbol came to represent a combination of things or ideas. Further, as this multidetermined picture

315

accreted ideational and associational content, the emphasis shifted from the realistic representation to the abstract significance. The given form might stand for an idea, an association; it became a sign of recalling a sound—an element of speech—and as such eventually a symbol of written language. It was said of Gaudier Brzeska, a sculptor keenly perceptive of meanings in form, that he could read Chinese writing to a certain extent without ever having studied the syllabary. On seeing the Chinese ideogram for a horse (fig. #339), he remarked, according to Ezra Pound, "Of course you can *see* it's a horse."[124]

#340

The specimen reproduced in figure #340 is taken from an address written on an envelope and reading literally, "Wien II." A noted Austrian interpreter of handwriting, Scherman, who worked only on an ideographic basis, saw in it immediately the image of a steamboat, with the outlines of a smokestack and its smoke, as well as the wake of the ship. This image, as it turned out, was indeed potent in the writer's unconscious; his wishful daydream was to cross the ocean. The specimen presented in figure #341 shows how such a pervasive wishful imagery—which in this case came to actual realization—may stamp the individual's script throughout life. This writer in his childhood was poor and supported himself by working as a "candy butcher"

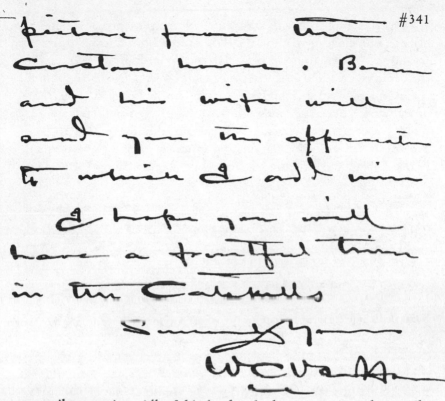

on railway trains. All of his boyhood phantasy centered on railroads; his daydreams were filled with images of locomotives and lines of rails cutting through unexplored wildernesses. The adult handwriting is patterned in parallel lines running like railroad tracks. Many of the word configurations suggest speeding locomotives, notably the word "the" in the first line. The effect of streamlined motion in this script arises from its extraordinary combination of functional and pictorial quality. In its individual features it yields an array of indices of mental speed, keen grasp of essentials, technological vision, and artistic imagination—adding up to basic creative drive and sustained practical purposefulness as the keynote of the graphic portrait of Sir William Van Horne, the builder of the Canadian Pacific Railway.

Clearly enough, even though pictorial imagery no longer has a place in our modern writing, the deep source from which it springs is still at work, and remains discernible in handwriting. Such imaginative creation lives itself out most overtly in the signature.

Often a signature embodies an image symbolic of the vocation of the writer. A painter may use the form of a palette (figs. #146, #260); a composer or conductor may use the image of a clef or a baton: such emblems appear for instance in the signatures of Franz Lehár, Johann Strauss, and Max Reger (fig. #342). The

(a)   (b)

(d)

#342   (c)

sword will appear as a favorite device of military men, as notably in the signatures of Napoleon (figs. #274a, #354, #355); the cross is an emblem often found in the signatures of ecclesiastics. Figure #343 shows a complex construction of strokes that might stand for the coils of a motor or the blades of a propeller; this is the signature of Charles Levine, who won the distinction of being the first transatlantic plane passenger. Figure #344 represents an excerpt from a letter written by a young air-force pilot, whose graphic gesture manifestly suggests the motion of flying. The

#343

318

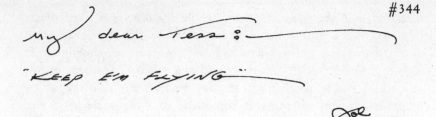

signature of Walt Disney (fig. #345) is full of animated details as ingenious as those of his well-known cartoon creations. The graphic thrusts and leaps reflect the same dynamism as the swift and playful antics of his little story creatures.

#345

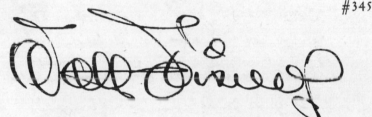

However, since subjective recognitions of this kind amount merely to tentative and suggestive highlights, they must be checked and confirmed on the basis of a thorough analysis of both text and signature. As P. M. Symonds acutely remarks:

A projective technique is not a test in the sense that it can be used to measure something. A projective technique is most valuable for throwing light on the meaning and underlying motivations of behavior. In my judgment every interpretation of a projective technique is frankly a guess, a hypothesis, a surmise which has to be verified by further evidence.[153]

CONGRUENCE OF SIGNATURE AND BODY SCRIPT

The implication is plain that we cannot detach the signature from the handwriting to which it belongs, but must examine and interpret it in the context of the whole pattern. It is particularly important to compare the expression of the signature with that of the handwriting in general. If the character of the signature is not congruent with the style and the essential features of the script as a whole, the indication may be that the role the writer plays in his own phantasy is somewhat at odds with his actual personality. But if the body of the writing and the signature accord in style and expression, and both are natural and balanced in size, emphasis, and arrangement, we may conclude that the writer is making a valid self-assertion (fig. #341).

#346

A small signature, paired with a larger body script, indicates underestimation of the self (fig. #346). This humility may be artificial, an attitude based on a desire to appear modest, or it may be a true expression of neurotic self-depreciation. There are signatures in which the capitals are smaller than the other letters. This symbolizes self-devaluation—an expression that as a rule is corroborated by other features of the handwriting, especially by the size of the capital *I* when standing for the personal pronoun (p. 163).

Inferiority feelings giving rise to a defensive behavior pattern may impel the writer to heighten or enlarge his signature or initials

#347

#348

beyond good measure (fig. #347). Figure #348 shows the signature of a physician who compensates his deficient self esteem
by emphasizing his professional standing with an oversized capital
D in his title. Often the signature as a whole is larger and more
ostentatious than the writer's general script; here the intention is
to impress people and to suggest stature and prestige (fig. #349).

#349

In the signature shown in figure #350, the aggrandizement of the initial of the given name serves the purpose of "front."

Relation of Given and Family Name

The proportional relation between the given and the family name is a direct expression of the writer's reaction to family ties and to parent-child relations. In the signature, the family name represents the social ego, whereas the given name speaks for the more intimate part of the ego. Balanced proportion between the given name and the family name within the signature as a unit reflects a harmonious interaction of private and social roles.

Overemphasis on the family name or on an acquired last name may indicate family pride or feelings of prestige and preoccupation with status. Amplification and embellishment of the given

#351

name suggests a narcissistic urge to attract attention. Figure #351 reproduces the signature of a man who forsook the business of his prominent and wealthy family in favor of an artist's life abroad. To express his inner gratification at having made this choice, he embellishes his first name and contrastingly simplifies and belittles his family name (p. 366). Figure #352 shows the style

adopted by an unprepossessing seamstress for writing her given
name, thereby acting out a wishful phantasy that postured her as
a melodramatic figure.

PERSONALITY CHANGES AND THE SIGNATURE

An individual's signature may change with changes in his life
situation. Jacoby demonstrates this phenomenon in the signature
of Benito Mussolini. The changes in size and emphasis in signatures
written respectively prior to, during, and after his ascent to
power record a progressive enlargement of self-esteem and self-
assertion. It is strikingly apparent that the signature expanded
concurrently with the increasing inflation of the personality and
the enhancement of its power over the environment. The process is
particularly to be noted in the initial M, which grows broader as
the writer moves from success to success.[70]

The signature of Napoleon Bonaparte is a mine for the graphologist.[108] For in its changes in the course of that extraordinary
life, it offers a series of key revelations packed with staggering
surprises.

#353

323

#354

Figure #353 presents his signature as a young sublieutenant of artillery signing his military oath of allegiance in 1791. The signature in figure #354 was penned at the height of consciousness of power. The mighty stroke underlining the name lifts the writer above the ordinary plane of life, emphasizing his stature. The forceful swing of the dense, sharp-edged terminal stroke expresses the pent-up life energy of the ambitious man who, when opposed, crushes his enemy. The autograph in figure #355, which belongs to the period just before the signing of the Peace of Tilsit (June 22, 1807), is even more impressive, reflecting a sensuous delight in the feeling of power. Here a single initial stands proxy for and actually fills up the space of a whole signature. The attitude expressed is obviously that this overwhelming *N*, mounted on a coiling spring of force and culminating in a titanic sword thrust, can stand for no one but Napoleon Bonaparte.

#355   #356

But after the retreat from Moscow there is a decisive change. In the pattern seen in figure #356, we have a protagonist losing ground, shuffling cautiously like a baffled boxer. The expression clearly heralds a dramatic reversal. The narrowness of the letters, and the self-covering strokes, especially in the meaningful *N*,

324

show consuming anxiety and tension. But the writer is not giving up. In the contraction the movement gathers force and rises up sheer as with some superhuman new access of strength. The end stroke is the most telling indicator of the drastic change in attitude. Instead of boldly inviting challenge as before, the signature now erects a barrier—a magic wall of defense against the uncertainties of the future—by means of the perpendicular double terminal stroke.

Figure #357 shows a signature on a military order written a year later, in October, 1813. Confusion reigns. The writer is unsure of himself; twice he almost scratches out his name, debating inwardly. In figure #358, we see him two weeks later, at Erfurt, desperately trying to conceal his feeling of defeat. He now puts into practice the actor's technique he learned from the tragedian Talma: harnessing all his remaining powers, he makes a supreme

#358

325

effort. By July 14, 1815, in the hand that appears in figure #359, we have the stark picture of a totally collapsed ego. Size has shriveled to the vanishing point, all firmness is gone. The features are now pressureless and pastose. This microscopic signature conveys a self-image drawn in to mousehole proportions.

ELABORATION AND APPENDAGES

The inclination that leads to elaboration of the signature runs a tremendous gamut in designs and styles. Almost every signature has some sort of embellishment; it may be anything from a simple end stroke to some one of those fanciful accessories which encircle, under- or overline, emphasize or adorn.

The simplest type of accessory is a dot. In general interpretation, a dot always registers some sort of retention. When the tracing of the signature itself begins with a dot, it indicates a deliberate concentration before the start (fig. #93). A dot appearing arbitrarily within the signature is a sign of some inhibitive mechanism at work (fig. #288). A dot following the signature reflects an impulse to come to an end, to cut off (figs. #212, #221). It may at the same time be symptomatic of distrust, a gesture of safeguarding.

Another simple accessory is the end stroke that finishes off the signature with a swing. The release of surplus energy it stands for may express a playful or an aggressive attitude. Playfulness expresses itself in an outswinging, easy, ascending, looping stroke (figs. #342a, #342d, #344, #345;) aggressiveness finds vent in downward curving strokes shaped like a scimitar (fig. #351) or spurting to the right, as in the signatures of Napoleon. When strokes of this kind turn leftward, cutting across the name, they manifest displaced aggression. The writer, instead of thrusting outward into the environment, is deflecting his belligerence back upon himself, in a gesture of self-destruction. An instance of this appears in figure #368 *c,* where also we may note another significant formation, the drooping end stroke, which marks a dwindling away of energy. Such a stroke registers, in greater or lesser degree, a dying out of movement, sometimes with visible breaks in the tracing (fig. #346). French graphologists have given this expression the name of *brisement douloureux de la vie* ("grievous break in life").

#360

A quite different meaning attaches to the stroke underlining the name (fig. #360). This stroke, whatever its quality, betokens ego emphasis. According as it is clear-cut and firmly drawn, it shows the degree of poise and firm footing possessed by the writer.

The encircled signature has a basic meaning. The circle or

#361

closed ring is a common symbol of anxiety, of the desire to enclose and shelter the self — to protect it from harm as in a magic circle. Encirclement may also indicate withdrawal. Figure #361 reproduces the signature of a writer who, although he maintained social relationships, was essentially unapproachable. His autistic trend appears to have been one manifestation of his schizoid personality pattern. A number of his descendants—the progeny of

327

#362

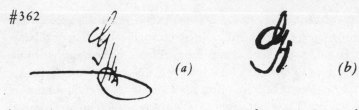

(a)　　　　　　　　　*(b)*

intersanguineous marriages over several generations—developed schizophrenic psychoses. Figure #362a shows the initial of one of this writer's grandsons, who never signed his full name. The initial, always followed by a certain cryptic pattern of lines, was not placed in the lower right-hand section of the page, but was shifted toward the left. The expression of withdrawal is reinforced by the graphic device itself—the three vertical lines constituting a part of the cryptic pattern represent a triple barrier against the world. Such an interpretation is supported by the expression of the G—a posture of rigidity, inhibition, and repulsion. In later life the writer developed schizophrenia with delusions of persecution. On his fiftieth birthday he left a note on his desk saying that he had gone to a certain mountain top to hang himself. The family rushed to the spot and found him very much alive, with a thick rope in his hand. It was learned that he had acquired the rope some twenty years before and kept it hidden in his closet. This event revealed the meaning of the enigmatic loop in his one-letter signature. It symbolized a hangman's noose, and as an image of a resolution of the problem of his hopeless life, it had enabled him to maintain a certain poise for decades.

An amazing recurrence of this symbolic gesture of schizophrenic withdrawal was found many years later in an identically formed initial (fig. #362b) appearing in the signature of the same man's great-grandniece, daughter of a schizophrenic mother. The girl had never seen nor known of any of the writing of her insane relative.[56]

Among more complicated patterns, some consist of jumbles of lines ostensibly as playful as the scribblings of children (figs. #9-11). The writer seems to take unconscious pleasure in adding such a flourish to his name, and though he may rationalize the gesture, he does not really know why he makes it. The explanation usually offered is that a complicated signature is more difficult to imitate than a plain one. Laymen are always surprised to be informed by experts that the genuine swing of a simple signature is inimitable, while an elaborately constructed pattern offers greater opportunity for successful imitation.

Other signatures of the complicated type can be shown—as has been done earlier in connection with handwriting in general —to embody definite images projecting the inner life of the writer. These reveal repressed wishes, unsuspected attitudes, dominating concepts fixed from early childhood on, or simple daydreams or other mechanisms of escape from reality.

#363

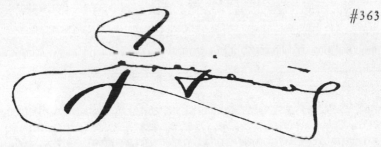

Figure #363 reproduces the signature of a provincial justice of the peace whose main job was to perform marriage ceremonies. He lived as a bachelor in a country town, and his public life was a model of order. In the initial capital we see the design of a ring, common symbol of wedlock. But it cannot be too often repeated that symbols are multidetermined, and that without knowledge of the writer's possible associations with the symbols he produces, no positive interpretation can be made. In this design, for instance, the graphologist may also see a common symbol of universal meaning, the male and female sexual organs in copulation.

In this fantastic capital *J,* the large upper-zone element floats above the middle zone in complete dissociation from an enormously inflated lower-zone loop. The bisected initial may be the projection of a sharply split body image. The middle zone as a whole is so dwarfed and sprawled out that it lacks all body and strength. Since symbolically this zone is the sphere of projection of the ego in its adaptation to reality, the proportional reduction of this zone as against the other two shows a total incapacity of the ego to cope with the phantasy activity manifested in the upper as well as in the hugely distended lower zone. The dimensions and the emphasis given to the lower zone disclose sexual urges of a violent and obsessive kind. These, since they are incompatible with the cringing ego (shrunken middle zone) and the writer's awareness of social and ethical demands (upper zone), hold the libido prisoner in the depths of the phantasy life. And when this celibate and respected civil servant died, his neighbors were shocked at sight of the obscene "pin-up" collection that entirely covered the walls of his bedroom.

PLACEMENT OF THE SIGNATURE

The location of the signature on the page is a significant index in itself, and therefore should be interpreted according to the principles that apply in analyzing the factor of location in any other feature of the handwriting. Convention places the signature in the lower right-hand section of the page. A signature shifted toward the extreme right betrays an impatient person consumed by nervous energy. Displacement toward the left suggests an attitude of withdrawal from the environment. When such displacement to the left is extreme, and the signature is written in a small and narrow hand, we have an expression of anxiety, of either temporary or permanent nature. Dropping of the signature far down on the page reflects a state of depression (figs. #346, #364); this dejected attitude will of course be expressed also in other features of the given script. In the farewell notes of suicides, the signature often appears very low at the left.[63]

It is clear that the signature has several distinct expressive functions. It speaks for the social personality, delineates the façade that the writer wishes to present to the world. At the same time, quite without awareness on his part, it illuminates the hidden aspects of his ego. But even though it furnishes these two major and pregnant avenues of exploration, the interpretation of the signature must be regarded as merely highlighting some significant aspects of the personality. The full portrait must be sought in a detailed analysis of both body script and signature.

SAMPLE ANALYSES
WITH USE OF WORKSHEETS

I. HANDWRITING OF A YOUNG WOMAN APPLICANT FOR A SECRETARIAL POSITION

This is a brief analysis made for the purpose of ascertaining to what extent the subject was qualified for a position as secretary and technical laboratory assistant in a doctor's office. The requisites specified, in addition to technical skills, were: (1) general reliability; (2) high ethical standards; (3) good general intelligence; (4) ability to get along with others; (5) punctuality; (6) perseverance.

Upon examination of the handwritings of all of the available small group of applicants, it was concluded that the personality traits disclosed in the handwriting of this subject most nearly approximated the stipulated personal qualifications.

MATERIAL (FIG. #365)

The material submitted for analysis consisted of a biographical record, including data on the professional background of the subject, written twice—in printscript and in a cursive hand. The excerpts here shown present a specimen in each style.

PROCEDURE

The graphic features are noted on the accompanying worksheet. Detailed analysis yields the following essential findings.

335

Experience : April 1948 - December 1949 -
Laboratory tech - clinical chemistry

Veterans' Administration hospital, Minneapolis,

Experience - April 1948 - December 1949 -
Laboratory tech - clinical chemist

Veterans' Administration hospital,

Minnesota.

#365

336

WORKSHEET

#365 Name A.B., SECRETARY & LAB-ASSIST. Age 26 Sex F   Predominant features ✳

		Marked	Moderate	Marked		Other salient features	Remarks
MOVEMENT							
Expansion: in height	extensive				limited		CAPITALS EXTENSIVE, FULL
in width	extensive				limited	✳	CONCEALING STROKES
Co-ordination	smooth				disturbed	✓	
Speed	fast				slow		
Pressure	heavy				light	✓	
stroke	sharp				pastose	✓	a's, o's FLOODED
	shaded				unshaded		
Tension	high				low		
stroke	rigid				flexible		
Directional trend	rightward				leftward		
terminal strokes	long				short		OCCASIONALLY LEFTWARD OR CUT
Rhythm	flowing				disturbed		OCC. SLIGHTLY DISTURBED | SHORT
FORM							
Style	pictorial				linear		
	natural				stilted		
	individual				conventional		
Letter shapes	fluid				rigid		
	diverse				uniform		
	elaborate				simple		
	ample				lean		
	curved				rectilinear	✓	TREMULOUS CURVES
loops	standard				irregular	✓	WAVERING
Connective forms	garland				arcade	✳	
	thread	—		—	angular		
Rhythm	balanced				uneven		
ARRANGEMENT							
Pattern, over-all	organized				disorganized		
rhythm	good				poor		
Margins: top	broad				narrow		
left	broad				narrow		
right	broad				narrow		
Alignment: lines	parallel				divergent		
	straight				undulating		
	ascending				descending		STEPPED; WORDS SINKING
	well-spaced				overlapping		
Word interspaces	adequate				inadequate		
Zonal proportions*	M < extensions				M > extensions		UPPER LOOPS OCC. BROKEN
	L < U				L > U		
	balanced				unbalanced		
Slant	rightward				leftward	✓	
	upright				fluctuating		
i dots	HIGH					✓	
t bars	LIGHT					✓	SHORT
SIGNATURE							
Congruence with text							
Emphasis on	given name				family name		
Placement							

* U — upper zone
M — middle zone
L — lower zone

The fact that a given quality is noted in the right- or the left-hand listing has no implication of positive or negative evaluation

GRAPHIC INDICES*	PERSONALITY TRAITS
pattern organized	desire for neatness, organization,
spacing clear	general efficiency
left margin large	
middle zone: degree of connected-	good average intelligence, sufficient
ness high	to organize everyday activities
	purposefully
forms ample	retentive memory
letter shapes conventional,	lack of imagination
legible	
trend rightward	adequate speed
writing line fluent	articulateness
upper zone: large	ethical sense
i dots placed high	
pressure slight	quiet, soft-spoken manner
t bars light	
capitals large, full, curved	deferential attitude

SIGNIFICANT TRAITS

a's *and* o's *closed*	introversion
terminal strokes occasionally curved	
leftward	
connective form: arcade	reserve
slant rightward	sensitivity
lower loops full-bodied; ascending	tendency to evade intimate rela-
stems not carried across base	tions
line	
upper loops occasionally broken or	susceptibility to fatigue
tremulous	
stroke pastose	proneness to passive acceptance
a's *and* o's *flooded*	
lines stepped	refusal to admit weariness or to
words sinking	complain

---

* The student is cautioned against taking any single graphic feature as an index of a specific character trait. Each feature must be evaluated in the light of its relation to all others in the script, and of the role it plays in the pattern as a whole.

ANALYSIS

General reliability	good
Ethical standards	high
General intelligence	average plus
Ability to get along with others	excellent
Punctuality	dependable
Perseverance	steady, despite tendency to fatigue

General characteristics and ability are judged to be satisfactory for the position in question. However, to assure steadily efficient performance, due regard must be given to certain fundamental traits. These are oversensitivity, refinement of feeling, and reserve, in addition to limitation of physical strength. Applicant should not be overworked, since she will never complain, admit fatigue, nor talk about herself.

II. HANDWRITING OF AN AMERICAN ARTIST

The handwriting here interpreted is that of a distinguished American artist, aged seventy and living in Paris at the time of writing.

MATERIAL (FIG. #366)

The specimen is part of a note taken from a series of letters, all similar in style and expression. The hand retains traces of the Spencerian penmanship of the latter half of the 19th century.

#366

WORKSHEET

#367   *Name* HENRY MOSLER   *Age* 70   *Sex* M   Predominant features ✳

		Marked	Moderate	Marked		Other salient features	Remarks
MOVEMENT							
Expansion: in height	extensive		•		limited		
in width	extensive		•		limited		
Co-ordination	smooth	•			disturbed		
Speed	fast	•			slow	✳	DYNAMIC
Pressure	heavy	•			light	✳	VIGOROUS
stroke	sharp	•		•	pastose	✓	OCC. FILLED-IN LOOPS
	shaded	•			unshaded	✳	SHADED CURVATURES
Tension	high	•			low		
stroke	rigid			•	flexible	✓	
Directional trend	rightward	•			leftward		
terminal strokes	long	•			short		OUTSHOOTING PINPOINT ENDINGS
Rhythm	flowing	•		•	disturbed		SOMETIMES DISTURBED
FORM							
Style	pictorial	•			linear		
	natural	•			stilted		
	individual	•			conventional		HIGHLY DEVELOPED
Letter shapes	fluid	•			rigid		
	diverse	•			uniform	✓	ARTISTIC
	elaborate			•	simple		
	ample		•		lean		
	curved		•		rectilinear		
loops	standard		•		irregular		
Connective forms	garland		•		arcade		
	thread			•	angular		SOME m's, n's, AND TRIANGULAR FORMATIONS
Rhythm	balanced	•			uneven		
ARRANGEMENT							
Pattern, over-all	organized		•		disorganized		
rhythm	good	•			poor		
Margins: top	broad		•		narrow		
left	broad		•		narrow		
right	broad			•	narrow		
Alignment: lines	parallel		•		divergent		
	straight		•		undulating		
	ascending		•	•	descending		INTERCHANGING
	well-spaced		•		overlapping		
Word interspaces	adequate		•		inadequate		GENEROUS SPACING
Zonal proportions✳	M < extensions			•	M > extensions		
	L < U			•	L > U		
	balanced		•		unbalanced		
Slant	rightward		•		leftward		
	upright	—		—	fluctuating		STEADY
i dots	COMMA-LIKE, PLACED FORWARD					✓	DISTORTED
t bars	EXTENDED	•				✳	COUPLED HIGH ABOVE WORDS (IN ROOF FORMATION)
SIGNATURE							
Congruence with text		•					
Emphasis on	given name		•		family name	✓	CAPITAL ORNATE
Placement	STANDARD	•					

✳   U —*upper zone*
M—*middle zone*
L —*lower zone*

The fact that a given quality is noted in the right- or the left-hand listing has no implication of positive or negative evaluation

OVER-ALL *IMPRESSION*	The script is highly developed, individualistic, strikingly vigorous and dynamic.
MOVEMENT	The dynamism of the hand is produced by an interplay of force and speed. The intensity of pressure— seen in the quality of the stroke—and the unhampered pace indicate spontaneity and forcefulness, i.e., a forthright discharge of life energy.
PRESSURE *stroke* *shading* *thrust of* *extensions* *coupling* *strokes* *co-ordination* *tension-release* *pattern* *pastosity*	The strokes are dark, sharp-cut, of varying thickness. The downstrokes are emphasized. Distinctive qualities appear in the controlled, springy curvatures with broad crescent-formed shadings, the hairline beginnings of first strokes in the words, the pin-point terminations of end strokes. There is a bold, balanced thrust in the upper and lower extensions and in the horizontal strokes, seen notably in streamlined coupling strokes, as in "the fall" and "I hope." These effects are due to heavy pressure exerted by a hand that has perfect command, so that it can intensify and relax pressure at will. Thus the writer, though maintaining high tension, is able to relax and to handle the pen as facilely as a paintbrush. This results in pastosity, warm, colorful strokes, and filled-in loops.
ARTISTIC *QUALITY* *diversity* *balance* *unity* *rhythm*	This variation in the texture of the stroke is a unique characteristic of the writing pattern, and a major contribution to its artistic quality. Other main factors contributing to the aesthetic effect are the imaginative diversity of the forms and their balanced distribution in a unified, rhythmic pattern.
PERSONAL PACE *impetus* *streamlining* *fluency* *swing*	These features reveal a man who moves under emotional tension, and whose impetus is not checked by overcontrol. Nervous impatience prevents elaboration of details. In his rushing forward movement, the writer is unwilling to slow down even on reaching the edge of the paper—e.g., in "compliments" (fourth line) parts of letters are omitted, and the force of an unavoidable sudden braking at the end of the word distorts the final *s,* while the surplus energy thus checked finds outlet in a stroke that

342

i dots

finally shoots with a horizontal forward thrust through the *t*. Moments of anger or irritation are signalized by *i* dots distorted into commas or asterisks.

ILLEGIBILITY

Occasionally entire words are illegible. Such negligence, as in the closing "Sincerely and Paternally Yours," also highlights the writer's defiance of convention and his insistence on doing as he pleases.

CONNECTIVE
FORMS
angularity

t *bars*

Willfulness and self-righteousness are indicated particularly in the acute angularity of some *n*'s and *m*'s, with their heightened first strokes, as well as in the triangular formations—as in the *f* in "fall"—and notably in the remarkable *t* bars placed extremely high over the stems. No other stroke in the handwriting is as clear an index of vigor, determination, and disposition to command as the *t* bars traced so firmly and extended so conspicuously to roof over a whole world. They are begun with heavy pressure that lessens as the movement proceeds and tails off at the end. This stroke symbolizes the writer's attitude toward his fellow men. It stems from a desire to exert power.

DIRECTIONAL
TREND

slant

LOOPS AND
OVALS

But as a counterbalance to the group of features expressing arbitrary and autocratic disposition, we have another significant group. The rightward trend of the movement, the rightward slant, the generous spacing, the warm pastosity, as well as the ample loops and the rounded *a*'s, *e*'s, and *o*'s, indicate a sensuous, fundamentally human approach, a genuine rapport with and sympathy for persons who have appeal for the writer. Thus the motive of domination is sublimated to protectiveness.

SIGNATURE
congruence

*relation of
given and
family name*

The signature in style and expression is congruent with the script as a whole. Thus it may be concluded that its individualistic character is the genuine self-assertion of a free and integrated personality.

The relation between the given and the family name is somewhat less balanced than that between the signature and the body script. The given name is emphasized by the size and ornamentation of the initial capital, recalling the flourishes of the Spencerian style, and by the two forceful end strokes. The family name is contrastingly plainer in design and written with less ebullience. This reflects the writer's attitude toward his family and toward himself. While he dwells with pleasure on his self-image, the reference to his clan induces a less vigorous response.

PERSONALITY SKETCH

The writer, at the age of seventy, is revealed as a vigorous and temperamental person of decidedly independent and spontaneous behavior. Energy and drive are the key to his relatively youthful dynamism. He moves quickly, with the impetus of a fighter. He appreciates and is at home with power, and derives considerable pleasure from asserting dominance. He wishes to see everything about him on a grand scale, and is not deterred by financial considerations in achieving this end. He is willful, impatient, and irritable, and his relations with other persons are seldom smooth and sometimes unpleasant. However, his ideas are generous and he has a genuine desire to help and protect others.

The subject reacts sensitively to color and form, and has highly developed artistic perceptions. He is continuously engaged in the artist's struggle for self-realization. Although extremely individualistic, and guided only by his own code of conduct, he has a strong desire for approval and recognition.

BIOGRAPHICAL DATA

The handwriting is that of a man who detached himself from the social milieu of his wealthy American family to live an artist's life in Paris. His paintings were the first works by an American ever to be purchased by the French government. The facts of his life are sufficiently known to supply definite confirmation of the graphological analysis.

III. HANDWRITING OF A DELINQUENT GIRL

The subject, Mary, was a young girl of 13 years and 6 months who was being seen once a week at the Treatment Clinic of the Manhattan Children's Court in New York City. After three months of therapy, a graphological analysis was undertaken in order to evaluate progress.

MATERIAL (FIG. #367)

This specimen is the manuscript of an original poem that represents a spontaneous expression of the subject's basic mood and her sentimental yearnings.

#367

WORKSHEET

MOVEMENT

	Marked	Moderate	Marked		Other salient features	Remarks
Expansion: in height	extensive			limited		HIGH CAPITALS & I'S
in width	extensive			limited		O'S, E'S DEFLATED, M'S, N'S
Co-ordination	smooth			disturbed		NARROW, CONCEALING STROKES
Speed	fast			slow		
Pressure	heavy			light		
stroke	sharp			pastose		
	shaded			unshaded		
Tension	high			low		
stroke	rigid			flexible		
Directional trend	rightward			leftward		
terminal strokes	long			short		BACKWARD, COUNTERCLOCKWISE
Rhythm	flowing			disturbed		

FORM

	Marked	Moderate	Marked		Other salient features	Remarks
Style	pictorial			linear		
	natural			stilted		
	individual			conventional		
Letter shapes	fluid			rigid		
	diverse			uniform		
	elaborate			simple	✳	CAPITALS OVERELABORATE
	ample			lean		
	curved			rectilinear		
loops	standard			irregular	✓	WELL-DEVELOPED
Connective forms	garland			arcade		JOININGS GARLAND, M'S, N'S
	thread			angular		ARCADES; I'S ANGULAR
Rhythm	balanced			uneven		

ARRANGEMENT

	Marked	Moderate	Marked		Other salient features	Remarks
Pattern, over-all	organized			disorganized	✓	
rhythm	good			poor		
Margins: top	broad			narrow		FOLLOWS POETRY PATTERN
left	broad			narrow		SLIGHTLY DECREASING
right	broad			narrow		
Alignment: lines	parallel			divergent		
	straight			undulating		RULED PAPER
	ascending	—		— descending		RULED PAPER
	well-spaced			overlapping		
Word interspaces	adequate			inadequate		NARROW
Zonal proportions*	M < extensions			M > extensions		M. UNDERSIZED
	L < U			L > U	✳	U. DOMINANT
	balanced			unbalanced		
Slant	rightward			leftward	✳	INCREASING TILT
	upright	—		— fluctuating		
i dots						FORMED
t bars	EXTENDED					DESCENDING, CURVED

SIGNATURE

	Marked	Moderate	Marked		Other salient features	Remarks
Congruence with text						
Emphasis on	given name			family name		
Placement						

---

*   U—upper zone
    M—middle zone
    L—lower zone

The fact that a given quality is noted in the right- or the left-hand listing has no implication of positive or negative evaluation

OVER-ALL IMPRESSION The handwriting reveals at first sight a spontaneous and impulsive nature. The general impression suggests precocious maturation—mental, sexual and emotional— in an adolescent. It shows further a lack of originality and formalistic emulation of a conventional writing style.

ARRANGEMENT The writing pattern ·is properly set upon the page. The words follow one another narrowly. The alignment follows the guidelines of the ruled paper. The *interlinear spaces* script does not depart from this visible base. The resulting interlinear spaces, though consistent and liberal in size, do not serve as a clarifying and structuring factor, since they are filled up with over-extended loops and stems, and with appendages of capital lerrers. This points to an inability to assimilate emotional experiences and to maintain enough *word inter-spaces* integrity to organize daily routine. The narrow word interspaces, on the other hand, are characteristic of an individual who does not keep her distance, who has no need for privacy, and who craves contact. They further suggest a fear of being left behind or *margins* left alone. The margins, in view of the fact that the script is in verse form and on ruled paper, are of minor importance. The left-hand margin, decreasing slightly toward the bottom of the page, shows a slowing down of writing speed, denoting a dying out of initial impulsiveness.

EXPANSION The showy expansion of the handwriting is intimately bound up with Mary's need for self-display and her desire to be the focus of attention and love. Special indicators of this attitude are the pretentious *height* height of the overelaborated capitals and the romantic feeling projected upon the ego-representative *capital* I capital *I*. Further characteristics are the outreaching initial and terminal strokes which first shoot forward, and—after this impetus is spent—swing backward in a released counterclockwise movement. The

347

relation of height to width	relation of height to width is somewhat unbalanced and inconsistent. The capitals and upper loops are ample, and their width appropriate to their height; the unizonal letters are less outspread and fluctuate
width	in size and width. Such letters as *o* and *e* are deflated, and the *m*'s and *n*'s show restriction: the distance between two strokes is less than the standard requirement. The narrowness is emphasized by up-and-down strokes running too close together. This results
concealing strokes	in strokes that cover and conceal each other, a feature that is an index of anxiety.
ZONAL PRO-PORTIONS *middle zone* *upper zone* *lower zone* *loops* *stems*	The writing line shows a dominant upper zone, an undersized middle zone, and a fairly balanced, well-developed lower zone. The middle zone tells of an ego oppressed and depressed by the outside world. The elements of the upper zone reveal a tendency to daydreams and illusions, a flight from the "pots and pans" of practical life. The elements of the lower area, especially the smooth loops, suggest aroused sexual urges that seek normal outlet. The overshooting, curved stems point to an imperative need for emotional gratification.
SLANT *increasing tilt*	This picture of the ego functioning is reinforced by the evidence of other features, such as the slant. The extreme rightward slope freely expresses the abandoned attitude of a spontaneous, sensitive young person who wallows in sentimentality, and whose approach to life is determined less by reason than by feeling. This excessive rightward slant and the increase in tilt toward the end of a word and toward the end of the writing line indicates uncontrolled behavior and low frustration tolerance. It also discloses a tendency to give up connection with reality and to falsify actualities to suit demand. This creates a need for substitute gratifications, and thus a disposition to drift into alcoholism or the use of narcotics.
PRESSURE	Another trait rounding out this personality picture appears in the writing pressure as seen in the stroke.

pastosity	The pen is guided over the paper with slight pressure, and manipulative skill conduces to an easy, sliding movement. The general tendency is to keep rolling along and to avoid unnecessary friction. The resulting stroke is pastose; it is almost uniform in width, and lacks sharpness and marked shading. It denotes a sensuous person who manages to indulge her inclinations without reticence.

CONNECTIVE FORMS
garland
arcade
angularity

The connective forms that join the letters are predominantly of garland type, whereas the linking of up-and-down strokes, as in the *n*'s and *m*'s, is effected by means of arcades. In contrast to these, an angular formation appears in some of the *l*'s. This mixture of forms reflects a striking ambivalence—relaxed mood alternating with fear, orientation toward people with withdrawal. The angular *l* formation is a gesture of cringing—of ducking away from danger.

CONTINUITY
connectedness

All the letters of long words are connected in one continuous movement, with automatic ease. The high degree of connectedness seen in the middle zone shows the subject's capacity for adaptive behavior, and ability to associate experiences on a common-sense basis. The smooth connectedness in the lower zone reflects facility in establishing socio-sexual relationships. The kind of connectedness seen in the upper zone indicates less favorable personality characteristics. The joinings contrived by means of overextended swirling strokes and superfluous flourishes reveal unbridled fantasy, activated without creative force. The forms produced lack aesthetic quality and originality; they are merely elaborate reproductions of the features of an outmoded style of penmanship. This shows the subject's limitations in discrimination and taste.

SUMMARY

The graphic indices here discussed, together with other features recorded on the worksheet, give the impression that Mary possesses mental ability above the norm for her chronological age. The handwriting further suggests an impulsive and emotionally labile disposition, and surrender to fantasy activity.

The graphological prognosis of evaluating progress and possible personality development was made with reservations. Mary's desire for overwhelming emotional experiences, and her lack of resistance to frustration, expose her to a compelling need for substitute gratification.

CLINICAL REPORT

Mary was first brought into court because of incorrigible behavior at home. She had been away from home for an extended period of time, during which she had become addicted to narcotics, indulged in sexual relations with an older man, and engaged in minor stealing episodes.

Very little was known of Mary and her relationship with her family up to the age of six, when her mother died. The girl was brought up by a maternal aunt. Her developmental history as described by the latter was uneventful. Her father had a cardiac condition and was described as an inadequate provider and heavy drinker.

The data obtained through projective techniques and clinic contacts revealed an oversensitive, overreactive adolescent who had great need of self-assertion, emotional display and warmth, but feared rejection and deprivation. She felt that she would not be accepted, and tried hard to rationalize her general anxiety and her frustrated need of dependence. Her lack of real warmth and of contact with an understanding female personality made identification and acceptance of herself in a female role quite difficult. She had been sexually stimulated and her interest in sex was strong, but her fear and ambivalence about it were greater.

Mary was a girl of superior intelligence (IQ 123) who, having been denied affection, warmth, and acceptance, attempted to find emotional satisfaction in any area in which she could perform well without too much risk of being hurt. Suggestible and emotionally starved, she was easily led into delinquent behavior, because on this level she could feel that she belonged to and was wanted in a group. She appeared to have good potential, which would serve her for a favorable development if she could obtain supervision of a constructive kind from a warm and understanding adult in a controlled milieu.

This analysis was undertaken in connection with judicial and private examination into the circumstances of a case tried in a criminal court in Budapest.

The sudden death of a young actress had occupied the newspaper headlines for days, and the question of whether she had died by murder or suicide prompted an investigation to establish the cause of the tragedy. The graphologist was asked by the court to examine questioned documents in the case, and the family of the deceased further requested an analysis of the girl's handwriting, for such disclosure as it might afford of a possible motive for suicide.

MATERIAL (FIG. #368)

The three specimens are respectively from writing produced by the subject at sixteen, eighteen, and twenty years of age. In Hungary it is customary for the given name to follow the family name, so that the full name appears here as "Forgács Anna."

#368(a)

Specimen *a* is from an employment application blank. It conforms strictly to the copybook round-hand standard. Though simple and natural, it is somewhat immature, and lacks the swing and stamina expectable in the hand of a sixteen-year-old office worker.

#368 (b)

Specimen *b* was written two years later, when the girl had left her position as a typist to begin a stage career. The striking change in the script reflects an attempt to adopt a mannered style in imitation of a so-called "society hand" favored by girls of privileged class. It is apparent that the effort overwhelms and inhibits the writer: the constrictive gesture to which she is forcing herself impedes any natural expressive movement.

Specimen *c*, produced after another interval of two years, evidences a startling disintegration. The accompanying worksheet sets forth the essential findings regarding this specimen, which is discussed in detail in the interpretative analysis that follows.

intézzem el nekem épp

A fényképek közül egye-

nek nem lesz rá szüksége,

a nagy tanulmány fejet (; az

között a decoltáltat (; adja

et és meleg üdvözlet

[signature]

#368(c)

WORKSHEET

#368   Name ANNA FORGÁCS   Age 20   Sex F   Predominant features ✳

		Marked	Moderate	Marked		Other salient features	Remarks
MOVEMENT							
Expansion: in height	extensive				limited	✳	IMMODERATE
in width	extensive				limited	✳	EXTREMELY NARROW
Co-ordination	smooth				disturbed		
Speed	fast				slow		
Pressure	heavy				light	✳	
stroke	sharp				pastose		EXTREMELY THIN
	shaded				unshaded	✓	
Tension	high				low		
stroke	rigid				flexible		BRITTLE
Directional trend	rightward				leftward		
terminal strokes	long				short	✓	CUT OFF OR FALLING DOWNWARD
Rhythm	flowing				disturbed		
FORM							
Style	pictorial				linear		
	natural				stilted		
	individual				conventional		MASK
Letter shapes	fluid				rigid		
	diverse				uniform		MONOTONOUS
	elaborate				simple		
	ample				lean		OVALS DEFLATED
	curved				rectilinear		
loops	standard				irregular		DEFLATED, NO HEADS
Connective forms	garland				arcade		MIXED
	thread				angular	✓	BASE OF a's & o's
Rhythm	balanced				uneven		
ARRANGEMENT							
Pattern, over-all	organized				disorganized		FLAT, CONSTRICTED
rhythm	good				poor		NO RHYTHM
Margins: top	broad				narrow		
left	broad				narrow		
right	broad				narrow		NO COMMON BASELINE
Alignment: lines	parallel				divergent		
	straight				undulating		
	ascending				descending		
	well spaced				overlapping		RESTRICTED, INADEQUATE
Word interspaces	adequate				inadequate		HAPHAZARD
Zonal proportions*	M < extensions				M > extensions		OVERSIZED
	L < U				L > U		U SHORT
	balanced				unbalanced		
Slant	rightward				leftward		
	upright				fluctuating		
i dots					WEAK		PLACED ABOVE STEM
t bars					SHORT		
SIGNATURE							
Congruence with text							IN BOTH NAMES
Emphasis on	given name —			—	family name		CAPITALS MUTILATED
Placement					LEFTWARD		

* U —upper zone
  M—middle zone
  L —lower zone

The fact that a given quality is noted in the right- or the left-hand listing has no implication of positive or negative evaluation

PROCEDURE

**OVER-ALL
IMPRESSION**

The pattern appears weak and flat, unimaginative
and rigid, disturbed and constricted. Spontaneity is
conspicuously absent, as well as any expression of
the youthful strength, the pulsating life, or the emotional glow of a young woman who has just experienced her first triumph in a successful stage
performance. This pattern is clearly a failure as a
true self-expression, because it does not spring from
genuine feeling. It also elicits no response in the be-
holder.

ARRANGEMENT

alignment

rhythm

The words are almost haphazardly deposited on the
page. The letters within the words have no common
base line. Irregular, inadequate spacing and intertwining extensions disturb the alignment and make
for a pattern in which there is no rhythm.

EXPANSION

height

width

*relation of
height to
width*

*concealing
strokes
loops and
ovals*

Observation is instantly drawn to the expansion of
the handwriting—its bizarre height, extreme narrowness, and unusual proportions (marked with asterisks
on worksheet). The immoderate height is an index
of pretentiousness, i.e., of a desire to impress people
and to attract attention; it is a mark of exhibitionism, a craving to bask in the limelight. The minimized width of the letters is an index of restraint
and constriction, of the writer's inability to take up
her alloted space. The disproportion reveals emotional conflict. The writer's urgent need to stand out
and be noticed is thwarted by self-consciousness and
anxiety—so much so that she cannot swing into
action but holds back in a frozen attitude.

Compression appears also in downstrokes and upstrokes running so close together that they partially
cover each other. From the same cause, loops and
ovals become lean and deflated, e.g., the *o* (fourth
letter) in the last word of the sixth line (*üdvözlet*)
takes the shape of an *i*. In the signature this happens also to the *o* in the family name, "Forgács,"
while the *a* of "Anna" (last letter), is reduced to a
tangle of overlapping strokes. The concealing strokes

reinforce the impression of self-consciousness and insincerity. The writer's natural impulses are covered over: what she says or does is never what she really wants to say or do.

ZONAL PRO-PORTIONS *middle zone* *lower zone* *upper zone* *t bars*	The middle zone is oversized, at the expense of the upper zone. This indicates inordinate ego involvement, concentration upon self with no attention to spare for others. The extremely long lower loops, falling into the depth, thin out without forming heads. This indicates that instinctual urges are dying out without fulfillment. The lean and relatively short upper loops point to a low level of aspiration. Thus another conflict is revealed in the discrepancy between the showy total height and the relative shortness of the upper extensions. It means that the writer strives toward purely narcissistic goals, without higher aims or gratifications. The extremely short horizontal strokes betray timid and futile striving. They also indicate lack of imagination and of self-confidence, preventing any planning ahead.
PRESSURE *stroke* *tension*	The stroke is as thin as a spiderweb. It has no body, no sharpness, no shading, and expresses no rhythmic interplay of muscular contraction and release. The slight energy exerted seems to be easily blocked; the writing movement becomes taut, the stroke becomes rigid and brittle. This indicates high tension, induced by anxiety and pent-up aggression.
ANGULARITY	This finding is supported by the angularity of the letter forms. Angles appear inappropriately, e.g., at the base in oval forms such as *a*'s and *o*'s. This results from restrained movement, and can be regarded as the incipient stage of the deflated oval. The pinpoint attrition of the forms at the base, together with the conspicuous lack of a firm base in words and lines in general, betrays defective equilibrium, both psychic and somatic.
CONNECTIVE FORMS	The manner of linking down- and upstrokes and of joining letters reflects increasingly insecure social behavior. Specimen *a* shows, notwithstanding its

357

immature adherence to copybook forms, a genuine trend to roundness of form and curving connections, and a flexible and pastose stroke, i.e., natural gestures of warmth and adaptability. In specimen *b,* the deep, narrow garlands betoken shyness and restraint, although the rightward slant and curved connections point to some compliance and passive receptivity. In specimen *c* mixed connective forms appear. Garlands are rare, appearing only in the *n*'s of the first two lines. Arcades predominate, denoting limited receptivity and increasing aloofness. Even more conspicuous are the angular connections, which, however, lack all regularity. These express a show of resolution, an effort to escape failure by obstinately refusing to admit error or defeat.

garland

arcade
angle

TERMINAL
STROKES

The terminal strokes never swing to the right; instead they are cut short, or sink down, or are turned to the left. Their connotation is the same as that of the end stroke of the signature (see below).

SIGNATURE
capitals

Conventionally, in Hungarian writing, the capitals in a signature are emphasized. Here, however, the initial *F* of the family name is mutilated, while the *A* of the given name is denied capitalization and written as a small letter. Thereby the writer expresses rejection of her social and personal being, in short, total selfnegation.

SYMBOLIC
GESTURES

The monotonous quality of the tracing is varied by two spontaneous strokes—the dynamic terminal strokes of the two names. These strokes represent highly symbolic gestures. Instead of the swing to the right that stands for a release of surplus energy and of possible aggressive impulse in the direction of the external world, the end stroke of "Forgács" turns leftward, against the name. It stands for a violent gesture suddenly breaking through rigidity as though to attack the name and annihilate it. The other end stroke grows out of the cramped, nullified final *a* of the given name. However, it shows an upsurge of energy, the writer's last attempt to lift herself by her bootstraps. But it is followed by the endless falling terminal stroke testifying to complete collapse. This end stroke is similar in dynamic and form to the downstrokes of the lower loops, which sink into the depth without completion. They reveal a glaring deficiency in the life energy as a whole, as well as a marked lack of sexual libido.

CASE HISTORY

Anna Forgács was the only child of an elderly lower-middle-class couple. Her mother was a shy little woman, her father a clerk forced to take much abuse from his superiors. He overcompensated his frustrations by playing the tyrant at home. Nevertheless Anna was loved and spoiled.

At the age of sixteen, after completing a commercial-school course, the girl obtained a job as a typist, but soon gave up this calling. Because of her good looks, her friends encouraged her to change over to a theatrical career. She enrolled in a dramatic workshop, and before long managed to get a part in a professional play.

Her childishly appealing way with men won her many beaux, but they tended to drift away after brief flirtations. One boy, however, courted her steadily. He was an idler, always seeking the spotlight in his group, getting involved in all sorts of extravagances, but lacking the funds necessary for such a life. He and Anna eventually became engaged.

The young man's brutal behavior and the girl's submissive acceptance of it shortly made them repugnant to all their friends. A newspaper gossip column once reported the following incident. A passer-by in a certain street, noticing a gay company of several couples, and hearing a sound of soft crying, turned around in time to see a young man hitting a frail girl. He interceded, knocked the bully down, and then turned protectively to the girl. She pushed him away and bent down to comfort her escort. "Don't bother," said the others. "She likes to be beaten up."

Anna married this boy, and some time afterward they went to spend their deferred honeymoon at an Alpine resort. Outsiders

359

saw them as a lovely pair, and there was much teasing about their romance. But the hotel chambermaids and some guests in neighboring rooms reported that they had heard Anna crying and her husband yelling at her.

The husband, boasting of his athletic prowess, proposed to climb a mountain peak. In full climbing regalia, he set off with Anna, who was to accompany him for a short distance. When she failed to return, the hotel personnel began a search for her. She was finally found in a ravine, with some minor bruises and completely hysterical. Since no accident had ever before occurred on the path the pair had taken, Anna was questioned at length when she was brought back to the hotel, but evaded explanation, responding only with an occasional nod of her head. On being asked whether she had been pushed off the cliff, she became violently disturbed and refused all answer.

Her husband returned shortly afterward, sunburned and in a gay mood, bringing with him a large bunch of mountain flowers. When he was told of what had happened, he ran up to Anna's room, and their neighbors later reported having heard crying and commotion.

Next morning the young man strolled about in good spirits, announcing to all concerned that Anna was feeling fine and resting quietly. That evening when the maid went to their room to straighten the beds, she found Anna dead, her hand gripping an empty package that had contained a drug.

An autopsy revealed remnants of poison in the girl's stomach. Moreover, it was discovered that shortly after their marriage Anna's husband had taken out an insurance policy on her life, with himself as beneficiary.

Was it suicide or murder? The grief-stricken husband offered evidence purporting to show that Anna was a hysterical girl and a drug addict, adding that he had repeatedly foiled attempts at suicide on her part, on several occasions by forcibly taking the drugs out of her hands. He revealed that soon after their marriage she had had to be taken to a private hospital. Investigation disclosed that on the occasion described, the doctor and nurse had suspected that the drug was not self-administered.

A complete study of the handwriting of the man, on the basis of specimens covering a period of years, disclosed him to be a moral imbecile; he was immature, abnormally egocentric, inefficient and unreliable, and given to excessively aggressive, attention-compelling behavior. The Doctor of Law diploma he bragged about was found to be a forged document. The trend of the evidence at the trial was against him, and even though there was no final proof of his guilt, he was indicted for murder.

SUMMARY

From the handwriting of Anna Forgács, it may be concluded that the girl was essentially self-oriented and consumed by narcissism. She had no interest in and no love for other persons, and was obsessed by her craving for outward success. Her weak ego was thwarted by lack of vocational and sexual satisfaction. Deeply frustrated, she had no appropriate resources for acting out resentment and hostility. Immobilized by constant inner conflict, she lived in a strait jacket of anxiety that blocked any possible release or happy abandon. This state of tension was associated with feelings of insecurity and isolation, guilt, and remorse. These sufferings proved to be more than she could endure; they forced her to make maladaptive compromises and to seek in erotic masochism a compensation for repressed aggressive reactions.

The inhibition of outward expression led her to turn aggressive feelings inward—against herself. Unconsciously she was moved to choose a brutal mate, a bully, as a tool for self-punishment and self-destruction. In her obsession she saw only one way of achieving success in terms of front-page claim to attention—by focusing the limelight upon herself as the heroine of a sensational mystery.

Though this may have been a case of suicide or murder in the ordinary sense, graphological analysis of the two main characters gives ground for the presumption that the girl brought about her own death by goading the man to carry out the act of destruction.

BIBLIOGRAPHY

1 ALEXANDER, Franz

Fundamentals of Psychoanalysis. *New York, 1948.*

2 Psychosomatic Medicine. *New York, 1950.*

3 ALLPORT, Gordon W., and VERNON, Philip E.

Studies in Expressive Movements. *New York, 1933.*

4 ANGYAL, Andras

Foundations for a Science of Personality. *New York, 1941.*

5 ARNHEIM, Rudolf

"Experimentell-psychologische Untersuchungen zum Ausdrucksproblem." Psychologische Forschungen, *XI, 1-32, 1928.*

6 BACHOFEN, Johann Jakob

Urreligion und antike Symbolik. *Leipzig, 1926.*

7 BALÁZS, Dezsö, and HAJNAL, Richard

Ember jellem irás [Man, Character, Handwriting]. *Budapest, 1946.*

8 BALDO, Camillo

Trattaro come da una lettera missiva si conoscono la natura e qualita del scrittore. *Bologna, 1664.*

9 BÁNÁTI FISCHER, Arpád

Lélek és irás [Soul and Writing]. *Budapest, 1937.*

10 BECKER, Minna

Graphologie der Kinderschrift. *Heidelberg, 1926.*

11 BENDER, Lauretta

"Psychological Principles of the Visual-motor Gestalt Test." Transactions of the New York Academy of Sciences, ser. 2, vol. XI, no. 5, 1949.

12 BENDETZ, Moric

Grafológia a gyakorlatban [Practical Graphology]. *Budapest, 1936.*

13 *Grafológai tanulmányok* [Studies in Graphology]. *Budapest, 1939.*

14 BINET, Alfred L.

"La graphologie et ses révélations sur le sexe, l'age et l'intelligence." L'année psychologique, X, 179-210, 1904.

15 BIRÓ, József

A modern grafológia [Modern Graphology]. *Budapest, 1930.*

16 BLAU, Abram

The Master Hand. *New York, 1946.*

17 BRANDON, O. H.

"Doodles International." Collier's, *May 22, 1948.*

18 BROOKS, Harry

Your Character from Handwriting. *London, 1930.*

19 BUSSE, Hans H.

Die Handschriftendeutungskunde. *Munich, 1896.*

20 CARUS, Carl Gustav

Symbolik der menschlichen Gestalt. *Dresden, 1895.*

21 CASTNER, Burton M .
"Prediction of Reading Disability prior to First-Grade Entrance." American Journal of Orthopsychiatry, V, 375-87, 1935.

22 CRÉPIEUX-JAMIN, J.
L'écriture et le caractère. *Paris, 1888.*

23 Les éléments de l'écriture des canailles. *Paris, 1924.*

24 DIEHL, A.
"Über die Eigenschaft der Schrift bei Gesunden." Psychologische Arbeiten, III, 1-61, 1899.

25 DELHOUGNE, A.
"Dreidimensionale Graphologie." Zeitschrift für Menschenkunde, *vol. VII, 1931.*

26 DOWNEY, June E.
"Judgments on the Sex of Handwriting." Psychological Review, XVII, 205-16, 1913.

27 Graphology and the Psychology of Handwriting. *Baltimore, 1919.*

28 *"Laterality of Function."* Psychological Bulletin, *vol. XXX, no. 2, 1933.*

29 DREVER, I.
"Notes on the Study of Handwriting." Experimental Pedagogy, *vol. II, no. 25, 1913.*

30 DUPARCHY-JEANNEZ, M.
Les maladies d'après l'écriture. *Paris, 1919.*

31 ELIASBERG, Wladimir
"Political Graphology." Journal of Psychology, XVI, *177-201, 1943.*

32 *"Graphology and Medicine."* Journal of Nervous and Mental Diseases, C, *381-401, 1944.*

33 ELIASBERG, Wladimir
"Forensic Psychology." Southern California Law Review, *vol. IX, no. 4, 1946.*

34 ENG, Helga
The Psychology of Children's Drawings. *New York, 1931.*

35 ERLENMEYER, D.
Die Schrift: Grundzüge ihrer Physiologie und Pathologie. *Stuttgart, 1879.*

36 FANTA, Otto, and
SCHÖNFELD, Willy
Graphologie als Wissenschaft. *Prague, 1935.*

37 FEUCHTWANGER, Erich, and
GOLDZIEHER ROMAN, Klara
"Handschriftenuntersuchungen an Hirnverletzten." Schweizerisches Archiv für Neurologie und Psychiatrie, *vol. XXXIV, no. 1, 1934.*

38 FLATAU, Theodor, and
GOLDZIEHER ROMAN, Klara
"Die graphologische Beurteilung der Stottererhandschriften." Medizinische Welt, *no. 25, 1929.*

39 FREUD, Sigmund
Psychopathology of Everyday Life. *New York, 1914.*

40 GALTON, Francis
Inquiries into Human Faculty and Its Development. *London, 1883.*

41 GERNAT, Alfred
Graphologische Praxis. *Villach, 1948.*

42 GERNAT, Alfred
Leitfaden zur Theorie und Praxis der Graphologie. *Vienna, 1949.*

43 GESELL, Arnold, *et al*
The First Five Years of Life. *New York, 1940.*

44 GÖTTEL, W.
"Experimentelle Beiträge zur Untersuchung des schnellen und des gestörten Schreibaktes." Archiv für die gesamte Psychologie, vol. LXXXIX, nos. 1-2, 1933.

45 GOLDSTEIN, Kurt
The Organism. New York, 1939.

46 GOLDZIEHER ROMAN, Klara
"Untersuchungen über die Schrift der Stotterer, Stammler und Polterer." Zeitschrift für Kinderforschung, vol. II, no. 1, 1922.

47 Irás és egyéniség [Handwriting and Personality]. Budapest, 1926.

48 "Untersuchungen über die Schreibgeschwindigkeit und ihre Hemmungen." Nachrichtendienst fur Charakterologie, vol. VI, no. 1, 1927.

49 "A hibásbeszédüek irása." [Handwriting in Cases of Speech Disability"]. Magyar gyógypedagógia, vol. IV, no. 6, 1928.

50 "Graphodyn." Zeitschrift für angewandte Psychologie, XI, 23-33, 1931.

51 "Az irás kisérleti vizsgálata" ["Experimental Investigation of Handwriting"]. Jövö utjain, no. 2, 1934.

52 GOLDZIEHER ROMAN, Klara
"Studien zur Schriftentwicklung." Die Schrift, vol. I, no. 5, 1935.

53 "Studies on the Variability of Handwriting: The Development of Writing Speed and Point Pressure in School Children." Journal of Genetic Psychology, XLIX, 139-60, 1936.

54 A balkezesség [Left-handedness]. Budapest, 1938.

55 GOLDZIEHER ROMAN, Klara
"A jobb-és balkezesség szerepe az ikrek irásában" [Right- and Left-Handedness in the Handwriting of Twins"]. Magyar Psychologiai szemle, vol. XV, nos. 1-4, 1942.

56 Ki vagy? Megmondja az irás. A grafológia kézikönyve [Who Are You? . . . A Manual of Graphology]. Budapest, 1944.

57 "Untersuchungen der Schrift und des Schreibens von 283 Zwillingspaaren." Schweizerische Zeitschrift für Psychologie und ihre Anwendungen, VI (suppl.), 29-55, 1945.

58 "Tension and Release: Studies of Handwriting with the Use of the Graphodyne." Personality, no. 2, 1950.

59 GOLDZIHER, Erzsébet
"Arany János a grafológia tükrében" [János Arany in the Mirror of His Handwriting"]. Emberismeret, vol. I, no. 1, 1934.

60 GOTTSCHALK, Louis A., SEROTA, Herman M., and GOLDZIEHER ROMAN, Klara
"Handwriting in Rheumatoid Arthritics." Psychosomatic Medicine, VI, 354-60, 1949.

61 GROSS, A.
"Untersuchungen über die Schrift Gesunder und Geisteskranker." Psychologische Arbeiten, II, 450-567, 1899.

62 HAACK, Theodora
"Über die funktionelle Asymmetrie des Auges." Zeitschrift für angewandte Psychologie und Charakterkunde, XLVIII, 415, 1935.

63 HAJNAL, Richard
"Utolsó üzenet" ["The Suicide's Last Letter"]. Emberismeret, vol. I, no. 2, 1934.

64 HARTGE, Margaret
"Die Schriftspannung." Die Schrift, *no. 3, 1935.*

65 HEISS, Robert
Die Deutung der Handschrift. *Hamburg, 1943.*

66 HILDRETH, Gertrude
"Reversals in Reading and Writing." Journal of Educational Psychology, *vol. XXV, no. 1, 1934.*

67 *"Developmental Sequences in Name Writing."* Child Development, *VII, 290-303, 1936.*

68 HIRT, Emil
"Untersuchungen über das Schreiben und die Schrift." Psychologische Arbeiten, *VI, 531-664, 1914.*

69 JACOBY, Hans
Handschrift und Sexualität. *Berlin, 1932.*

70 Analysis of Handwriting. *New York, 1940.*

71 Self-Knowledge through Handwriting. *New York, 1941.*

72 JOHNSON, A., SHAPIRO, L. B., and ALEXANDER, F.
"Preliminary Report on a Psychosomatic Study of Rheumatoid Arthritis." Psychosomatic Medicine, *IX, 295, 1947.*

73 JOSEY, Charles C.
"The Place of Psychology in the Development of Values." Personality, *no 1, 1950.*

74 JOTEYKO, I.
"Recherches expérimentales sur la significance de l'écriture en miroir." Revue psychologigue, *no. 12, 1909.*

75 KANFER, Alfred
"Physiology and Pathology in Handwriting." In Mendel, H. O., Personality in Handwriting. *New York, 1947.*

76 KIPIANI, V.
Ambidextrie. *Paris, 1912.*

77 KLAGES, Ludwig
Die Probleme der Graphologie. *Leipzig, 1910.*

78 Ausdrucksbewegung und Gestaltungskraft. *Leipzig, 1913.*

79 Einführung in die Psychologie der Handschrift. *2d ed. Heidelberg, 1923.*

80 Der Geist als Widersacher der Seele. *Leipzig, 1929.*

81 Die Grundlagen der Charakterkunde. *8th ed. Leipzig, 1936.*

82 Handschrift und Charakter. *18th ed. Leipzig, 1940.*

83 KOMAI, T., and FUKUOKA, G.
"A Study of the Frequency of Left-Handedness and Left-Footedness among Japanese School Children." Human Biology, *VI, 33, 1934.*

84 KRAUSS, R.
"Über graphischen Ausdruck." Zeitschrift für angewandte Psychologie, *no. 48 (suppl.), 1930.*

85 KROEBER-KENETH, L.
"Die Leserlichkeit der Handschrift." Industrielle Psychotechnik, *vol. XII, nos. 4-5, 1935.*

86 LANDIS, C.
Sex and Development: A Study on the Growth of the Sexual and Emotional Aspects of the Personality. *New York, 1940.*

87 LEGRÜN, Alois

"Zur Deutung von Kinderkrit-
zeleien." Zeitschrift für Kinderforschung, XLVII, 236-49, 1938.

88 LESSING, Theodor

Charakterologie. Halle, 1926.

89 Einmal und nie wieder. Prague,
1935.

90 LEWIN, Kurt, and
GOLDZIEHER ROMAN, Klara

"Das allgemeinmotorische Ver-
halten des Stotterers." Berlin,
1929 (unpublished).

91 LEWINSON, Thea, and
ZUBIN, Joseph

Handwriting Analysis. New York,
1942.

92 LEWINSON STEIN, Thea

"Handwriting in Chronic Arthritis." Rheumatism, vol. I, no. 2,
1938.

93 LEWINSON STEIN, Thea

"Dynamic Disturbances in the
Handwriting of Psychotics. Amer-
ican Journal of Psychiatry, vol.
XCVII, no. 1, 1940.

94 MACHOVER, Karen

Personality Projection in the
Drawing of a Human Figure.
Springfield, Ill., 1949.

95 MARGUERITE, R., and
MANHEIM, M. I.

Vincent van Gogh im Spiegel
seiner Handschrift. Basel, 1938.

96 MASLOW, A. H.

"The Expressive Component of
Behavior." Psychological Review,
vol. CVI, no. 4, 1949.

97 MITTELMANN, Béla

Principles of Abnormal Psychology. New York, 1941.

98 MEAD, Margaret

"Trends in Personal Life." New
Republic, CXV, (no. 12), 345-
48, 1946.

99 "The Application of Anthropo-
logical Techniques to Crossna-
tional Communication." Transactions of the New York Academy
of Sciences, ser. 2, IX, 133-52,
1947.

100 MELOUN, H. A., et al

"Handwriting Measurement and
Personality Traits." Character and
Personality, II, 322-30, 1924.

101 MENDEL, A. O.

Personality in Handwriting. New
York, 1947.

102 MENDELSOHN, Anja

"Graphologie und Psychoanalyse."
Die Schrift, no. 1 (suppl.), 1939.

103 MENDELSOHN, Anja
MENDELSOHN, Georg
Der Mensch in der Handschrift.
Leipzig, 1928.

104 MEYER, Adolf

Ideen und Ideale der biologischen
Erkenntnis. Leipzig, 1934.

105 MEYER, Georg

Die wissenschaftlichen Grundlagen
der Graphologie. 4th ed. Jena,
1943.

106 MICHON, J. H.

Les mystères de l'écriture. Paris,
1872.

107 La méthode pratique de graphologie. Paris, 1878.

108 Histoire de Napoléon Ier d'après
son écriture. Paris, 1879.

109 MILES, W. R.

"Ocular Dominance Demonstrated
by Unconscious Sighting." Journal
of Experimental Psychology, no.
12, 1929.

110 MÜLLER, W. H., and
ENSKAT, Alice

Theorie und Praxis der Graphologie. *Rudolstadt, 1949.*

111 MURPHY, Gardner

Personality. *New York, 1949.*

112 NÉMETH, Peter, and
GOLDZIEHER ROMAN, Klara

"Züllött fiatalkoruak," etc.
["Studies of Handwriting in Juvenile Delinquents"]. Magyar gyógypedagógia, *nos. 4-6, 1933.*

113 NEWCOMB, Theodore M.

Social Psychology, *New York, 1950.*

114 NEWMAN, H. A.,
FREEMAN, F. N., and
HOLZINGER, K. J.

Twins: A study of Heredity and Environment. *Chicago, 1937.*

115 NINCK, J.

"Napoleon I. und seine Mutter." Zeitschrift für Graphologie. *vol. I, No. 2, 1930.*

116 OSBORN, Albert S.

Questioned Documents. *Albany, 1929.*

117 ORTON, Samuel T.

Reading, Writing and Speech Problems in Children. *New York, 1937.*

118 PASCAL, I.

"Handwriting Pressure: Its Measurements and Significance." Character and Personality, *XI, 234-54, 1943.*

119 PETER, Herbert

In Böhme, Albrecht, Psychotherapie und Kastration. *Munich, 1935.*

120 POPHAL, Rudolf

Grundlegung der bewegungsphysiologischen Graphologie. *Leipzig, 1939.*

121 Zur Psychophysiologie der Spannungserscheinungen in der Handschrift. *Leipzig, 1939.*

122 Die Handschrift als Gehirnschrift. *Rudolstadt, 1949.*

123 Das Strichbild. *Stuttgart, 1950.*

124 POUND, Ezra L.

Foreword, in Fenollosa, E. F., The Chinese Written Character as a Medium for Poetry. *London, 1936.*

125 POWERS, Edwin

Graphic Factors in Relation to Personality. *Dartmouth, 1930* (unpublished).

126 PREYER, Wilhelm T.

Zur Psychologie des Schreibens. *Hamburg, 1895.*

127 PULVER, Max

Trieb und Verbrechen in der Handschrift. *Zurich, 1934.*

128 Symbolik der Handschrift. *3d ed. Zurich, 1940.*

129 Der Intelligenzausdruck in der Handschrift. *Zurich, 1949.*

130 RANSCHBURG, Paul

Pathopsychologie der Störungen des Lesens, Schreibens und Rechnens im Kindesalter. *Munich, 1924.*

131 RIEGER, Anton

"Über Muskelzustände." Zeitschrift für Psychologie, *vol. XXXI, no. 32, 1903.*

132 ROBACK, A. A.

"Writing Slips and Personality." Character and Personality, I, 138-48, 1932.

133 ROGUES DE FURSAC, J.

Les écrits et les dessins dans les maladies nerveuses et mentales. Paris, 1905.

ROMAN, Klara G., see GOLDZIEHER ROMAN, Klara

134 ROSENZWEIG, Saul

"An Outline of Frustration Theory." In Hunt, J. McV. (ed.), Personality and the Behavior Disorders, vol. I, chap. 11. New York, 1944.

135 RUESCH, J., and FINESINGER, J. E.

"Muscular Tension in Psychiatric Patients: Pressure Measurements in Handwriting as an Indicator." Archiv für Neurologie und Psychiatrie, L, 439-49, 1934.

136 SAUDEK, Robert

Psychology of Handwriting. London, 1925.

137 Experiments with Handwriting. New York, 1929.

138 "Das zentrale Nervensystem und der Schreibakt." Jahrbuch der Charakterologie, VI, 277 - 303, 1929.

139 "Zur psychodiagnostischen Ausdeutung des Schreibdruckes." Zeitschrift für angewandte Psychologie, XXXIX, 433-49, 1931.

140 "Zur Psychologie der amerikanischen Handschrift." Zeitschrift für Menschenkunde, VI, 361-96, 1931.

141 SCHILDER, Paul

The Image and Appearance of the Human Body. New York, 1935.

142 SCHLAG, Oskar R.

"Anmerkungen eines Graphologen zur Handschrift von Ernst Jünger." Schweizerische Zeitschrift für Psychologie und ihre Anwendungen, suppl. 18.

143 SCHNEICKERT, Hans

Leitfaden der gerichtlichen Schriftvergleichung. Leipzig, 1918.

144 SCHÖNFELD, Willy

Die graphologische Intelligenzbeurteilung. Prague, 1933.

145 SCHÖNFELD, Willy and MENZEL, K.

Tuberkulose, Charakter und Handschrift. Prague, 1934.

146 SCHULMANN, Adolf

"Heilpädagogische Wertung von Schriftuntersuchungen an Sprachkranken." Zeitschrift für Kinderforschung, IV, 439-44, 1934.

147 SEELIGER, Max

Handschrift und Zeichnung. Leipzig, 1920.

148 SEEMAN, Ernest, and SAUDEK, Robert

"The Handwriting of Identical Twins." Character and Personality, I, 22-40, 268-85, 1933.

149 SMITH, James J.

"A Medical Approach to Problem Drinking." Quarterly Journal of Studies on Alcohol, X, 251-57, 1949.

150 SONNEMANN, Ulrich

Handwriting Analysis. New York, 1950.

151 STEIF, Antal

"Ikrek megegyező firkálásmodja" ["Similarity of Scribbles in Twins"]. Magyar psychologiai szemle, III, 51-66, 1939.

152 STRACKE, Hans

"*Über die Beeinflussung der Handschrift durch Ausführung einer Nebentätigkeit,*" *etc.* Archiv für die gesamte Psychologie, *vol. LXXXIX, no. 1, 1932.*

153 SYMONDS, Percival M.

"*Current Trends and Developments in the Field of Projective Techniques.*" Personality, *no. 1, 1950.*

154 TEILLARD, Ania

L'âme et l'écriture. *Paris, 1948.*

155 TELTSCHER, H. O.

Handwriting, the Key to Successful Living. *New York, 1944.*

156 THEISS, Herbert

"*Experimentelle Untersuchungen über die Erfassung des handschriftlichen Ausdrucks durch Laien.*" Psychologische Forschung, *vol. XV, no. 3, 1931.*

157 THORNDIKE, E. L.

"*Handwriting.*" Teachers College Record, *IX, 83-175, 1910.*

158 WACHHOLDER, Kurt

Willkürliche Haltung und Bewegung. *Munich, 1928.*

159 WASHBURN, Margaret F.

Movement and Mental Imagery. *New York, 1916.*

160 WEISS, Deso A.

"*Organic Lesions Leading to Speech Disorders.*" Nervous Child, *vol. VII, no. 1, 1948.*

161 WERTHEIMER, Max

"*Über Gestalttheorie.*" Symposion, *no. 1, 1925.*

162 WIESER, Roda

Der Rhythmus in der Verbrecherhandschrift. *Leipzig, 1938.*

163 WILE, Ira S.

Handedness, Right and Left. *Boston, 1934.*

164 WITTLICH, Bernhard

Angewandte Graphologie. *Berlin, 1948.*

165 WÖLFFLIN, Heinrich

"*Über das Rechts und Links im Bilde.*" Münchner Jahrbuch der bildenden Kunst, *no. 5, 1928.*

166 WOLFF, Werner

"*Die Gestaltsidentität in der Charakterologie.*" Psychologie und Medizin, *IV, 32-44, 1929.*

167 WOLFF, Werner

"*Über die Faktoren charakterologischer Urteilsbildung.*" Zeitschrift für angewandte Psychologie, *XXXV, 385-446, 1930.*

168 Expression of Personality: Experimental Depth Psychology. *New York, 1943.*

169 WOLFF, Werner

Diagrams of the Unconscious. *New York, 1949.*

170 WOLFSON, Rose

A Study in Handwriting Analysis. *New York, 1949.*

171 WOLTMANN, Adolf

"*Mud and Clay.*" Personality, *no. 2, 1950.*

I N D E X

A

Aberrations, 56
Abnormality, 12, 112
Abstract thinking, 83
Accentuations, 273
Adaptability, 219, 230
Adaptation to reality, 137
Additions, 47
Address, location of, 309
Adjustment, 283
   socio-erotic, 231
Adjustments, initial and terminal, 46
Adornments, 28, 84
Aesthetic sense, 289
Age, chronological, 116
Age in handwriting, 5, 115
Aggressiveness, 18, 21, 61, 169, 218,
   262, 269, 280, 282, 327
Alignment, 292 ff.
   downward, 298
   upward, 298
   irregular, 300
   variability of, 297
Ambition, 142
American writing, 99
   feminine, 99
Ampleness of letter forms, 81, 82
Amplification of given name, 322
Anal type, 160, 161
Analytical psychology, 11
Ancient Greek writing, 144
Angularity, 93, 161
Antisocial acts, 140
Anxiety, 21, 73, 77, 235, 280, 302
Arrangement, 126, 127, 289 ff.
   leftward, 296
   of total pattern, 143
Arthritis, rheumatoid, 281
Artificiality, 15, 86

Association of speaking, reading,
   writing, 42
Associative conditioning, 42
Associative processes, speed of, 240
Attention, capacity for, 48

B

Balance, 121
Base line, 136, 137
Beginning of letter, 142
Biological egotism, 168
Biocentric, 8
Blockage, 54, 72, 253
Body image, 28, 140, 165, 166
Body of script, 136, 289, 313
Brain writing, 6, 108
British writing, 97
Brisement douloureux de la vie, 327
Business hand, 45

C

CAPITAL LETTERS, 161 ff., 246,
   274
   emphasis on, 275
   as personality projection, 165
   oversized, 161 ff.
   oversized in signature, 321, 322
Capital "I," 77, 163 ff., 320
Carelessness, 81, 308
Character of writer, 7
Characterology, 7, 8
Checker motif in doodles, 32
Cheerfulness, 21
Children, abnormal (*see also* Hand-
   writing of), 12
Chinese writing, 143, 144, 316
Chorea, 58
Circle formation, 77, 327
Clinical observation, 9, 10

371

Clinical psychology, 15, 17
Complexity, 84
Compliance, 187
Compulsive features, 77
  ideas, 37
  neurosis, 36
  tendencies, 32
Concentration, 50, 244, 262
Conflicts, 56, 61 ff., 280, 291
Confusion, 84
  emotional, 293
Congruence of signature and body
  script, 319 ff.
Connectedness, 223, 228 ff.
CONNECTIVE FORMS, 126, 199 ff.
  Angular, 126, 199, 214 ff., 285,
    288
  Arcade, 126, 199, 203, 207 ff.,
    218, 220
    narrow, 211
    shallow, 210
    topheavy, 210
  Double curve, 199, 200, 216
  Garland, 16, 199 ff., 213, 214
    broad, 204
    flattened, 205
    looped, 207
    pseudo, 206
    shallow, 205
    underslung, 205
  Mixed, 218 ff.
  Threadlike, 126, 199, 200, 216 ff.
Connection, streamlined, 225
Contemplation, 142
Continuity, 221 ff., 235, 284
Contraction, 16, 77
Control, 244, 285
Co-ordination, 52, 55, 57, 125
  *of visual, auditory, and motor
    functions*, 44
Creative imagination, 103
Creativity, 140, 317
Critical sense, 269
Cruelty, 269
Cursive writing, 44, 45, 199

D

Daydreams, 317, 329
Defiance, 187

Delinquency, 16
  juvenile, 12, 78, 262
  sexual, 268
Delinquent constellation, 16
Depression, 85, 206, 250, 296, 297,
  308, 309
Depth, 136, 140
Depth psychology, 11, 17
Determination, 263
Developmental stages, 41, 47
Developmental standards, 53
Deviations from standard letters, 47
Differentiation pattern, 16
Differentiation of writing features,
  119
Direction, 125, 134, 140 ff.
  change in, 47
  from left to right, 23
  from top to bottom, 23
Directional trends, 40
Disconnectedness, 223, 228 ff., 233
Discouragement, 296
Disguise, 86
Dishonesty traits, 15
Discharge of feeling into movement,
  29
Discrimination of brightness, 48
Disorder
  developmental, 56
  functional, 72
  incipient, 57
  pituitary, 115
  thyroid, 115
Disorganization, 234
Disproportion between height and
  width, 275
Disturbance
  emotional, 73
  in adolescence, 77
Doodles, 29 ff.
  association in, 30, 32
  as symbols, 29
  interpretation of, 32
Dot, 134, 250
Drawings, 28, 40, 150
  drawing a man, 40
Dreams, 140
Dream analysis, 32
Drives, 8, 142

Drug addiction, 268, 269
Duality of right and left, 145
Ductus, *see* stroke
Dysfunction
  endocrine, 115
  muscular, 282

E

Economy, 160, 289
Effort, 285
Ego emphasis, 327
Ego expression, 137
Elaboration, 47, 80 ff., 85
Elation, 250
Emotional balance, 47
Emotional content, hidden, 274
Emotional disturbance
  in adults, 276, 277
  in puberty, 72
Empathy, 107, 109, 122
Emphasis, 163, 251, 273 ff.
Empirical criteria, 284
End of letter, 142
Endurance, 262
Energy, 263
  expended and unexpended, 278,
    280
  psycho-sexual, redirection of, 271
Enlargement of unizonal letters, 149
Ethics of graphologist, 132
Excitability, 183, 190
Excitement, 297
Expansion, 125, 157
  of graphic pattern, 147 ff.
  pseudo, 160, 161
  vertical and horizontal, 150 ff.
Expansive personality, 289
Experimental investigation, 9
Expression, unity of, 7
Extension, 7
Extensors, 178, 278
Extraversion, 141, 157, 171, 309
Eye-hand control, 42 ff.

F

Fan phenomenon, 288
Fatigue, 270, 288; 296, 297; systemic,
  232

Feeblemindedness, 250, 303
Fence motif, 36
  in doodling, 33
Fixation, 142, 193
Fixation span, 43
Flexors, 178, 278
Flight of ideas, 232, 250
Flightiness, 263
Fluency, 221 ff., 234 ff.
Formality, 209
Form, 125, 127
  balance of, 289
Forms
  broken, 72
  half-completed, 85
  jutting, 72
  tremulous, 72
  meaning of, 5
Form level, 8, 123
Form niwo, 8
Fragmentary writing, 233
Frigidity, 269

G

Gaps in lines, words, or letters, 25,
  251, 302, 303
Generalizations, 228
Genital development, retardation of,
  70
German writing, 148
Gestalt theory, 15, 40
Graphic indices, 119, 127
  interpretation of, 129
  ordering of, 127
  of speed, 247
Graphological studies
  in America, 13 ff., 43
  in France, 4, 5
  in Germany, 6 ff.
  in Great Britain, 15
  in Hungary, 11, 12
  in Switzerland, 11
  of personality patterns, 283
Graphology
  application of, 10
  experimental, 17
  motor-physiological, 10
  practice of, 104

373

Graphologist
  qualifications of, 108
  ethics of, 132
Graphodyne, 12, 64, 73, 74, 223, 236, 239, 279 ff., 283
Graphometer, 185
Grip pressure, 278
Guilt feelings, 73

H

HANDEDNESS, 145 ff., 194, 213, 214, 234
  left-handedness, 52, 53, 64, 194 ff., 286
  right-handedness, 194 ff.
HANDWRITING
  confused, 55
  deficient, 56
  disturbed, 56, 72
  large, 151, 154
  mature, 67
  mechanical, 86
  over-relaxed, 285
  small, 153, 154
  stylized, 270
  ungainly, 55, 56
  untidy, 56, 60
  cultural patterns in, 90
  elements of, 4
  as expressive movement, 13
  national characteristics of, 92
  teaching of, 41
  of alcoholics, 188, 189
  of architects, 208
  of artists, 266
  of children, 48 ff.
  of school children, 42 ff., 64, 150, 222, 223, 262
  of high school girls, 262
  of disabled persons, 15
  of twins, 12, 213
  of identical twins, 53, 197, 198
  in adolescence, 60
  in puberty, 60, 61
  (*see also* puberty)
Handwriting analysis
  of children, 48 ff.
  in diagnosis of speech disorder, 239

  in vocational and medical fields, 10
Handwriting interpretation
  validity of, 17
Harpoon formation, 285, 286, 288
Haste, 244
Hebrew writing, 144, 145
Hieroglyphic characters, 143
Height of letters, 135, 147, 148
  of unizonal letters, 150
Homosexuality, 187, 193, 268, 277
Hysteria, 216
Hypomania, 250

I

i dots, 217, 223
  antenna-like, 288
  built-in, 226
  high-placed, 149, 170, 172
  hooked-up, 232
  position of, 248
  round, 284
  stretched, 285, 287
Identification with the letter form, 136
Ideogram, 144
Illegibility, 85, 276
Illusions, 140
Images, 28, 136
  archetypal space image, 137
  compulsive images, 79
  meaning of, 122
  symbolic of vocation, 318, 319
Imagery, 317
  concrete, 83
  graphic, 229, 315 ff.
  language of, 317
  pictorial, 318
Imaginative associations, 225
Imaginative projection, 314, 315
Imagination, 140
  ideographic, 79
Imbalance, state of, 280
Immaturity, organic, 78
Impulsiveness, 263, 293
Incoherence, 295
Indecision, 295
Individuality, 23, 86
  graphic, 60

374

of graphical expression in children, 47
Inertia, 206, 263
Infantilism, 78, 161, 315
Inferiority feelings, 63, 168
Informality, 209
Inhibition, 72, 160, 214, 235, 279, 286
Initial adjustment, 245
Initial delay, 246
INITIAL LETTER
    break in, 252
    dwarfed, 163
    emphasis on, 162
    first stroke of, 169
    tall stems in, 171
Insecurity feelings, 173
    revealed in slant, 62, 302
Insincerity, 212, 214, 295
Instability, 36
Instinctual urges, 175
Integration
    capacity for, 127, 289
    of word forms, 64
    of writing pattern, 231
Intelligence, perceptive, 50
Interpretation of graphic features, 119
    of personality traits, 119
Interruptions (*see also* Gaps), 223, 227, 247
Interspace
    inadequate, 302
    overlarge, 301
    size of, 301
Introspection, 142
Introversion, 141, 157, 171, 309
Intuition, 8, 17, 108, 109, 111, 122, 123, 128, 228, 230
Irritability, 288
Isolated trait, 4

J

Joinings (*see also* Connective forms)
    location of, 229
    retracing of, 233
    soldering of, 233
Jumble of lines, in doodles, 21

L

Lability, 169
Laterality (*see also* Handedness), 198
    deviation in, 40
Leanness of letter forms, 82, 85
Lebensstörung, 9
Left-handedness, *see* Handedness
Leitmotif, 317
Libido
    physical, 263
    psychic, 263
    sexual, 270
LINE, 134 ff.
    broken, 295
    concave, 297
    convex, 298
    downward, 296
    serrated or stepped, 297, 298
    straight, 294
    tottering, 294
    undulating, 295
    upward, 296, 297
Lines
    bunched together, in doodles, 36
    crossed, 36
Logic, 228, 231
LOOPS, 140, 148, 150, 170, 178 ff.
    cramped, 288
    crooked, 72
    disconnected, 231
    lean, 288
    oddly formed, 182, 183
    overshooting, 72
    twirled, 72, 73
    υ turn of, 178
    Lower loops, 173 ff., 177 ff.
        broken into triangles, 287
        indices of tension in, 287
        overlarge, 273

M

Maladjustment, 56, 235, 263
Mania, 190
Material demands, 140
MARGINS, 289
    bottom margin, 308
    diminishing, 306, 307
    left-hand, 303, 304

insufficient, 306
right-hand, 304, 305
top, 306, 308
Masochism, 268
Matching method, 13
Maturation, 12, 41, 64, 72
   physiological, 67
   sexual, 115
   socio-sexual, 68
Meaning, fixed, 14
Measurements, 14 ff., 150, 284
Medical history of writer, 118
Mental development, 28, 47
Mental retardation, 263
Mirror writing, 195, 196
Misspellings, 55, 115
Monotony, 59, 126, 170, 183
Motor behavior, types of, 10
Motor co-ordination, 47
Motor development, 52, 54
Motor functions, development of, 43
Motor intelligence, 52
Motor pattern, 178
Motor play, 21
MOVEMENT, 5, 23, 124 ff.
   angular, 21
   automatic, 44
   blocked, 237
   circling, 21
   continuous, 47, 222 ff.
   discontinuous, 224
   downward, 284
   expressive, 8, 284
   of fingers, 43
   flow of, 243
   free, 21
   language of, 121
   left-ward, 14, 284
   loose, 21
   measurement of speed, 236 ff.
   modulation of, 46
   pattern of, 178
   probing, 250
   restrained, 21
   rhythm of, 247, 284, 289, 299
   right-ward, 141, 284
   sequential, 21, 222, 223
   skilled, 53
   spastic, 237, 285

   sweeping, 21
   tense, 21
   two-handed, 52
   upward, 284
Movements
   correspondence in, 5, 8
   internal consistency of, 14
Muscle contraction, 43
Muscle tonus, 238, 278, 282, 285, 298
Muscular rigidity, 279

N

Name writing, 41, 311
Narcissism, 64, 322
Narrowness of letters, 137, 158, 286, 302
Nationality of writer, 118
Naturalness (see also Spontaneity), 15
Negativism, 56, 194
Neurotic conflicts, 282
Nodules, 73, 276
Non-objective modes of expression, 83
Nonsense pictures, 29
Normality, 112
Norms, establishment of a scale for, 66
Numerals, 100, 308, 309

O

Objective methods, 16
Objectivity, 228
Obsession, 302
Obstinacy, 216
Occupation of writer, 118
Omissions, 47, 115
Optimism, 297, 298
Order, sense of, 293
Organization, 50
   lack of, 300
   spatial, 289
Orientation
   confused, 52
   directional, 143
   in time, 142
Outlines
   blurred, 257, 269
   broken, 285

ragged, 257
sharp, 269
Oval letter parts
   deflated, 148
   inflated, 148
   flooded, 276
Over-all impression, 119
Over-all pattern, 320
Overconnection, 231
Overcontrol, 183
Overemphasis on family name, 322

P

Pace
   acceleration of, 248
   dynamics of, 242 ff.
   personal, 53, 240 ff.
Palmer system, 45, 46, 96
Paper, 266
   quality of, 260
   ruled, 294
Pastosity, 267, 268
PATTERN OF WRITING, 6
   impersonal, 86
   individuality of, 25, 90
   linear, 82, 315
   pictorial, 83, 315
   professional, 99 ff.
   shallow, 235
   stereotyped, 50
   tangled, 286
   vocational, 90 ff.
Pattern vision, 48
Parent-child relation, 322
Pauses, 251, 301
Penmanship, 46
   training in, 43, 96
   types of, 15, 86 ff.
Pen types, 257 ff.
Perception, "global," 40
Periodicity, 243, 247
   rhythmic, 284
Perseveration, 232
Personal style, consistency of, 88 ff.
Personality make-up, 119
Personality picture, 129, 132
Personality traits, 130, 131
Pessimism, 296 ff., 309
Phantasy activity, 140, 232

Pictorial writing, 143, 144
Point pressure, 278
Precision, 81
Pre-school child, 40
PRESSURE (*see also* stroke), 7, 9,
   14, 23, 67, 236, 254 ff., 261 ff.
   in adolescence, 74
   breakdown in puberty, 75
   as discharge of libido, 263
   displaced, 277 ff.
   exerted in movement, 125
   heavy, 255, 256
   fluctuations in, 279
   location of emphasis, 274
   weak, 21
Pressure board, 15
Printscript, 43 ff., 96, 277
Projection, 136
   creative, 38
   of body image, 165 ff.
   of hostility, 35
   in signature, 314 ff.
   unconscious, 137
Projective techniques, 11, 15
Protest, 193
Psychic energy, 263
Psychoanalysis, 15
Psychograms, 38
Psychometric techniques, 9
Psychosomatic disturbances, 235
Psychosomatic state, 280
Psychosomatic studies, 282
Puberty, changes in writing during,
   64, 69 ff., 150, 303

Q

Qualitative aspects, 16
Quantitative aspects, 15, 16

R

Rage, 297
Ratings (*see also* Measurements), 14,
   16
Reading difficulties, 52
Recall, 48
Receptivity, 203
Regression, 28, 140, 142
Regularity, 125

377

Relatedness, 301, 302
Release (*see also* Tension-release),
    16, 28, 250, 278 ff.
  *balance between release and con-
    traction,* 147
  unconscious, 29, 134
Repetition, 14, 22
Repression, 28, 38, 73, 285
Reserve, 304
Responsiveness, 203
Resultants, theory of, 5
Retention, 284
Reticence, 207
Retouching of loops and stems, 172
Reversals, 51
Rhythm (*see also* Movement), 8, 28,
    66, 121, 242
  balance of, 16
  distribution of, 126
  disturbance of, 272, 302
  of form, 126
  inner, 83
  of movement, 125
  periodicity of, 125
  theory of, 16
  unevenness of, 126
  of writing pattern, 243
Right-ward writing trend, 144
Ritual gesture, 77, 306
Rorschach inkblot test, 11, 32, 265
Rounded letter shapes, 92

S

Sacré Coeur handwriting, 86
Sadism, 161, 267, 273
Sadness, 21
Scales
  system of, 16
  for analysis of writing, 284
Schizoid pattern, 170, 327
Schizophrenic traits, 50, 59, 276, 328
School children, experimental and
    statistical studies with, 264 ff.
School of fixed signs, 5
School-model letters, 47, 148, 200
Scratching technique, 144
Scribbles, 21 ff., 40
  diversity of pattern, 24, 25
  interpretation of, 23

Seizure state, 303
Self-assertiveness, 167
Self-confidence, 170
Selfconsciousness, 157, 160, 248, 304
Self-depreciation, 320
Self-destruction, 37, 327
Self-esteem, 164
Self-expression of children, 22
Selfishness, 142
Self-reliance, 187
Semitic writing, 143
Sensibility, 168
Sex behavior, 177 ff., 183
  clues to, 174, 175
Sex characteristics, 61
Sex differences, 67, 68
Sex differentiation, 116
Sex glands, 115
Shading, 136, 255, 270, 284
Shyness, 207
SIGNATURE, 17, 28, 29, 63, 311 ff.
  ascending line in, 299
  changes in, 323 ff.
  congruence with body script, 320
  consistency of pattern, 312, 313
  dot in signature, 326
  elaboration of, 326
  encircled, 327
  endstrokes, 264, 326, 327
  enlarged, 321
  expression of, 320
  expressive functions of, 331
  family likeness in, 313, 314
  family name, 311
  final appendage, 311
  flourish in, 29
  given name, 315
  jumble of lines, 29, 311, 328
  location of, 330
  margin under, 306
  middle name, 311
  ornamentation, 311
  projection in, 314
  *relation of given name and family
    name,* 322
  speed in writing, 241, 242
  of suicides, 330
  symbolic imagery in, 229, 318 ff.,
    330

undulating stroke in, 327
"Signs," 4, 14, 28, 127; "sign"
    reading, 110
Silent speech, 44, 234
Simplification, 47, 80, 84, 100; of
    family name, 322
SIZE
    of letters, 147, 150
    ascendant and descendant grada-
        tions of, 155
    evaluation of, 166
    of spaces between letters, 157
Skill, manipulative, 80
SLANT, 184 ff.
    degree of, 187
    fluctuations in, 63, 187, 192 ff.
    left-ward, 186 ff.
    extreme left-ward, 193
    in left-handedness, 196 ff.
    right-ward, 185, 218
    upright hand, 185 ff., 192
Slips of the pen, 115
Slowness, 304
    extreme, 250
Sluggishness, mental, 250
Smeariness, 160, 267, 268
Snake as symbol, 33, 34
Social relationships, 137
Society hand, 87
Soldering, 221, 233
Spacing, 291 ff.
    interlinear spaces, 289, 293, 308
    word interspaces, 289, 300 ff.
Spasm, 279
Specimen collection, 111, 112
Speech disturbances (*see also* Stutter-
    ing), 54, 55, 234 ff.
SPEED, 7, 9, 14, 47, 53, 64, 67,
    240 ff., 260
    affected by writing situation, 250
    determined by temperament, 244,
        245
    deviations from average, 250
    excessive, 250
    fluctuations in, 241
    indices of, 247, 248
    of movement, 125
    regular, 250
    significance of, 15

Spencerian system, 148
Sphere of abstraction, 137
Spirals, 37
Spontaneity, 28, 86, 248
Standard values, 12
Statistics, 15
Stems, 140, 170
    tracing of, 178 ff.
    upper and lower, 150
Stereotypy, 220
Stimulus words, 115, 251
Stinginess, 160
Strain, mental, 280
Stratosphere, 137, 173, 269
Streamlined forms, 47
STROKE, 135
    blurred, 270
    broken, 221
    broken connecting, 55
    circular, 40
    concealing, 206, 212
    continuity of, 224
    course of, 131
    diffuse, 21
    downstroke, 43, 255
    downstroke ending in spearheads,
        275
    forceful, 21
    horizontal, 135, 156, 306
    interrupted, 224
    pastose, 256, 265, 266
    qualities of, 254 ff.
    rigid, 269, 285, 287, 288
    sharp, 269
    showy, 264
    sideward, 155, 156
    smoothness of, 248
    springboard, 155, 169, 246
    soldered, 250
    terminal, 155
    terminal dagger-like, 267
    terminal, right-ward, 219
    underlining, 156
    of uniform width, 255
    upstroke, 42, 255
    tremulous, 273
    vertical, 135
    weak, 270
    zigzag, 21

379

Stubbornness, 85
Stuttering (*see also* Speech disturbances), 54, 55, 235, 238
Style, 80 ff., 126
  consistency of, 103
  of life, 87
  stilted, 86
Surélévation, 162, 169
Swallowtails, 260, 261
Swellings, 72, 276
Swoops, 72, 276
Symmetry, 22, 23, 28
Symbols, 315
  of anxiety, 327
  conditioned, 42
  symbolic gestures, 28, 136
  symbolic meaning of writing pressure, 266
  symbolism of writing space, 134
Syndrome, 119
Synthesis, 119, 132

T

t bars, 223
  broken, 72
  coupled, 266
  high-placed, 149, 172
  hooked-up, 232
t stems
  lopsided, 72
  twisted, 72
Tension, 8, 61, 73, 85, 169, 244, 250, 278
  hypertension, 281
  low, 296
  muscular, 281
  phenomena of, 10
  relief from, 270
Tension-release, 207, 283 ff.
  balance of, 287
  interplay of, 283
  muscular, 46
  pattern of, 279
Terminal letter, 155
Test situation, 113
Time measurements, 241
Theory of personality, 8
Therapeutic use of graphological findings, 54

Threadlike finish, 155
Thriftiness, 291
Tracing
  evenness of, 46
  firmness of, 46
Trait psychology, 13
Triangles, 27, 28

U

Unconscious motivation, 15
Uniformity, 4, 220
Unrest, 293

V

Visual acuity, 48
Visual form perception, 48
Visual-mindedness, 83, 234

W

Wavy line, 213, 283
Western writing, 143
Whorls, 21
Width of letters, 135, 148
  excessive, 157
Withdrawal, 142, 214, 327, 328
Word endings, 285
Worksheet, 128, 129
WRITING
  development in school children, 12
  development of writing symbols, 315
  difficulties, 52
  disturbances, 235
  efficiency, 52
  Gothic style, 200
  on envelope, 308
  field, 134
  line, 293
  pattern as a whole, 119
  pattern disorganized, 268
  space, 289
  symbolic meaning of space, 11, 134, 135
  systems, 92 ff.
  techniques, 143
  tools, 254
WRITING ZONES, 137 ff.

Lower Zone, 140 ff., 149, 171 ff.
  connectedness in, 231
  height of, 148
Middle zone, 137, 141, 167 ff.
  diminution of, 169
  fluctuations in, 168
  height of, 148, 170
  joinings in, 229, 230

Upper zone, 137, 138, 142, 149,
  156, 170 ff.
  disconnectedness in, 230
  height of, 148
  joinings in, 230
  overextension into, 137
  oversized elements in, 173
  oversized letter forms in, 171

INDEX OF AUTHORS

ALEXANDER, Franz, 282
ALLPORT, Gordon W., 13, 14, 132
ANGYAL, Andras, 8
ARNHEIM, Rudolf, 14, 88
BACHOFEN, J. J., 146
BALÁZS, Deszö, 12, 251
BALDO, Camillo, 3
BECKER, Minna, 23
BINET, Alfred, 5, 115
BRANDON, Henry, 34
BROCA, Paul, 234
BUSSE, Hans H., 7
CRÉPIEUX-JAMIN, J., 5, 115, 162
DOWNEY, June E., 13, 110
DUPARCHY-JEANNEZ, M., 232
ENSKAT, Alice, 10
ERLENMEYER, D., 7
FANTA, Otto, 11
FLANDRIN, Abbé, 4
FREUD, Sigmund, 140
GESELL, Arnold, 28
GOLDZIHER, Erzsébet, 12
HAJNAL, Richard, 12
HARDWICK, Gladys, 43
HEISS, Robert, 10
JACOBY, Hans, 233
JANET, Pierre, 5
JUNG, C. G., 35, 36
KLAGES, Ludwig, 6 ff., 16, 123, 126,
    207, 216, 228, 283
KRAEPELIN, Emil, 9, 288
KROEBER-KENETH, L., 8
LESSING, Theodor, 7, 9
LEWIN, Kurt, 235
LEWINSON, Thea S., 16, 284
MACHOVER, Karen, 28, 165

MASLOW, A. H., 296
MEAD, Margaret, 96
MENDEL, A. O., 194
MENDELSOHN, Anja, 36, 37, 38
MENZEL, Karl, 11
MEYER, Georg, 7
MICHON, Jean Hippolyte, 4, 5, 127
MUELLER, W. H., 10
NÉMETH, Peter, 12
NEWCOMBE, Theodore, 250
NINCK, J., 264
OSBORN, A. S., 15, 86, 112
PASCAL, J., 263
POPHAL, Rudolf, 10, 222, 287
POWERS, Edwin, 14
PREYER, Wilhelm, 6, 108
PROSPER, Alderisius, 3
PULVER, Max, 11, 134, 137, 155, 167,
    173, 209, 263, 270, 308
RIEGER, Anton, 10, 222
SAUDEK, Robert, 14, 15, 195, 247
SCHERMANN, Rudolf, 316
SCHILLER, Paul, 22
SCHLAG, Oskar, 11
SCHÖNFELD, Willy, 11
SEELIGER, Max, 88
SONNEMANN, Ulrich, 17
SYMONDS, P. M., 319
THEISS, Herbert, 109
UDINE, Jean d', 66
VERNON, Philip E., 13, 14, 132
WACHHOLDER, Kurt, 10
WITTLICH, Bernhard, 10
WOLFF, Werner, 14, 17, 34, 266
WOLFSON, Rose, 16, 284
ZUBIN, Joseph, 16, 284

ABOUT THE AUTHOR

Klara Goldzieher Roman (1881–1962) was internationally known as a psychologist and handwriting expert. Born in Budapest, she graduated from the Hungarian Royal State Institute for Abnormal Psychology in 1928, then did extensive research at the University of Berlin and at the Heckscher Foundation, Munich. In 1930, she founded the Institute for Handwriting Research, Budapest, where she studied thousands of normal and abnormal children. In 1933, she was appointed as a handwriting expert to the Royal Hungarian Criminal Courts and the Court for Juvenile Delinquents.

Emigrating to the United States in 1946, Mrs. Roman first lectured at the New York State Psychiatric Institute, then won a research appointment to the Institute for Psychoanalysis and the Institute of Psychosomatic Research and Training, both in Chicago. In 1948, she joined and remained for fourteen years on the faculty of the New School for Social Research in New York City, teaching the only college-accredited courses on graphology in the United States. From 1951 to 1956, she was Research Consultant to the Treatment Clinic of Manhattan Children's Court and an Affiliate of the National Hospital for Speech Disorders. Following a lecture tour in Europe, in 1961 Klara Roman was appointed Clinical Psychologist and Graphologist on the staff of the Children's Health Council of the Mid-Peninsula, Palo Alto, California. Returning again to Europe in 1962 to lecture, she completed her last work, the *Encyclopedia of the Written Word,* which was published posthumously in 1968.

Her book, *Handwriting,* published first in 1952, remains a classic in its field.